# Karl Jaspers on Truth and Dialogue

## Contemporary Studies in Idealism

***Series Editor***: Paolo Diego Bubbio, University of Turin



The *Contemporary Studies in Idealism* series features cutting-edge scholarship in the field of classical German Idealism and its legacy. "Idealism" is considered both in a historical and in a theoretical sense. The series features projects that center upon Kant and the post-Kantian Idealists (including, but not limited to, early German romantic thinkers Fichte, Schelling, and Hegel) or upon other related forms of nineteenth-century philosophy—including those often considered to oppose Idealism, such as those of Kierkegaard and Nietzsche. The scholarship also seeks to critically assess the legacy of Idealism in the twentieth and twenty-first century. The series uses the resources of classical German Idealism to engage in contemporary debates in all sub-fields of philosophy.

### Recent Titles in the Series

*Karl Jaspers on Truth and Dialogue: A Rethinking of His Philosophy of Universal Communication*, by Anton Hügli

*Schopenhauer's Buddhism: A Historical-Philosophical Inquiry*, by Laura Langone

*Kant in Context: The Historical Primacy of the Transcendental Dialectic*, by Daniel Patrick Kelly

*Kant's Struggle for Autonomy: On the Structure of Practical Reason*, by Raef Zreik

*Happiness in Kant's Practical Philosophy: Morality, Indirect Duties, and Welfare Rights*, by Alice Pinheiro Walla

*Schopenhauer and the Nature of Philosophy*, by Jonathan Head

*Nietzsche and Adorno on Philosophical Praxis, Language, and Reconciliation: Towards an Ethics of Thinking*, by Paolo A. Bolaños

*Hypotyposis in Kant's Metaphysics of Judgment: Symbolizing Completeness*, by Byron Ashley Clugston

# Karl Jaspers on Truth and Dialogue

## A Rethinking of His Philosophy of Universal Communication

Anton Hügli

LEXINGTON BOOKS

*Lanham • Boulder • New York • London*

Published by Lexington Books
An imprint of The Rowman & Littlefield Publishing Group, Inc.
4501 Forbes Boulevard, Suite 200, Lanham, Maryland 20706
www.rowman.com

86-90 Paul Street, London EC2A 4NE



British Library Cataloguing in Publication Information Available

**Library of Congress Cataloging-in-Publication Data**

Names: Hügli, Anton, author.
Title: Karl Jaspers on truth and dialogue : a rethinking of his philosophy of universal communication / Anton Hügli.
Description: Lanham : Lexington Books, [2025] | Series: Contemporary studies in idealism | Includes bibliographical references.
Identifiers: LCCN 2024043545 (print) | LCCN 2024043546 (ebook) | ISBN 9781793649126 (cloth) | ISBN 9781793649133 (ebook)
Subjects: LCSH: Jaspers, Karl, 1883-1969. | Communication—Philosophy
Classification: LCC B3279.J34 H88 2025 (print) | LCC B3279.J34 (ebook) | DDC 193—dc23/eng/20241011
LC record available at https://lccn.loc.gov/2024043545
LC ebook record available at https://lccn.loc.gov/2024043546

∞™ The paper used in this publication meets the minimum requirements of American National Standard for Information Sciences—Permanence of Paper for Printed Library Materials, ANSI/NISO Z39.48-1992.

Motto: We only come closer to the One when there is unity in the world[1]

1. See ChT 55.

# Contents

# Preface

I believe that with this book I can achieve what I once set out to do as a young student of philosophy: to finally understand what Jaspers' philosophizing is all about. Basically, I would have had the best conditions for doing so. I came to Basel to study when Jaspers had just given his farewell lecture, his students (although he never really wanted to have students) were sitting in the philosophy chairs, dissertations were being written about him all around me, and he was well known to the public too. But what I read in Jasper's writings and heard interpreted seemed to me diffuse and dark. This gave me no peace. I came to the conclusion that there was so much Kierkegaard in Jaspers that one could only really understand him if one had studied Kierkegaard. And not in a translation, but in the original. So Copenhagen and the Kierkegaard scholars there became my next stop, and Kierkegaard became the subject of my dissertation and various other works. The further study of Jaspers, however, I left to my friend Hans Saner, who, as Jaspers' assistant and administrator of his estate, had the best prerequisites for this and was fully committed to the task, which found its institutional form in the Karl Jaspers Foundation, founded by Jeanne Hersch in 1973: To promote the work and thought of Karl Jaspers and to make his works and writings, his estate and his correspondence accessible to the public.

After completing my dissertation, so-called existential philosophy in general, and Jaspers in particular, no longer seemed to me to be a philosophical project worth pursuing. I was much more fascinated by analytic philosophy, which was now beginning to triumph outside the Anglo-Saxon world. I hoped that it would give me the clarity and rationality of philosophizing that I had missed in Jaspers. So Oxford, then the Eldorado of analytical philosophy, became my next stop, and a decision-theoretical investigation of the possibilities and limits of conflict ethics became the subject of my habilitation thesis. This, however, only caused me more discomfort. In the end, I had had enough of specialized works that only specialists read, but also enough of a philosophy that, turning away from the history of philosophy, believed that it could only satisfy itself.

I now immersed myself in research on the history of philosophy, or more precisely, the history of concepts, and became a collaborator and co-editor of the *Historical Dictionary of Philosophy (Historisches Wörterbuch der Philosophie)* and other lexical and philosophical-historical works. I now saw it as my task to make philosophy communicable in the diversity of its manifestations and effective in its spiritual leadership. A special opportunity for life effectiveness arose when, as a professor of philosophy, I was appointed director of the Teacher Training Institute in Basel. Now I could practice philosophy as a pedagogical enterprise, not only in theory but also in practice.

It was only in this way that I realized the extent to which philosophy requires communication and is designed for communication. This insight led me back to Jaspers. In his philosophizing I began to see everything that had become important to me in the meantime: the Kierkegaardian motif of existential seriousness, but also the breadth of his philosophizing, trained by Kant, which leaves nothing out and tries to understand and examine even the most remote thoughts. This is done with the help of the logical means that have been developed in philosophy over the centuries, and which in turn are subject to the methodical requirement of becoming aware of what one is doing with each mental step.

In this new openness to Jaspers' philosophizing, it took little persuasion when Hans Saner asked me to support him in his Jaspers projects. I became a member and soon, as Reiner Wiehl's successor, also president of the Karl Jaspers Foundation. When Hans Saner's intellectual powers were already beginning to decline, we were still able to initiate the large-scale project of an Annotated Complete Edition of the Works of Karl Jaspers, which is now being realized by the Academies of Science in Heidelberg and Göttingen at the University of Heidelberg since 2012 and at the University of Oldenburg since 2016. The conferences organized by the Foundation brought me into contact with Jaspers scholars from the various national Jaspers Societies in Europe, the USA and Japan. An indispensable companion for me was Kurt Salamun, who with his Jaspers monograph and as president of the Austrian Karl Jaspers Society with his yearbooks published since 1988 has probably made the greatest contribution to Jaspers research in Europe, along with Hans Saner.

However, research on Jaspers has now received a decisive boost with the start of the Complete Edition. On behalf of the Jaspers Foundation, Georg Hartmann spent many years meticulously processing and archiving Karl Jaspers' estate, which had been handed over to the German Literature Archive in Marbach by Hans Saner. His numerous finds from the estate have become a new and indispensable source for all further research. The workshops and discussions in connection with the edition were equally valuable to me. They allowed a close exchange with the volume's editors, who have become true experts: Dirk Fonfara, Oliver Immel, Dominic Kaegi, Bernd Weidmann, and once again Georg Hartmann. My special thanks go to them, but no less to my colleagues on the Board of Trustees, who took on the role of working group leaders in the editorial work: in Heidelberg Thomas Fuchs and Jens Halfwassen, who unfortunately passed away all too soon, and his successor Markus Enders, and in Oldenburg Reinhard Schulz.

Thanks to this continuous dialogue with the Jaspers scholars mentioned here by name, and with many unnamed colleagues who would also deserve to be mentioned, I believe that I have gradually come to understand better what Jaspers was trying to say. In my own lectures and articles, and in the conference proceedings that I have edited, I have tried to make my understanding understandable to others. This book is an attempt to synthesize these various attempts and to recall Jaspers' philosophy in its entirety for myself and thus for my readers. Ultimately, however, it is not about me and my relationship to Jaspers, as this personal preface might suggest. I would not have undertaken this work if I were not convinced that Jaspers' thought has not only not lost its relevance for today's world, but that it is especially necessary in view of today's global, but increasingly uncommunicative communication. Of course, certain contents of Jaspers' work may be time-bound, but what remains indispensable for the future is the attitude expressed in his philosophizing: his honesty and his unconditional will to truthful communication.

No book without a publisher to bring it to the public. So I am grateful to Bloomsbury and the former Lexington publishers for their belief in this book, to my editor, Jana Hodges-Kluck, for her understanding and patience with my many requests for deadline extensions, and last but not least, to Crystal Branson and Anjaly George, who were in charge of its completion and production.

Writing for an English-speaking audience has been no small challenge. It begins with Jaspers' idiosyncratic terminology, which is not easy to convey even to a German-speaking audience; it continues with his abstract writing style, which offers little opportunity for visualization and leaves it to the reader to fill in and concretize the content, and it leads to the main obstacle: as someone who is not socialized in the English language, making a writing and thinking that is tied in a special way to the German language comprehensible to an English-speaking audience. Thanks to the intensive dialogue with deepL, I hope to have produced a text that, at least linguistically, does not cause too much offence. Filiz Peach, as a thorough reader familiar with Jaspers, has tried to protect me from many terminological and other errors. I would like to thank her for this.

# Abbreviations

## *(Letters Concern the German Edition)*

A — *Antwort. Zur Kritik meiner Schrift "Wohin treibt die Bundesrepublik?"* München: Piper, 1967.
*The Future of Germany. Selection.* Translated by E. B. Ashton with a Foreword by Hannah Arendt. Chicago, IL; London: University of Chicago Press, 1967.

AB — *Die Atombombe und die Zukunft des Menschen. Politisches Bewußtsein in unserer Zeit.* München: Piper, 1958.- 6. Aufl. Neuausgabe München, Zürich: Piper, 1982.
*The Future of Mankind.* Translated by E. B. Ashton. Chicago, IL: The University of Chicago Press, 1961.

AnPo — *Aneignung und Polemik. Gesammelte Reden und Aufsätze zur Geschichte der Philosophie*, edited by Hans Saner. München: Piper 1968.

AP — *Allgemeine Psychopathologie. Ein Leitfaden für Studierende, Ärzte und Psychologen.* Berlin: Springer, 1913. - 4. völlig neu bearb. Aufl. Berlin; Heidelberg: Springer, 1964.
*General Psychopathology*. Translated from the Germans 7th Edition by Julius Hoenig and Marian W. Hamilton. Manchester: Manchester University Press, 1962. Toronto: University of Toronto Press, 1963. Chicago, IL: University of Chicago Press, 1968. Baltimore, MD: Johns Hopkins University Press, 1997.

Ant — «Antwort.» In: *Karl Jaspers*, herausgegeben von Paul A. Schilpp, 750–853. Stuttgart: Kohlhammer, 1957.
«Reply to my Critics.» Translated from the original German by Paul Arthur Schilpp and Ludwig B. Lefebre. In *The Philosophy of Karl Jaspers*, 747–869.

Aut “«Philosophische Autobiographie.” In *Karl Jaspers*, herausgegeben von Paul A. Schilpp, 1–80. Stuttgart: Kohlhammer, 1957. Erweiterte Neuausgabe, München 1970.

Philosophical Autobiography. From the original German manuscript translated by Paul Arthur Schilpp and Ludwig B. Lefebre. In: *The Philosophy of Karl Jaspers*. Edited by Paul Arthur Schilpp. (La Salle, IL: Open Court Publishing Company, 1974). 1–94. Enlarged with a New Section on Heidegger in the second edition (La Salle, IL: Open Court Publishing Company, 1981).

ChT *Chiffern der Transzendenz*, edited by Anton Hügli and Hans Saner. Basel: Schwabe 2011.

De *Descartes und die Philosophie*. Leipzig: de Gruyter, 1946, 4. Aufl. Berlin, 1966.

E *Erinnerungen an Karl Jaspers*, edited by Klaus Piper and Hans Saner. München: Piper, 1974.

Einf *Einführung in die Philosophie. Zwölf Radiovorträge*. Zürich: Artemis, 1950.- München: Piper, 1953. Neuausgabe München: Piper, 1971.

*Way to Wisdom*. Translated by Ralph Manheim. London: Gollancz, and New Haven, CT: Yale University Press, 1951.

Ent *Die Frage der Entmythologisierung*. Karl Jaspers, Rudolf Bultmann. München: Piper, 1954. - Neuausgabe mit einer Einführung von Heinrich Ott, München; Zürich: Piper, 1981.

*Myth and Christianity. An Inquiry into the Possibility of Religion without Myth*. Karl Jaspers, Rudolf Bultmann. Translated by Norbert Guterman. New York: Noonday Press, 1958.

Ex *Existenzphilosophie. Drei Vorlesungen*. Berlin, Leipzig: de Gruyter, 1938. - 4. Aufl. Berlin; New York 1974. Neue kommentierte Ausgabe, edited by Dominic Kaegi, in: *Schriften zur Existenzphilosophie*, 99–160. Karl Jaspers Gesamtausgabe I/8. Basel: Schwabe, 2018.

*Philosophy of Existence*. Translated and with an Introduction by Richard F. Grabau. (Editor’s note: John R. Silver). Philadelphia, PA: University of Pennsylvania Press, Oxford: Blackwell, 1971.

FW *Freiheit und Wiedervereinigung. Über Aufgaben deutscher Politik*. München: Piper, 1960. Neuausgabe mit einem Vorwort von Willy Brandt, München; Zürich 1960.

GP *Die großen Philosophen. Erster Band*. München: Piper, 1957. Neuausgabe München; Zürich: Piper, 1988. Neue kommentierte Ausgabe, edited by Dirk Fonfara, Karl Jaspers Gesamtausgabe I/15.1, 15.2, Basel: Schwabe, 2022.

*The Great Philosophers*. The Foundations. The Paradigmatic Individuals: Socrates, Buddha, Confucius, Jesus. The Seminal Founders of Philosophical Thought: Plato, Augustine, Kant. Edited by Hannah Arendt. Translated by Ralph Manheim. New York: Harcourt, Brace & World, and London: Hart-Davis, 1962.
*The Great Philosophers*. The Original Thinkers: Anaximander, Heraclitus. Parmenides, Plotinus, Anselm, Nicholas of Casa, Spinoza, Lao-Tzu, Nagarjuna. Edited by Hannah Arendt. Translated by Ralph Manheim. New York: Harcourt, Brace & World, and London: Hart-Davis, 1966.

Selected chapters of these two volumes are also published as:

*Anaximander, Heraclitus, Parmenides, Plotinus, Lao-tzu, Nagarjuna*. New York: Harcourt, Brace, Jovanovich, 1974.
*Anselm and Nicholas of Cusa*. New York: Harcourt, Brace, Jovanovich, 1974.
*Kant*. New York: Harcourt, Brace and World, 1962.
*Plato and Augustine*. New York: Harcourt, Brace & World, 1962.
*Socrates, Buddha, Confucius, Jesus*. New York: Harcourt, Brace, Jovanovich, 1990.
*Spinoza*. New York: Harcourt, Brace, Jovanovich, 1974.

GPN 1 *Die großen Philosophen. Nachlaß 1*: *Darstellungen und Fragmente, edited by* Hans Saner. Unter Mitarbeit von Raphael Bielander. München; Zürich: Piper, 1981.

GPN 22 *Die grossen Philosophen. Nachlass* : *Fragmente, Anmerkungen, Inventar,* edited by Hans Saner. München; Zürich: Piper, 1981.
*The Great Philosophers.* Volume 3: Xenophanes, Democritus, Empedocles, Bruno, Epicurus, Boehme, Schelling, Leibniz, Aristotle, Hegel. Edited by Michael Ermarth and Leonard H. Ehrlich. Translated by Edith Ehrlich and Leonard H. Ehrlich. Foreword by Michael Ermarth. New York; San Diego, CA; London: Harcourt Brace & Company, 1993.
*The Great Philosophers*. Volume 4: The Disturbers. Descartes, Pascal, Lessing, Kierkegaard, Nietzsche. Philosophers on Other Realms. Einstein, Weber, Marx. Edited by Michael Ermarth and Leonard Ehrlich. Foreword by Michael Ermarth. New York; San Diego, CA; London: Harcourt Brace & Company, 1994.

GPhil *Grundsätze des Philosophierens,* edited by Bernd Weidmann, Karl Jaspers Gesamtausgabe, II/1, Basel: Schwabe, 2019.

GSZ *Die geistige Situation der Zeit.* Berlin: de Gruyter, 1931.—13. Aufl. 1979.

HS *Hoffnung und Sorge. Schriften zur deutschen Politik 1945–1965.* München: Piper, 1965.

IU *Die Idee der Universität.* Berlin: Springer, 1923.—Neufassung 1946 und (mit Kurt Rossmann) 1961. Berlin; Göttingen; Heidelberg: Springer, 1961.
Neue kommentierte Ausgabe, edited by Oliver Immel, in: *Schriften zur Universitätsidee*, Karl Jaspers Gesamtausausgabe I/21, Basel: Schwabe, 2016.
*The Idea of the University.* Edited by Karl W. Deutsch. Preface by Robert Ulich. Translated by Harold A. T. Reiche and H. F. Vanderschmidt. Boston, MA: Beacon Press, 1959.

KlSch *Kleine Schule des philosophischen Denkens.* München: Piper, 1965.
*Philosophy is for Everyman: A Short Course in Philosophical Thinking.* Translated by Richard F. C. Hull and Grete Wels. New York: Harcourt, Brace & World, 1967.

MW *Max Weber. Deutsches Wesen im politischen Denken, im Forschen und Philosophieren.* Oldenburg: Stalling, 1932.- 2. Aufl. unter dem Titel: *Max Weber. Politiker, Forscher, Philosoph.* Bremen: Storm, 1946. Mit einem neuen Vorwort München: Piper, 1958.
*Max Weber as Politician, Scientist, Philosopher.* Translated by Ralph Manheim. In: *Karl Jaspers: Three Essays.* Leonardo, Descartes, Max Weber (New York: Harcourt, Brace & World, 1964), pp. 187–274.
*Max Weber: Politician, Scientist, Philosopher (1932).* Translated from the German by Robert J. Whelan. In *On Max Weber.* New York: Paragon House, 1989, 29–135.

N *Nietzsche. Einführung in das Verständnis seines Philosophierens.* Berlin; Leipzig: de Gruyter, 1936.—4. Aufl. Berlin; New York 1981.
Neue kommentierte Ausgabe, edited by Dominic Kaegi und Andreas Urs Sommer, in Karl Jaspers Gesamtausgabe I/18. Basel: Schwabe, 2020.
*Nietzsche: An Introduction to the Understanding of His Philosophical Activity.* Translated by Charles F. Wallraff and Frederick J. Schmitz. Tucson, AZ: University of Arizona Press, 1965.

NPL *Nachlaß zur Philosophischen Logik.* Herausgegeben von Hans Saner and Marc Hänggi. München; Zürich: Piper, 1991.

PGO *Der philosophische Glaube angesichts der Offenbarung.* München: Piper, 1962.—3. Aufl. München; Zürich: Piper, 1984.
Neue kommentierte Ausgabe, edited by Bernd Weidmann, in: Karl Jaspers Gesamtausgabe I/13. Basel: Schwabe, 2016.

PA *Philosophische Aufsätze.* Hamburg: Fischer, 1967.

Ph *Philosophie.* 3 Bde. (Bd. I: *Philosophische Weltorientierung.* Bd. II: *Existenzerhellung.* Bd. III. *Metaphysik.)* Berlin: Springer, 1932.—4. Aufl. 1973.
Neue kommentierte Ausgabe, ediert von Oliver Immel: Karl Jaspers Gesamtausgabe I/7.1/7.2 /7.3. Basel: Schwabe, 2022.

*Philosophy*. 3 vols. Translated by E. B. Ashton. Vol. 1: Introduction to Philosophy/Philosophical World Orientation, 1969, vol. 2: Existential Elucidation, 1970, vol. 3: Metaphysics, 1971. Chicago, IL and London: University of Chicago Press, 1969–1971.

PG *Der philosophische Glaube*. Zürich: Artemis, 1948.—6. Aufl. Neuausgabe. München: Piper, 1974.
Neue kommentierte Ausgabe, edited by Bernd Weidmann, Karl Jaspers Gesamtausgabe, I/12. Basel: Schwabe, 2022, 9–108.
*The Perennial Scope of Philosophy*. Translated by Ralph Manheim. New York: Philosophical Library, 1949 and London: Routledge & Kegan Paul, 1950.

PW *Die Psychologie der Weltanschauungen*. Berlin: Springer, 1919.—6. Aufl. Berlin; Heidelberg; New York: Springer 1971. *Psychology of Worldviews*. Paperback-Ausgaben nach der 6. Aufl.: München; Zürich: Piper, 1990 und 1994.
Neue kommentierte Ausgabe, edited by Oliver Immel: Karl Jaspers Gesamtausgabe I/6, Basel: Schwabe, 2019.

PhW *Philosophie und Welt. Reden und Aufsätze*. München: Piper, 1958.
*Philosophy and The World: Selected Essays and Lectures*. Translated by E. B. Ashton. Chicago, IL: Henry Regnery Co., 1963, Reprint 1989.

Prov *Provokationen. Gespräche und Interviews*. Edited by Hans Saner. München: Piper, 1969.

Sch *Schelling. Größe und Verhängnis*. München: Piper, 1955. Neuausgabe. München; Zürich: Piper, 1986.
SchW *Schicksal und Wille. Autobiographische Schriften*. Edited by Hans Saner. München: Piper, 1967.

UZG *Vom Ursprung und Ziel der Geschichte*. Zürich: Artemis, und München: Piper, 1949.—8. Aufl. Neuausgabe. München: Piper, 1983.
Neue kommentierte Ausgabe, edited by Kurt Salamun, in: Karl Jaspers Gesamtausgabe, I/10, Basel: Schwabe, 2017.
*The Origin and Goal of History*. Translated from the German by Michael Bullock. New Haven, CT: Yale University Press, and London: Routledge and Kegan Paul, 1953.

VE *Vernunft und Existenz. Fünf Vorlesungen*. Groningen: Wolters, 1935.—5. Aufl. und Neuausgabe. München: Piper, 1973.
Neue kommentierte Ausgabe, edited by Dominic Kaegi, in *Schriften zur Existenzphilosophie*, Karl Jaspers Gesamtausgabe I/8, Basel: Schwabe, 2018, 3-98.
*Reason and Existence*. Translated with an introduction by William Earle. London; Toronto; New York: Noonday Press, 1955, Routledge & Kegan Paul, 1956.

VuD *Vom unabhängigen Denken. Hannah Arendt und ihre Kritiker. Nachgelassene Fragment,* edited by Georg Hartmann, Karl Jaspers Gesamtausgabe, II/6. Basel: Schwabe, 2022.

VÜK *Ausgewählte Verlags- und Übersetzerkorrespondenzen,* edited by Dirk Fonfara, Karl Jaspers Gesamtausgabe III/8.1, 8.2, Basel: Schwabe, 2018.

VWZ *Vernunft und Widervernunft in unserer Zeit. Drei Gastvorlesungen.* München: Piper, 1950.—3. Aufl. Neuausgabe München: Piper, 1990.

W *Von der Wahrheit. Philosophische Logik. Erster Band.* München: Piper, 1947.—4. Aufl. Neuausgabe. München; Zürich: Piper, 1991.
*Tragedy is not Enough.* Translated by Harold A. T. Reiche, Harry T. Moore, and Karl W. Deutsch. The Bibliography, Notes and Index were prepared by Harold A. T. Reiche. Boston, MA: Beacon Press, 1952 and London: Gollancz, 1953.
*Truth and Symbol.* From Von der Wahrheit. Translated with an Introduction by by Jean T. Wilde, William Kluback and William Kimmel. New York: Twayne Publishers, and London: Vision Press, 1959.

WErz *Was ist Erziehung? ein Lesebuch.* Herausgegeben von Hermann Horn. München; Zürich: Piper, 1977. 3. Aufl. München 1982.- Neuausgabe 1992.

WF *Das Wagnis der Freiheit. Gesammelte Aufsätze zur Philosophie,* edited by Hans Saner. München; Zürich: Piper, 1996.

WGP *Weltgeschichte der Philosophie. Einleitung,* edited by Hans Saner. *World History of Philosophy.* München, Zürich: Piper, 1982.

## CORRESPONDENCE

BJA *Hannah Arendt/Karl Jaspers: Briefwechsel 1926–1969,* edited by Lotte Köhler und Hans Saner. München; Zürich: Piper, 1985.
*Hannah Arendt, Karl Jaspers. Correspondence 1926–1969.* Edited by Lotte Köhler und Hans Saner. Translated from the German by Robert and Rita Kimber. New York; San Diego, CA; London: Harcourt, Brace, Jovanovich, 1993.

KorrPhil
Korrespondenzen Philosophie, edited by Dominic Kaegi and Reiner Wiehl. Göttingen: Wallstein, 2016.

# Introduction

## WHAT IT SHOULD BE ABOUT

Communication tools and channels are multiplying daily and worldwide. Never before in the history of mankind have there been so many ways to connect with other people as there are today. However, it seems that the willingness to talk and listen to each other has never been as low as it is today. It is not only the connection between the living that is in danger of breaking down but also the communication with the history of mankind, with the dead that has been cast into the sea. People insist on their unquestionable opinions, plunge into irrational delusions, and wage a campaign of destruction against all those who disagree. The inability to communicate extends to all areas of life: from the realm of public services, vaccination or non-vaccination, for example, to social and political problems, to ideological and religious questions. In any case, it seems hopeless to ever reach an understanding on these issues. They open up not only rifts but also chasms.

This lack of communication is more detrimental than all the other dangers that threaten humanity today because it is driving forward every other disaster that hangs over humanity like a portent; first and foremost, climate change, the loss of biodiversity, and the danger of humanity's nuclear self-destruction, which has not been averted for a long time. For how are we to counter these dangers if we cannot talk to each other and form a common will?

*The question of all questions is, therefore: Is global understanding possible at all? If so, under what conditions? And in what ways?*

This question lies beyond the horizon of any science. Whoever tries to answer it will always be confronted with another, even deeper question, the question of what kind of beings we humans are, and what is and what is not possible for us. This is a philosophical question. Not just one among others, but the question in which all philosophical questions converge. Among contemporary philosophers, there is one in particular who has linked the question of what it means to be a human being with the question of the possibility of communication: Karl Jaspers. He suffered more than any other philosopher from the lack of communication. For him, the will to communicate became a driving force behind his philosophizing, and making communication possible became the goal of his philosophical work. As a result, he enabled us to sharpen our awareness of the extent to which communication has been part of philosophy from the very beginning: in that philosophy urges to communicate, wants to express itself, and wants to be heard.[1]

Even if we do not know where it will lead us when we engage with Jaspers's philosophy, we can at least expect that our efforts might be worthwhile in exploring his valuable insights. We may feel like Jeanne Hersch after her first Jaspers lecture: "I understood nothing," but I understood "that there was something to understand here."[2] The aim of this book is to set out on a journey of understanding together with the reader.[3] The main text is aimed at readers who—with or without prior philosophical knowledge—are prepared to engage with philosophical thought processes. These should be understandable and comprehensible on their own without having to look up every second word in encyclopedias or consult works on the history of philosophy and be constantly reminded of one's own lack of knowledge. In the endnotes, those familiar with Jaspers should be shown on the one hand why Jaspers can certainly be understood in the way he is presented in the main text, and on the other hand what his sources are and where there are connections to other authors.[4] To deepen the understanding, however, the text itself also refers here and there to authors who were influential for Jaspers, in particular Kant and Kierkegaard, Plato and Plotinus.

When reading the book, the reader may notice that certain themes recur throughout the book. However, these are not repetitions but new perspectives on earlier themes that arise from new approaches and new contexts. A circle, as it were, that spirals into ever greater depths of thought.

## THE WILL TO UNDERSTAND AND TO BE UNDERSTOOD

Communication begins when we feel addressed and try to meet that demand.[5] We can also be addressed by a face, a gesture, or a landscape, but being addressed is only a metaphor for the claim that one person makes on another. For man, at least according to one of his oldest definitions, is distinguished from all other living beings by the fact that he has language and can speak (*zoon logon echon*). Of course, there are ways of understanding that are not on the linguistic level, such as understanding feelings, intentions, moods, physiognomies, and the like. But let us focus on linguistic understanding for now, that is, understanding what is written or said. And to begin with, let us leave aside the question that will still occupy us: Can we understand anything at all—be it already verbalized or non-verbalized—if we cannot say what we have understood?

The ability to understand presupposes *the will* to understand and to be understood. Everything else depends on this condition, and it, in turn, depends on the very first condition: that we allow ourselves to be addressed at all, that is, that the person addressing us is not indifferent to us but *is* significant and important. If we cannot understand each other, it may simply be that we do not want to understand each other. But assuming that we do want to understand each other, what else could prevent us from doing so?

Of course, at this point, we could list all the sources of misunderstanding and incomprehension that actually exist: that we live in different worlds, that we do not speak the same language or speak unclearly, that we have not listened carefully, that we give different meanings to words, that we are not talking about one and the same thing but about different things or contradicting each other, and so on. Suppose, however, that all these barriers to understanding had been removed, that the communicator had said everything he wanted to say, and that the receiver had understood everything that was said, that is, the communication had been successful. Could we then say that all that needs to be said has been said, and all that needs to be understood has been understood? That may well be true. But the important question is: Are there things that cannot be communicated—not just for external reasons, but in general?

The thesis that there are such things has a long and venerable tradition. Mysticism and *Negative Theology* have always proclaimed that God has neither a name nor attributes, and that He transcends all understanding. He is incomprehensible, inconceivable, inexpressible, and therefore incommunicable. Just when the will to communicate is at its greatest, we realize that what we want to communicate cannot be communicated. But God was not the only one of whom this was claimed to be true. Since the eighteenth century at the latest, at least since Herder—although it cannot be traced back to him—people speak of the individual as *ineffable*, as inexpressible and unspeakable. Goethe thought he could derive a world from this word[6] and Schiller translated it into the verse: "When the soul speaks, ah! the soul no longer speaks."[7] In the spirit of this Schiller quote, the non-communicability thesis has been and continues to be advocated in a wide variety of philosophical camps, from Schopenhauer and Bergson to Moritz Schlick and the Wittgenstein of the *Tractatus*.[8] In the tradition of *Negative Theology*, as we shall see, Jasper himself stands explicitly, and in the second tradition, at least implicitly. But even the thesis that there is something incommunicable needs to be understood first.

How do we even know that there is such a thing as the unspeakable? On the one hand, we would have to know that this unspeakable X exists at all, and on the other hand, that not only up to now but—in principle—also in the future, it will never be possible to say what it is. In this respect, it would be different from all the other things that are assumed to exist, but of which we do not know what they really are, such as quarks and black holes, or the Loch Ness monster.

The very categorization itself, that it should be noncommunicable, sounds paradoxical. Because at least this seems to be expressible: that it is not expressible. And in order to know what we are talking about, we have to be able to identify the incommunicable in some way, be it with a name, a label, or a way of pointing, either linguistically or with linguistic analogies.

Should we not rather say that whatever exists, whether it is real, possible, or impossible, whether it is expressible or not, exists for us at least in language? In this sense, everything is in language, and where language ends, our world ends. But language never ends, for where is its limit? It is like the endless horizons of the sea: behind each horizon, there is another horizon. The present horizon is that which has already been spoken, but behind and beyond it lies the space into which no language has yet penetrated: the space of the unspoken, the space not yet shared. But is this space really unlimited?

Even if it is true that everything that exists *for us* is in language, it is also true that language is not everything that exists. Language is not a closed universe; it has an open side, toward what we call reality. The window to reality opens with every sentence that does not itself refer to words and sentences but to the world of things that are independent of us, that support us, and whose resistance we encounter. Whenever we try to say what these things are like, we open the window to reality. It is nothing more than an attempt. The fact that things are not always what we think they are is a fundamental experience in dealing with language. We can be deceived, and we are deceived.

When we make statements, the question always arises: Are we really saying how things are? Is what we say true? In the case of truthful communication that is not based on deception, we claim to say what is true. Or at least, since we can always deceive ourselves, we claim to say what we believe to be true. This modified claim shifts from what a person says to how he or she relates to us—and to themselves: Whether they are being truthful (to us and to themselves). Whoever seriously wants to communicate can only do so with the will to be truthful and with the expectation that the other person wants to be truthful as well.

This already indicates why it might be crucial for communication to turn to a philosophy that, like the existential philosophy of Karl Jaspers, centers on the question of the Self: What kind of person do I want to be?

## NOTES

1. Cf. Einf 18–27, Ph 2, 55.

2. Jeanne Hersch, "Karl Jaspers als Lehrer," in *Erinnerungen an Karl Jaspers*, ed. Klaus Piper, Hans Saner (München; Zürich: Piper 1974), 60.

3. This book aims to introduce the reader to the philosophical thought of Karl Jaspers, but it does not contain an account of Jaspers's life and work. Anyone looking for such an account is referred to the relevant monographs of Hans Saner (*Jaspers,* (Reinbek: Rowohlt, 1970)) and Kurt Salamun (*Karl Jaspers. Physicist, Psychologist, Philosopher, Political Thinker* (Berlin: Palgrave Macmillan (Springer), 2022)) or the lexical overview by Anton Hügli ("Jaspers, Karl (1883–1969)," in *Bloomsbury Philosophy Library,* 2020. (https://www.bloomsburyphilosophylibrary.com/article?docid=b-9781350962200&tocid=b-9781350962200-0007&st=Karl+Jaspers)).

4. There is no such thing as a Jaspers's philosophy; there is only a Jaspers philosophizing. Therefore, you can start at any point and make it the center temporarily. (Jaspers calls this *Standpoint Mobility (Standpunkt Verschieblichkeit*). It is the same procedure that Hans Saner (*Kant's Weg vom Krieg zum Frieden,* Bd. I: Konflikt und Einheit. Wege zu Kants politischem Denken (München: Piper, 1967), 32) chose for his Kant book and is therefore praised by Jaspers. See VuD, 122f.: Jaspers quotes Hans Saner:

> The interpretation is based on: "the scheme of an infinite process towards a goal, which is set in the idea, that is driven towards the goal through the medium of resistance. Since this process is infinite, any point in it can become the center (. . .) Kant as a thinker is infinite process, not one of its static points. Inquiry must be allowed to make each of the static points the center, the early Kant of physics as well as that of the critique of the opus postumum."

5. To allow oneself to be addressed is a demand that runs through Jaspers's work. He is therefore suspicious of the *ataraxia* sought by the Stoics, the imperturbability of the soul, which is based precisely on remaining indifferent to what affects us. The flip side of this attitude is vulnerability: to be affected not only by what happens to me but also by all those whose fate I allow to affect me.

6. Johann Wolfgang von Goethe, "An Lavater" (20. 9. 1780), in *Gedenk-Ausgabe*, ed. Ernst Beutler, Bd. 18 (Zürich: Artemis, 1977), 533.

7. Friedrich Schiller, "Musenalmanach für das Jahr 1797," Nr. 84, in *National-Ausgabe*, Bd. 1, 302.

8. More about this: Anton Hügli, "Mitteilung, Mitteilbarkeit, indirekte Mitteilung," in: *Historisches Wörterbuch der Philosophie*, Bd. 5 (Basel: Schwabe, 1980), 1424–1431, 1430/31.

# Chapter 1

# A First Approach to Karl Jaspers

## THE INDISPENSABILITY OF COMMUNICATION FOR THOSE WHO WANT TRUTH

Why the need to claim truth for oneself and for others? In the struggle for existence, it can certainly be advantageous to evade this claim, to deceive others in order to assert one's own interests and to conceal reality. The necessity of insisting on the claim to truth becomes apparent only when we seriously want to know what is really true. For there is only one way to test whether what we believe to be true is true: by measuring our judgment against that of others.[1] This requires us to state what we believe to be true and why we believe it to be true and to see if others can contradict us with good reasons, or point out things that we have overlooked or failed to notice or were not aware of. These others are not just those who happen to be available, but in principle anyone who can speak and understand—and who, like us, wants to know the truth. In fact, it should extend to everyone, present or absent, because there could still be someone who might come through the door and prove us wrong. This is the reason why, where the truth is important to us, we demand publicity for our judgments. Anyone who wants to should be able to answer. Therefore, anyone who wants to should have the opportunity to learn about my judgment. What has not yet been falsified can be considered to be true. This is true even if we refer to direct perception and our own experience. As soon as we try to communicate what we have experienced or perceived, what we have directly experienced or perceived becomes indirect or communicable and, like everything that is communicated, is in need of verification. Everything so-called given, everything factual is, as Goethe says, already theory.

It is a necessary condition for the examination of truth that those to whom I submit my judgment for examination are themselves truly seekers of truth. As seekers of truth, we cannot exist without communication with other seekers of truth. The will to truth drives us toward one another. This does not mean that what everyone believes to be true must be true, because we could all be wrong. It simply means what has become a core principle of Jaspers's philosophizing: No truth without communication. Truth, according to Nietzsche's sentence often quoted by Jaspers, begins with twos. What unites them is the solidarity of those who seek the truth. It is not the only kind of solidarity between people, but it is essential for any other kind of solidarity. It also leads us best to the center of Jaspers's philosophizing.

The most painful experience for those who seek the truth is when the other person withdraws or stops communicating, either because he is not interested in the truth or because he believes he already has the truth. This is the deepest divide between people: the divide between those who want the truth and those who do not. It is this divide that is so noticeable today. The category of those who do not want the truth includes not only the bullshitters who simply talk as they go along, regardless of what is true and what is not true, but also those for whom the only thing that counts as true is what benefits their interests or the interests of the power on whose side they stand, be it the party, the state, or whoever.

The solidarity of those who are willing to seek the truth is a very abstract form of solidarity. In it, the other appears only in one way: as a mirror of reality, as a consciousness that focuses on the objects of this world and tries to grasp them, just as I do. The less this consciousness is clouded by the subjectivity of the individual, by sympathies and antipathies, by prejudices, idiosyncrasies, and the like, the more suitable it is as a mirror of reality. What we seek in our search for truth is the universally valid truth that applies to all, as it is imposed on us by empirical facts and the stringency of logic, reflected in an impersonal consciousness that is identical for all. We, as cognizant subjects, are then, ideally, no more than a thinking ego, purified of all individual differences of feeling, sensation, and thought.

Like Kant, Jaspers too, calls the state of consciousness of such a subject reduced to cognition—*Consciousness in General (Bewußtsein überhaupt). Consciousness in General* is the mode to which we aspire as soon as we are awake. For if we want to know how things are—whether it was a train that just passed by or just a noise in my dream—we have to make them the object of our thought and cognition in the mode of *Consciousness in General*. Terminologically, this focusing of consciousness on an object is called *Intentionality*. The intentional relation between thought and object is unique, radically different from any other relation in the world, be it causal, logical, instrumental, or whatever. It is as if we were looking at the world together from a placeless point. The view from nowhere, as the American philosopher

Thomas Nagel has called it.[2] This image, however, only hides the puzzle we are facing here.

The more we think about the relationship of *Consciousness in General* to the objects of our thought, the clearer it becomes what was already hinted at in the discussion of the relationship between language and reality. The object to which we are directed from the perspective of *Consciousness in General* becomes an object that is separate from us, a counterpart that is alien to us. What we grasp is merely the way it appears to us—under this distanced gaze. It is as if there is a great divide running through the world: here is *Consciousness in General*—there is everything that can become its object, such as the realities of our sensory world, the contents of our thoughts and fantasies, as well as ideal objects, numbers, for example, or geometric shapes. And the one is never without the other: No consciousness without an object to which it is directed, no object that would not be an object for a consciousness, in short: no subject without an object and no object without a subject.

Jaspers calls this basic finding of our thinking existence the *Subject-Object-Split (Subjekt-Objekt-Spaltung)*. It is also commonly referred to as the *Subject-Object-Relation*. The crucial idea for Jaspers is that in this relationship the object is always meant as an object that is different from the subject, as something other than itself. This creates a split. He describes it in part as follows: "That which we think, of which we speak, is always other than ourselves, is that to which we, the subjects, are directed as to an opposite, the objects."[3] When we make ourselves the object of our thinking, we divide ourselves; we are an object and at the same time a thinking ego that carries out this thinking, but can never become an object itself, because it is always the precondition of every becoming-object.[4] Whenever we are awake and conscious, this split is there. According to Jaspers, the realization of this enigmatic phenomenon is one of the most momentous philosophical discoveries of all time. It can be found in Indian and Chinese thought as well as in Greek thought, but it was Kant who brought it to complete clarity.

The *Subject-Object-Split* is accompanied by a second split. Every object we think of is distinct from that which does not belong to that object but is related to it. What we can think is therefore always particular, never everything at once, never a whole that does not have another whole opposite to it. Even when we try to think of Being as such, we still separate it from Non-Being. In other words, we can only think in terms of distinctions: here instead of there, left instead of right, this instead of that, form instead of matter, identity instead of contradiction, and so on. The world as it appears to us has, as Jaspers says, an *Antinomic Structure*.

What do these divisions mean in terms of the will to communicate? They confront us with the fact that we can never say what the total Being is. Whatever we call this ultimate Being, whether we say it is matter or energy or life or spirit, it is always something particular within the whole of Being, but not *Being itself*. Even the *World*, as the epitome of the objects of our cognition, cannot be the ultimate whole, because something always remains outside of it: the thinking ego that makes the world its object. But even this thinking ego cannot be the last being, because the world continues to exist as that with which the thinking ego is confronted. The thought of the *World* as a whole is not already the *World* itself; in this thought, too, there is the contrast between the one who thinks and the content of the thought. Only that which simultaneously embraces both sides of this division, the *World* and the thinking ego, can be truly comprehensive. Jaspers logically calls this being the *Encompassing (das Umgreifende).*

But the paradox of the concept of *Encompassing* is that although we can think of it, we can never say what it actually is. The history of philosophical thought knows innumerable names for the *Encompassing*: the Primordial, the First, the Real Being, the Divine, but these are only names that say nothing and always fail to denote what they seek to denote. For as soon as we try to define the *Encompassing*, distinctions come into play again; the *Encompassing* is again delimited from that which it is not, and as such is no longer the *Encompassing*. This is the painful experience of the mystic. He may succeed in overcoming the *Subject-Object-Split* and experience in the *unio mystica* that complete unification of subject and object in which the ego is extinguished, everything objective disappears, and he sinks into the *Encompassing*. He can experience this sinking as if he were only now fully awake, and as if what we call wakefulness, the life in the *Subject-Object-Split*, was like a deep sleep. But when, after returning to the state of consciousness, the mystic tries to say what he has experienced, he lacks the words or has too many, because no word can reach the point where he found himself.

Considerations such as these, with which we try to approach the idea of the Encompassing—Jaspers calls them the *Basic Operation (Grundoperation)*—make us aware of the boundary that insurmountably surrounds us and in which we are trapped. To reach this limit, however, we need the radical will to abandon all knowledge of objective realities and to penetrate to the point where there is nothing more to recognize and know. This is the attitude with which philosophy begins: to be able to distinguish between what one knows and what one cannot know. Philosophy, one might say, begins with the knowledge of the difference between knowing and not knowing. It is boundary consciousness.

Boundary consciousness can fundamentally transform us. What we take to be the ultimate reality, the material, spatio-temporal world in which we live, is not *Being itself*. But *Being itself* is not another being that stands opposite this world as a second world, as dualistic thinking imagines the relationship between time and eternity. Rather, it is the primordial ground or background from which the phenomena of reality appear to us. As appearances, they are not illusory but the only way in which Being can show itself to us. For us, there is nothing other than these phenomena, and in this respect, we are and remain trapped in them. If we try to recognize more precisely what appearances we are dealing with and attempt to bring them to light even better, we never have anything other than mere appearances and never have Being as *Being itself.* Once we realize that we are always within Being and not somewhere outside of it as an observer, we also become aware that what exists is always more than what appears to us and what we can know—even the being that we ourselves are.

According to Jaspers, we are always more than we know and can know about ourselves. And this has unforeseen consequences. It is the best weapon against all assertions of the kind that man is *nothing more than*: nothing more than matter, than a neurophysiological system or than a product of evolution as some naturalistic philosophers suggest. All that the various human sciences, from biology and physiology to psychology and sociology, are able to grasp are always only particular manifestations of man, but never man himself. It is important to be aware of this limit of knowledge in today's world, which, blinded by the progress of science, all too easily falls prey to scientific superstition, the illusion that a scientific explanation already explains the human being as such, such as the brain mythology prevalent today, which knows only neurophysiological explanations for everything that moves in the human being.[5]

The fact that man is more than he can know about himself means that he cannot be explained by his history, by his biology, or by himself. He is rooted in a Being that encompasses and permeates him, and that must have its foundation in an even more comprehensive Being. And when he wonders what that Being is, he can only try to shed light on it from his position as a shut-in, just as the person trapped in the cave can only form an image of his position and the position of his cave from within. As philosophizing cave dwellers, however, we can try to capture in concepts what the *Encompassing* might be.

## THE IDEA OF THE ENCOMPASSING AND THE WAY WE BECOME AWARE OF WHAT IS

What is this encompassing *Being* from which and through which we exist? As soon as we try to determine it, we realize that the one thing we are trying to grasp is never one thing. Is that which encompasses us the cosmos, the *World*? Is it life, from which we also come? Is it society? Is it history? Consciousness? Instead of the one encompassing *Being*, we find ourselves in different *Modes of Being*. And we live in all of them simultaneously, but in different ways, depending on which of these *Modes of Being* dominates us. The dominant *Mode of Being* determines what we take to be true and how we communicate with each other. This is because each *Mode of Being* has a different concept of truth and a different form of communication. Whatever appears to us appears within the respective *Mode of Being*. It emerges from it, so to speak. In this sense, Jaspers's term for what is encompassing is also *Origin*. There are as many ways of grasping things as there are kinds of *Origins* from where we encounter things and out of which we live.[6]

The differences in the *Modes of Being* are evident in how we find ourselves in and become aware of the *Encompassing*. The most fundamental distinction is between the *Encompassing* that we ourselves are and the *Encompassing* that is not ourselves but the epitome of what surrounds us and what we call the *World*. The crucial difference between these *Modes of Being*: The *World* has no knowledge of itself; it does not know that it is and does not know what it is. There is knowledge of the *World* only to the extent that man recognizes it, that is, to the extent that the *World* penetrates and finds an echo in the *Encompassing* that man himself is.

According to an old metaphor, man is the mirror of the *World*. But this metaphor illuminates only one aspect, which is the split between the original and the reflection. It would be much more accurate to say that being in the *World* and being human are intertwined; man is in the *World* and can be nowhere else but in the *World*, and the *World* is in him. This means he himself is part of the *World*, and to the extent that he is aware of himself, he is also always aware of the *World* in which he finds himself. Therefore, the best way to access the different modes of *Encompassing* is to pay attention to the different modes of becoming aware and open up access to ourselves and to the World.

Becoming aware must be understood comprehensively here: as being conscious of what is. Consciousness is indispensable in every way of becoming aware. What does not enter consciousness is for us as if it were not. But this is not enough: there must be a correspondence between what is in consciousness and what consciousness is intentionally directed toward. I can only have become aware of a train passing by if a train actually passed by. The most general concept of such a correspondence is truth. The reference to truth is already evident in the word "becoming aware": I can only speak of becoming aware if what I perceive *is* actually (in truth) as I perceive it. But how does this correspondence come about?

One thing is certain: the correspondence between what is and what we "perceive" does not come about by itself; it requires an effort on the part of consciousness. The deceptive must be fended off, the unclear and confusing clarified, the indeterminate defined, the distant visualized. But this is only possible if there is a counter-movement, so to speak, on the side of *Being*:

what is must come to us, it must, to use another metaphor, step out of the hidden into the open and disclose itself. Truth, then, appears on the side of consciousness as evidence, and on the side of being as revelation—as *Unconcealment*, *aletheia*, as the Greek word for truth says.

These two movements, from consciousness to *Being* and from *Being* to consciousness, never occur separately. Neither is without the other. When we introspectively pay attention to what is happening to us, we realize that we experience ourselves either in the mode that we are active, that is, we are working toward something we are trying to achieve, or in the opposite mode, in which we encounter obstacles and resistance that stand in our way. This is true whether we are paying attention to internal processes, such as thinking or imagining, or whether we are responding to things or people in the external world.

Thus, we experience ourselves either as active, as the origin of activity, or as passive, as affected by the resistance of things. Because we experience ourselves in these two modes, we can also distinguish between what emanates from us and depends on us and only on us, and what happens to us and thus proves to be a reality independent of us.

In every awareness, there is always both the active and the passive. But activity precedes passivity: only by doing something can we experience resistance and make reality tangible. This interplay of activity and passivity also explains the difference between what we call objective and what we call subjective. Objective is the part of what we perceive that can be experienced in a passive mode. Subjective is the part that comes from our activity.

However, as far as our activity is concerned, the question is always in which direction we are moving: toward the truth by trying to bring in as much objectivity as possible, or away from the truth by becoming further entangled in errors and delusions. In order to become aware of reality, subjectivity and objectivity must find each other, just as a question ideally finds its answer. The question can come from both sides, the objective and the subjective. Asking questions is indeed an activity; it is the activity that stands at the beginning of all cognition. But every resistance it encounters (in the form of lack of an answer, for example) in turn becomes a question itself for the questioner as to how he wants to counteract this resistance. This is also the basic form of any communication: from speech and counter-speech to response to counter-speech and response to response, and so on.

This dialectic of question and answer shows that becoming aware is never a single, final event, but a process that (in principle) cannot be completed. And because we never know where we are in this process and in which direction we are heading, whether toward the true or even deeper into error and deception, the false is the constant companion of the true. Only one answer is true, but many are untrue. In struggling against the untrue, we need to find the one answer that is true, and we'll never get there, except in trivial cases. But to make sure that we are really moving toward this goal, we need to see if others want to join us on this journey. As long as I remain closed within myself, I will never know where I stand, but together with others, who are also willing to find the truth, I might. This is the point we were already at, and which is now becoming even clearer: *no truth without communication, without sharing what I believe to be true.*

The need to communicate with others can also be made clear in other ways: I have to translate what I think I have perceived into a language for myself, that is, I have to communicate it to myself, so to speak. But whatever language I use for this communication, it will never be my private language; it will always be a language that I share with others, first perhaps that of my parents, later that which I have learned from others, and which I will use correctly only if I can make others understand what I want myself to understand. But how can I learn this if not by connecting with others in communication? This begins in the most everyday contexts and continues through every form of truth-seeking.

So far, we have been talking about truth in the abstract. Now it is time to become more concrete. Depending on the context, the *Mode of Being*, as we said at the beginning of this paragraph, the concept of truth has different meanings and requires different forms of communication.

## NOTES

1. See W 372–375.
2. Thomas Nagel, *The View from Nowhere* (Oxford: Oxford University Press, 1986).
3. Einf 29.
4. Einf 29.
5. Cf. KlSch 26ff.
6. W 26.—*Origin* is the English word for what in Greek is called *arché*. Jaspers thus places himself in the tradition of those thinkers who, after Aristotle, posed the question of the primordial ground of all *Being*, which was not conceived, as in the myths of the origin of the *World*, as a temporal beginning, but as that which permanently underlies all reality and determines and dominates it (Aristotle, *Metaphysik,* 983b 6–13). The first of these thinkers was Thales of Miletus, but probably the greatest was Anaximander, who thought of the primordial ground as the *apeiron,* as the infinite, unlimited, and indeterminate—and thus as the absolute other to the *World* determined by the interplay of opposites. The philosophy of *Origin* takes three different forms in the tradition of metaphysics. Jens Halfwassen ("Karl Jaspers als Metaphysiker," in *Jaspers. Stationen seines philosophischen Wegs,* ed. Anton Hügli (Basel: Schwabe, 2021), 173–192, 180f.) explains them as follows:

> (1) Since Aristotle, the question of essence has led to the development of *Ontology* as a metaphysics of Being, which examines *Forms of Being* (ideas, categories, modalities, transcendentals) (. . .) (2) Since Plato, the insight into the unity of origin and the whole leads to the development of *Henology* as a metaphysics of the One, which conceives of the One itself as the Absolute (*anypotheton, apolyton*), to which everything real is related in its origin, which, however, in its absoluteness, can only be conceived from the negation of that which is founded in it, and thus leads to the discovery of the transcendence of the Absolute, to the *Beyond of Being* (*epekeina tes ousias*), as Plato says. (. . .) (3) The insight into the excellent relation of thought to the origin, to the whole and to the essence leads—in the beginning already with Plato and Aristotle, but only completed with Plotinus—to the development of *Noology* as a metaphysics, which discovers the non-objectivity of the mind in the power of negation and consequently thinks the mind (nous) as the original and basic form of *Being* (. . .).

As Halfwassen convincingly demonstrates, Jaspers's metaphysics stands in the Platonic tradition of the metaphysics of unity. More on this in chapter 9.

## *Chapter 2*

# The Modes of Encompassing and Their Different Sense of Truth

### THE ENCOMPASSING OF THE CONSCIOUSNESS IN GENERAL

Let us return to the different ways of understanding based on the way we become aware of them. We will look at three questions: What kind of *Being* opens up? What kind of truth is implicated? And what kind of communication is involved?

What are these different ways of becoming aware, of becoming aware of what is? When we reflect on how we experience reality, we realize that there is awareness of *Being* through experience, through cognition, and through action.

Cognition has already been mentioned. And rightly so. No matter how we become aware of *Being*, *Being* would not exist for us if we did not also have an awareness of it. Everything that exists for me exists only through the medium of "I think." I think that this and that is the case, and that is equivalent to saying to myself inwardly that this and that is the case. All this is cognition: consciousness, thought, language.

Starting from cognition, we have encountered one of the fundamental *Modes of Encompassing* without fully grasping it in its encompassing nature: *Consciousness in General*, through which we can objectify *Being* and thus recognize it at all. It is comprehensive for two reasons. First, because *Consciousness in General* is anchored in the consciousness of each individual, it encompasses—in its wholeness—the totality of all individual consciousnesses, but it is not already present as such in any of these individual manifestations. Second, *Consciousness in General* is comprehensive because it always encompasses both the cognizing subject and the object it cognizes.

Kant put this interlocking of subject and object in the act of cognition most clearly: everything that exists for us appears in our own forms of perception of space and time. The categories in which we think of what appears to us, for example, when we say that something is cause, substance, reality, and so on, are created by the thinking subject and are the condition of possibility for things to appear to us at all. The object (as appearance) can only exist as it appears to us. The forms of perception and the categories of understanding form, so to speak, the bracket with which the encompassing consciousness binds the recognizing subject and the recognized object.

It is extremely important to make this clear in order to avoid a fundamental misunderstanding. The *Subject-Object-Split* is not a split between consciousness and a being that faces it, but a split that passes through consciousness. Everything that appears to us at all enters into this split. It is an object that appears only through the imposition of our minds, a subject-object, so to speak. *Being* as such, which would be *Being* itself and not a mode of appearance of *Being*, is not a given of any kind (how could it be), but a construct, an objectless boundary concept with the help of which we try to conceive a world that would no longer be a world of appearances.

Consciousness is unique among all forms of understanding in that there is no consciousness without the knowledge that we have that consciousness. When I see a tree, I know that I am seeing a tree; when I speak a sentence, I know that I am speaking. In everything we experience, think, and do, we are also aware that we are experiencing, thinking, and acting. Our awareness is not only awareness of objects but also awareness of ourselves, self-awareness. From this self-awareness, we can turn ourselves and our cognition into an object and reflect on how an object can come to us and how we can come to the object, and whether there are other, better ways to access the object in question.

This reflection on our actions leads to what Jaspers calls *Methodological Consciousness*: the awareness that it depends on us, on the nature of our activity, how deeply we penetrate the phenomena of this world. *Methodological Consciousness* is an indispensable prerequisite for all scientific knowledge and, as we shall see, to an even greater extent for philosophy. Scientific results are dead property unless one also knows how they were obtained. What they mean becomes clear only to those who can comprehend or even recreate the movement that led to their realization.[1]

I think, I have consciousness, I am aware of myself. But how can I be sure? If I were to be an isolated, solipsistic ego, I would never be able to know anything about myself. Just as I can only experience my own reality and the reality of the *world* by acting upon it and thereby experiencing its resistance, I can only experience what I am myself through the echo I find in the consciousness of the other. If I want to become aware of myself as a thinker, I must communicate myself to the other person and seek his recognition and approval. Whoever thinks that he is already complete and that he alone has the truth has already robbed himself of the possibility of coming to himself and to the truth. I am as dependent on the other person as he is on me. I need his judgment to test my own judgment; I need the interaction with the other and his questions to awaken me from my slumber. Just as the other person needs my judgment, my acknowledgment, and my questions.

However, it is never just about the one other, but about the many others. The all-encompassing nature of consciousness opens up to us only when we seek it where it appears—in the countless others. But can it really be everyone else without distinction? Obviously, there are differences in rank. If we want consciousness in its purest form, purified as much as possible from subjective limitations, we must choose those thinkers in whom thinking is most clearly expressed: focused on the issue and the issue alone, committed to the methodology of collective inquiry. All subjectivity must disappear. Each individual is then no more than the thinking "I" identical with all the others. The content of their consciousness is that of all the others: that which is general and valid for all—the *universally valid.*

This also brings us to the understanding of truth within *Consciousness in General*: what is considered true is what is right for everyone, what is inherently obvious, what is imposed by its evidence on everyone who has understanding and understands it. This is independent of time and person: the fact that two and two equal four is and remains timelessly true throughout all time. When I become certain of the correctness of this equation, I am a pure thinking self, fully *Consciousness in General*. Performing the arithmetical operation forces me to believe that the matter is and must be as I think it is. This is why Jaspers speaks of *Compelling Knowledge*.

But being forced to believe that something is true is no guarantee that it is true. You can be led to a wrong conclusion by good arguments, or you can be persuaded by arguments that are not valid. Truth, in the simple sense that things are as we are forced to believe them to be, is and remains an idea that can never be caught up with.

For Jaspers—and we want to agree with him here—the accuracies of *Consciousness in General* include not only descriptive judgments, judgments about what is the case, but also prescriptive judgments, judgments that say what should be the case. The epitome of such correctness is the *Categorical Imperative*, with which Kant gives us an answer to the question of the principles of our actions: whether we can want the principles we choose to follow to become general laws followed by all. The demand of the *Categorical Imperative* only becomes a compelling insight for us if we disregard our individual inclinations and interests and become a thinking ego seeking agreement with every other thinking ego. Here, however, we must distinguish between the correctness of our moral judgment—whether I am prescribing to do what I can also want according to the law—and the question of whether I am willing to make my judgment true. The correspondence that makes the demand of the categorical imperative true is, in contrast to the descriptive judgment, no longer that between thinking and being, but between being and thinking: that what I do corresponds to what I ought to do.

## THE ENCOMPASSING OF *DASEIN*

In order to have consciousness, we must first be there, being in the *World.* We do not have to make ourselves the object of our thoughts in order to become aware of what it is like for us to be there: We are "life" and experience directly what it means to be alive through our bodily sensations, our feelings, our vitality, our drives and impulses, our fears and hopes, and our search for happiness. We make an immediate distinction between the inner world in which we live and the environment that surrounds us, affects us, and to which we react. Only that which enters into the whole of the inner world and the surrounding world is real for us. And yet we would like to go beyond that, to see the whole of our *Dasein.* But all that we are, we are only in and through our *Dasein.* We see ourselves as a link in the infinite chain of all living creatures that come into being and pass away, as a disappearing part of an immeasurable planetary and cosmic event that we cannot escape, and in the face of which we ask ourselves, "Why does it exist at all? Why is it even here? And why are we here?"

As part of all living creatures, we are individual beings with self-will and individual distinctiveness who are concerned with self-preservation and self-improvement. What is true in the service of *Dasein* is what enhances one's life, and what is untrue is what harms, limits, or paralyzes it.[2] The concept of truth in *Dasein* is that of pragmatism; that is, what is useful is true. The highest standard is usefulness in life, usefulness as a means to an end. What is an end depends on the particular situation of *Dasein* and the interests of *Dasein.* And as the situations change, so do the purposes. No purpose is a final purpose; what is useful in one situation may be harmful in the next. Therefore, there is no universal truth; what is true, that is, what is useful, is only true for that moment and that state of *Dasein.* Nothing is absolute.

As beings determined by *Dasein,* we unite when our interests converge and fight when they collide. In order to avoid the struggle that endangers *Dasein,* a form of communication must be found that enables common action through compromise. But the communication of *Dasein* itself is also in the service of the interests of *Dasein* and must prove its usefulness according to the situation.

While *Consciousness in General* is concerned with bringing to bear all the reasons that speak in favor of a cause and allowing itself to be guided only by generally understandable reasons, the communication of *Dasein* sees the other either as a useful ally to be kept on one's side or as a possible enemy to be weakened and fought against: by persuasion, by cunning and concealment, by exploiting one's social position, by playing with one's own power and vitality. It is not the truth that counts, but the effect. The communication of *Dasein* is therefore always in tension with the truth of *Consciousness in General*, with its claim to universality.

This tension between *Dasein* and *Consciousness in General* comes to a head when it comes to the moral claim to unconditionality and universality. Where the interests of *Dasein* dominate, there are no absolutes; what is valid is only what is useful to the individual or the particular community. A certain degree of commitment and continuity is created only by habits and conventions that are of general interest to all members of a community of *Dasein*.

Consciousness in the service of the interests of *Dasein* becomes the driving force of everything that can be calculated and planned and that people have produced to secure and promote their *Dasein*, such as houses, tools, weapons, machines—in short, the very creation of the entire field of economics and technology as the epitome of the material foundations of our *Dasein*. But the material basis is not everything; there is also that which goes beyond it, which we call *Culture*, a term that is not easy to understand. Jaspers uses another name for it. He calls it, in the tradition of German idealism, *Spirit (Geist)*. This makes the difficult seem even more incomprehensible. Perhaps it will become clearer if we borrow from other thinkers with an eye to what Jaspers meant.

## THE ENCOMPASSING OF *SPIRIT*

We humans would not be able to achieve what constitutes our culture if we did not move in a completely different *Mode of Encompassing* than the *Encompassing of Dasein*. It is the encompassing that arises and has arisen from the fact that human beings act together and create a new reality through their collective action, namely, states and institutions, laws, works of art, poetry, sciences and professions, and the like. They are what they are because, and only because, human beings want them to be. Their objectivity is therefore fundamentally different from that of the products of technology, which require a material independent of human beings and are the result of its processing. They are products of the human imagination. Although they require a material basis to come into existence, they are not what they are because of their material nature.

An obvious example is the invention of money: embossed pieces of metal, and later printed or written pieces of paper, are declared by a certain society to be a means of payment that can be exchanged for goods at will. At the latest with the transition to paper money, the material nature of money no longer bears any relation to its function as a medium of exchange. It is worthless in itself and acquires its value only through the *fiat* of an agency created and authorized specifically for this purpose,[3] which, through this miraculous declaration, transforms pieces of paper into dollar bills, for example. The authorization of this agency, however, is in turn based on a *fiat* issued by other agencies that are authorized by the *fiat* of further agencies to issue such authorizations, and so on. The rules by which this is done constitute the corresponding reality. Issuing a bill of exchange, making a purchase: these are actions and the results of actions that can only exist within the monetary economy and nowhere else in the world. The individual *fiat* by which these realities are constituted (e.g., the writing of a piece of paper, which then counts as a bill of exchange) can only take place in the name of, or with the authorization of, a collective, to whom then applies what the authorized persons or instances decree. No *fiat* stands alone, each *fiat* in turn refers to others. These reference systems form a meaningful, self-contained whole. In the case of money, for example, such a whole is the entire financial system, with all the institutions and actors involved in the circulation of money, and in keeping it going with their transactions.

As socialized beings, we find ourselves in an encompassing system of such wholes whose reality consists only in the fact that they are created by *Fiats*. They are the *third Mode of Encompassing*. Jaspers refers to this *Mode of Encompassing* with the German word *Geist*, and, following Hegel's use of language, he calls the principle inherent in these wholes *Idea (Idee)*.[4] Thus, for him, there is the *Idea* of the university, the *Idea* of democracy, the *Idea* of the doctor, the *Idea* of law, the *Idea* of marriage, and so on. *Ideas* are the principle that creates unity in the whole to which they belong; only by looking at them can we determine what is a meaningful feature within that whole. An *Idea* is present in every part of the whole it permeates, without ever itself being directly graspable or attainable as a plannable goal.

*Ideas* go hand in hand with a completely different concept of truth and reality: what is true is what corresponds to the *Idea*, and only what is true is also real. In this sense, one can speak of a true or real doctor, a true or real friend. In contrast to the truth of *Consciousness in General* (scientific truth), which is only given when our ideas correspond to its object, the truth of the *Spirit* is that the object must correspond to the *Idea*.[5] However, what is not true in the sense of the *Idea* can certainly have phenomenal reality. One could argue that not everyone among real existing doctors is actually a true doctor, and not everyone among real existing friends is actually a true friend.

Anyone who is part of a whole permeated by an *Idea*, and who seriously wants to participate in that wholeness, must be guided in his actions by that *Idea*. He recognizes this *Idea* as valid for himself and is bound to all others who also participate or have participated in it and are or were committed to its realization. Only what contributes to the realization of the *Idea* is true. If social conditions change, the respective concretization of the *Idea* will also change, new people may enter this whole and create new realities, but these changes in the realization of the *Idea* are not arbitrary and random; they are—in the light of the *Idea*—meaningful in themselves. As an example: the *Idea* of the university remains valid over time, but the real existing university has a different form under different historical conditions. This can come more or less close to what the *Idea* demands. Like all existence in space and time, however, no form will ever fully correspond to its *Idea*, never be the full realization of the *Idea*.

Explicating the *Idea* and making it a reality again and again is the never-ending task of all those who are in the service of an *Idea* of the *Spirit*.[6] Their communication is also based on the *Idea* and finds meaning and significance through it: in the selection, emphasis, and relatedness of what one does and says.[7] The *Idea* determines which purposes we can set for ourselves and what can be considered a reason in argumentation. In the light of the *Idea*, what is said and done becomes understandable and makes sense.[8] This applies not only to those who follow the *Idea* themselves but also to outside observers who try to understand the motives behind thoughts and actions within a community committed to the *Idea*. The only difference between the perspective of the participants and the perspective of the observers is that the observers do not place themselves under the claim of the *Idea,* and that the demands arising from it therefore have no *prescriptive* (action-guiding) force for them.[9]

*Ideas* are valid only for the historical communities that belong to them, not in themselves. As diverse as the *ideas* of the *Spirit* are, so diverse are the communities belonging to them with their truths.

The communities determined by *Ideas* are forces in *Dasein*. They have an endurance of their own and are therefore in a state of tension or even in open conflict with other powers. This struggle can become a matter of choice for the individual: Which of the conflicting *Ideas* that I follow do I ultimately feel committed to? For example, the judge who has to judge his own son and is now in conflict between his role as a father and his role as a judge.

It would be self-deception to think that one's attitude and actions are good simply because one is in the service of an *Idea*. *Ideas* themselves need legitimation. The question of whether the *Idea* I have been following unquestioningly is really the *Idea* I want to live for confronts me with a conscious decision. But what is the basis of my will and my decision? When I decide here, where do I stand? It would have to be a place that does not lie in any of the *Modes of Encompassing* considered so far: neither in *Dasein*, nor in *Consciousness in General*, nor in *Spirit*. It would have to be an *Encompassing* that again encompasses and at the same time transcends all these *Modes of Encompassing*. But what would it be like? How should we conceive of it?

## THE LIMITS OF OUR BEING IN THE WORLD

*Dasein*, *Consciousness in General*, and *Spirit* are modes in which we find ourselves in the *World*. They are part of the *World*. What appears in them are objective realities that can be investigated, just as everything in the *World* can be investigated. But as *Modes of Encompassing*, they are not objects in the *World* for us. Analogous to the limit of all objectification, which is the limit of *Consciousness in General*, there are also limits to the other two modes of our being in the *World*. None of these modes of our being in the *World* can claim to be the only one, and none is reducible to the other. In fact, there are interdependencies: without *Dasein*, there would be no *Consciousness in General*, without *Consciousness in General*, there would be no *Spirit*. This creates a hierarchy. Every higher *Mode of Encompassing* is always more and different from the one below. Thus, our existence in the *World*, as soon as it becomes concrete, proves to be divided into different modes of *Being*. This is why any philosophy that tries to reduce the world to a single principle is untrue: both *Materialism*, for which the *World* is nothing but matter, and *Idealism*, for which the world is nothing but *Spirit*. Whatever our attempt to grasp matter, everything we say about it is from the perspective of *Consciousness in General*, which is as immaterial as the relation of *Intentionality*, of being directed toward objects in the *World*, which cannot be compared to any kind of correlation in the physical world. And whenever we search for *Spirit*, we will encounter the Spiritless, which has never been grasped by the circular movement of an *Idea*, but flows into the infinite and the accidental.

The fundamental error of these monist theories is that they want to make statements about the ultimate *Being* of the *World*, ignoring the fact that we are only ever dealing with appearances in the *World*, but never with the *Being* of the *World* itself. However, once we have become aware of the phenomenal nature of the world, the tradition of philosophy that believes it can come up with *ontological* theories, theories about what *Being* is, independent of ourselves, becomes obsolete. The differences in the *Modes of Encompassing*, as we need to remind ourselves once again, are not differences in the *Being* of the *World*, but differences in the way we find ourselves in the *World* and place ourselves in the *World*. These different attitudes are most evident in language, in our use of personal pronouns. Wilhelm von Humboldt was the first to point out their systematic significance.[10] He distinguishes between

(1) the observing attitude of the third person toward states and processes in the objective world;
(2) the self-reflective attitude of the first person singular toward one's own experiences;
(3) the attitude toward the second person that we adopt when participating in conversations or joint practices;
(4) the attitude of the first person plural, of a person who says "we," distinguishing themselves as a member of a collective from non-members.

These distinctions can certainly be related to Jaspers's *Modes of Encompassing*. The first attitude corresponds to Jaspers's *Consciousness in General,* with its objectification of the *World.* In the second attitude, the self-reflective one, I become aware of myself in the *Encompassing* of *Dasein.* The fourth attitude is the dominant one in the *Encompassing* of the *Spirit.* The third posture of an I toward a You belongs to both *Consciousness in General* and the *Encompassing* of the *Spirit.*[11]

Nevertheless, there is a difference between attitudes and *Modes of Encompassing*. One chooses attitudes, and what is chosen is a matter of arbitrary decision, which is why neither can be traced back to the other.[12] But it would be wrong to speak of a choice in relation to *Modes of Encompassing.* We cannot simply choose which *Mode of Encompassing* we want to live in. We are always in them. As long as we are alive, we are *Dasein, Consciousness in General*, and *Spirit.* In a sense, however, there can still be a choice. We can decide which of these *Modes of Encompassing* should determine our lives. For example, we can ask ourselves whether we want to listen only to the voice of *Dasein* and be determined only by our interests in *Dasein*, or whether we want to commit to the life of the *Spirit* and become absorbed in following an *Idea.* Or we can choose not to choose at all and drift through life, driven by one motive or another, a life without coherence or continuity. The choice we are talking about here is not the choice between this and that preference, as we constantly have to make in our everyday life, between going home or staying at the office, for example, but the choice of what should be the most important thing in my life, what gives my life any meaning at all. This is a life choice, if you will, an answer to the question of what this life is for and what I want to do with my life. It is the kind of answer that the young Kierkegaard hoped to find to his life's question, and which was impressed on the mind of Jaspers, who was awakened by Kierkegaard:[13]

> What I really need is to come to terms with myself about what I should be doing [. . .] it is important to understand my purpose, to see what the Deity really wants me to do; it is important to find a truth that is truth for me, to find the *Idea* for which I want to live and die.[14]

With renewed passion, Kierkegaard has taken up the question that can become, for every human being, the primordial question to which the offers of the salvation of the religions promise an answer. Socrates places it at the center of philosophy, and Plato visualizes it in the final myth of his *Politeia*, which deals with the fate of human souls after death. The souls gathered in the afterlife are asked to choose their *daimon*, their way of life for the next life, before the next cycle of the world begins.[15] According to Socrates' commentary, this myth is meant to show how important it is to prepare for this choice and to "pursue justice and reason in every way" already in the present life.[16]

Choosing one's own *daimon*, choosing the *Idea* for which one wants to live and die: these phrases hint at what we need to examine more closely. Whoever chooses here chooses who he wants to be, not just for the here and now, not just in this or that role, but—as it were—for eternity. Instead of choosing life, one could just as well speak of choosing oneself: You choose yourself (not someone else) and you choose who you want to be.[17]

## NOTES

1. This insight was decisive for Jaspers as a psychopathologist. It was the principle that he followed in his *Allgemeine Psychopathologie*: "To develop and organize knowledge according to the methods by which it is gained, to recognize knowledge and thereby to clarify things" (Aut 26).

2. W 608.

3. The Oxford philosopher of law, H. L. A. Hart, drew attention to the peculiar nature of such *fiats* as early as the 1940s. As Hart points out, there are a number of expressions which, despite their indicative form, are not used to describe things or persons but to attribute something to them: titles, rights, and responsibilities, for example. When I say, "This is my book," I am not giving a description of the book but claiming ownership of the book. And when I say, "Miller is my agent," I am not making a statement about Miller's qualities, but authorizing him to make certain decisions on my behalf. In contrast to *descriptive* judgments, Hart calls such judgments *ascriptive*. His paradigm is the judgment of a judge who, as a recognized authority, assigns or denies responsibilities and rights on the basis of recognized rules. (See H. L. A. Hart, "The Ascription of Responsibility and Rights," *Proceedings of the Aristotelian Society,* 49 (9/1948), 171–194.)

In contemporary literature, this phenomenon is discussed primarily under the concept of *Collective Intentionality*, following John R. Searle. (See, for example, *Mind, Language, and Society. Philosophy in the Real World* (New York: Basic Books, 1999), ch. 5.) The basic structure of *Collective Intentionality* is as follows: For every X that is in and constituted by context Z, it is true that it is Y. For example, for every object (X) that serves as a means of payment in economic transactions, it is true that it has a certain value (Y).

4. Jaspers uses the term *Idea* in both the Hegelian and Kantian sense. For him, as for Kant, the *World, Freedom,* and *God* are *Ideas* of *Reason.* Their content cannot be caught up with; they are an "infinite task which, in the anticipatory presence of its content, pushes itself unfinished into the open." Jaspers therefore describes them as *open* in contrast to the *closed Ideas* of the *Spirit* (see PGO 115).

5. W 615.

6. As a member of the university, Jaspers, therefore, considered it necessary to remind the internal and external public of the *Idea* of the university at decisive turning points in his time and to express the demands arising from it for the current situation. This happened for the first time in 1923, then again in 1946, and 1961 (IU).

7. W 647.

8. This is in contrast to the understanding of what is directly experienced or to the understanding of a mental expression (AP 258).

9. See, for example, W 614: "The *Idea* is valid for us as an objective that approaches us, and yet it is nowhere compellingly demonstrable for everyone. For it is valid only for the subjective *Idea* through which its reality is grasped."

10. I owe this reference to Jürgen Habermas, whose systematization of the ways of communication itself is also based on these distinctions (cf. *Auch eine Geschichte der Philosophie* (Berlin: Suhrkamp 2019), Bd. 2, 780).

11. The more precise location of the *you*-relationship will be discussed in connection with the concept of *Existential Communication.*

12. If the *Modes of Encompassing* are misunderstood as *Modes of Being,* the transition from one Mode to the other must appear as a mysterious leap. This is a misunderstanding to which even Jaspers occasionally succumbs when he emphasizes the leaps (the riddle of transitions) that exist between the *Modes of Encompassing.* Cf. W 68: "The essence of consciousness cannot at all be derived from the consciousness of *Dasein.*"

13. Cf. Jaspers, for example, on the importance of knowing what one wants unreservedly: "This is how I would like to have lived forever," and to act in such a way that we say: "That this is done in the *World* is the will of *Transcendence.*" That is just a *Chiffer,* not a reality. What is important is that I act in such a way that I say: "What I can achieve is only that I know what I want, that I know what I want to live for. Blessed is the man who succeeds in reaching the point where he knows what is worthwhile" (Prov 53). Jaspers thought of himself as someone who knew what he wanted: I want *Reason* in the world. But I cannot say that God wants *Reason* to be in the *World,* at most: "God wants *Reason* to be represented in the *World*; we do not know what will come of it; I am one of those who are supposed to represent *Reason.* Then I am in the situation that only man can be in, that he knows what he wants, and that he relates this will to his *Transcendence,* and that he is aware that it has in some sense an eternal meaning" (54). "It is crucial to know what one wants, where one stands, what one wants to live for, what gives dignity to life" (55). These reflections are obviously inspired by Kierkegaard, who made the problem of life choice the starting point of his philosophizing, which was decisive for modernity.

14. Søren Kierkegaard, *Tagebücher,* vol. 1 (Düsseldorf: Diederichs, 1962), I A 75, p. 16.—On the problem of the choice of life as it is seen by Kierkegaard, see Anton

Hügli, "Søren Kierkegaard—Der Einzelne, das Ethische und die Freiheit." In *Klassiker der Philosophie heute*, ed. Ansgar Beckermann and Dominik Perler (Stuttgart: Reclam, 2004), 439–458.

15. Plato, *Politeia*, Werke, ed. Gunther Eigler, vol. 4 (Darmstadt: Wissenschaftliche Buchgesellschaft, 1971), 617 d 4.

16. Plato, *Politeia*, 621.

17. Jaspers calls it the *Original Choice* (W 326).

## *Chapter 3*

# Choosing One's Self

## *An Approach to the Concept of* Existence

### WHERE ARE WE WHEN WE ASK THE QUESTION OF SELF-CHOICE? AND WHO IS THE EGO ASKING THE QUESTION?

Several questions arise: What kind of ego is it that poses the question of self-choice? Where does it stand in Jaspers's *Modes of Encompassing*? When and under what conditions can the question of self-choice arise at all? What are the implications of this choice? What does it mean for communication between human beings?

The *Modes of Encompassing* also differ in that it is always a different "I." When I say "I" in the *Encompassing of Dasein*, "I" can mean two things: (1) What I know directly about myself in every act of thinking: not who I am or what I am, but just that I am.[1] In conversation, I use this word to position the place from which the speech emanates in relation to the other I-sayers: that it is I who is speaking and not the other person or a third party. (2) By "I" I can also refer to the phenomenal part of me that shows up in the psychological-reflective posture, that is, the I as the source of my feelings and sensations, which cannot be further defined. In the *Subject-Object-Split*, it is the part of me that is objectified by me as consciousness. In both senses of "I" in *Dasein*, the singularity of the I is remarkable. There is one and only one I in one and the same place in the context of the spatiotemporal events of *Dasein*. And the pain I feel is a pain that only I feel and no one else. So the I of *Dasein* is an absolute singularity, unique and incomparable. Comparable only in that everyone else is also an absolute singularity. In this respect, being singular is not an attribute that belongs to me and me alone. We can also attribute the quality of being within ourselves to animals. And wonder what it would be like to be a bat.

And what about the ego in *Consciousness in General*? In fact, *Consciousness in General* is fragmented into many minds and has reality only in them. But as far as we are pure consciousness, having reached the point in the cognitive process where we think we know and know the reasons we base ourselves on, everything individual becomes indifferent: everyone can be represented by everyone else. We are one and the same identical point, focused on one and the same fact.

In the *Encompassing of Spirit*, the ego becomes more concrete; it appears in certain roles within the respective community and in the service of the respective *Idea*: as a mother, as a worker, as a citizen, as a professor, as a soldier, and so on. But as a role-bearer, it may be replaced by other role-bearers: it is not its individuality that counts, but what it can achieve in its role.

But where is the ego that could decide which *Mode of Encompassing* should take precedence in a case of conflict? And with which task can it fully identify? It would have to be an ego that is not absorbed in any of these different *Modes of Encompassing*: neither the ego of *Dasein*, nor the impersonal ego of *Consciousness in General*, nor a role ego in the *Encompassing of Spirit*. It can only be the I that I am in the end if I can transcend and break through all these *Modes of Encompassing*.

Again, it is a borderline thought that we are thinking here. Through it, we become aware that the *Modes of Encompassing* described so far still lie on this side of the boundaries of the *World* as it appears to us. Even if, as *Modes of Encompassing*, they can never be grasped in their entirety, even if our cognition never comes to an end, everything that appears in these *Modes of Encompassing* lies within the objectively recognizable *World*. This distant and constantly shifting boundary is, if you will, *immanent Transcendence*. Therefore, in the search for our true selves, we must also think beyond these shiftable boundaries within the recognizable *World*, to where all objectification ends—in a transcendent space that transcends the *World*. The last I would be an I that would encompass both the cognizing and the cognized I, and thus be completely identical with me. What emanates from this I would have to be my *Origin*, and only there would I be myself. Only as this self could I make a new beginning in the objective *World* determined by causalities and defy the causalities that determine me in my *Dasein*. Only as this self would I be free. Jaspers calls the mode of being of this self *Existence* (*Existenz*).

But how can I even access this true self if I can never leave the objective *World*? Is it not an empty concept? A phantasmagoria?

## *EXISTENCE* AS AN EXPERIENCE OF BORDERLINE SITUATIONS

Access to the transcendent self opens up not only when I try to approach it by thinking—as a borderline concept that can never be caught up with—but also when I come existentially to the border of my existence. Jaspers tried to shed light on what this means with the concept of the *Borderline Situation (Grenzsituation)*.[2] His basic formula for what it means to exist in the sense of *Existence* shows how important this concept is to him: "Experiencing *Borderline Situations* and existing are the same thing."[3] It is therefore important that we clarify what he means by a *Borderline Situation*. A certain kind of situation, apparently. But what is a situation?

Nothing seems clearer than this—and that is probably why it is so difficult to grasp. Wherever we are and for as long as we are, we are in a situation: in the here and now, entangled in a spatially and temporally determined context of things and events. Which face the situation shows me depends on my interests and goals, and results from the way I am connected to my environment through my body and my senses. I realize how steep a mountain is when I climb it and how beautiful the view is when I reach the top.

In every situation, the question arises: What does it mean to me? Is it good or bad? Is it beneficial or detrimental to my interests? With each of these questions, I see new opportunities for action, but also new risks.

Situations are constantly changing. A new event is breaking in—an expected one, such as nightfall, or an unexpected one, such as the appearance of another person or a sudden change in the weather. When new situations arise, I can change them to my advantage, for example, by taking shelter from the storm, or I can be forced to accept a situation as it is and wait for a better one.

No situation repeats itself, so each one is absolutely individual, unique, and the opportunities it offers are gone once and for all if I do not seize them. Of course, this does not exclude the possibility that situations may be similar in their general characteristics. There are recurring types of situations: the general situation of being on a mountain hike, the typical situation of being caught in a thunderstorm. Every rule of behavior is based on such a generalization of the situation: for example, the rule that if you are caught in a thunderstorm, you should avoid tall trees only makes sense under the tacit assumption that there are recurring, relevantly similar situations. All learning, planning, and calculating is based on recurring patterns of situations. But the following applies to every situation in which I am involved: it always has individual characteristics, if only because of its spatial and temporal specificity, and is unique in the sense that there is one and only one person who met me at a certain fork in the road on June 10, 2022, at 4:15 pm.

Being in a situation is one thing; knowing the situation is another. In fact, we never know what situation we are in. We may think we are healthy, but cancer may have eaten away at our colon, or we may think we are happy, but one of our children may have just been in an accident. We often do not know what situation we might be in until after the fact, and it is not uncommon for others to know how we are doing much better than we do. In short, situations are never fully predictable. But one thing is certain: I can never get out of a situation without being in the next one. Being in a situation never ends. Therefore, as long as I live, no situation—no matter how bad it is for me—will be my last. But if no situation is the last, then where is the *Borderline Situation*?

## Borderline Situation and Ground Situation

If we want to get to the *Borderline Situation*, we must not look for it among the individual situations. It is not a situation that exists for a moment and then disappears; it is not just one of countless others. Nor is it what we might better call an exceptional or extreme situation, such as hanging from a rope on a mountain in mortal danger.

The basic characteristic of a *Borderline Situation* is that we cannot get into it and we cannot get out of it, because no matter how we turn, we are always already in it. That is why the *Borderline Situation* is also insurmountable, unchangeable, not like a barrier that we can get over in the end, not like something terrible that we can survive in the end, but an absolute wall that we come up against.

But what kind of situation can that be? I have already given one example: the fact that we are always in situations and cannot be anywhere but in situations. Jaspers mentions other such situations: that I cannot live without struggle and suffering, that I inevitably incur guilt, and that I must die. We cannot escape these situations; they are necessarily linked to our *Dasein* in the *World*, they are part of the *condition humaine*, to use Pascal's words. But they elude our gaze. The individual, concrete situations in which we find ourselves are like the waves on the surface of a body of water, but the *Borderline Situations* are the bottom in the depths above which all this takes place. As long as we drift on the waves of ever-changing situations, they remain hidden from us. They are *Ground Situations (Grundsituationen)*, but not yet *Borderline Situations*.[4] They only become *Borderline Situations* when we become aware of the *Ground Situation*.

## The Borderline Situation as Ground Situation Becoming Conscious through Philosophical Detachment from the World

How do we come to see the *Ground Situation*? It requires a different attitude: the readiness and willingness to gain the greatest possible distance from ourselves and to see ourselves as part of the whole *World* that encompasses us. This is a very special kind of distance. It is the one that constitutes philosophy and with which philosophizing begins.

We can see the difference more clearly if we compare the way we distance ourselves in everyday life or in science with philosophical distance. We expect even small children to take the first step toward everyday self-distancing. It starts with learning language. When a child learns to speak, it acquires the ability to free itself from its egocentric attachment to the individual situation, to the peg of the moment, as Nietzsche would say. As soon as it can use names, Mom and Dad, Hans and Willi, and knows how to work with labels, that is, with expressions like "that dog over there," "that woman from before," it is no longer attached to the particular situation when it speaks. The child can now refer back to past situations and anticipate future situations.

But if it is true that we are always in situations, we can ask ourselves: What situation are we in when we think and speak, distancing ourselves from ourselves in the concrete situation? This question may sound strange, and it becomes even more puzzling the longer we think about it. Of course, someone who speaks is with his body in a certain place and situation, in a lecture hall, at a beer bar or wherever, and of course he usually has a concrete counterpart with whom he speaks and to whom he speaks, even if this counterpart is only himself. But we realize how insignificant and indifferent the immediate situation is for our speech and thoughts at the latest when we are writing or talking on the phone. When we speak, our thoughts are somewhere else entirely, namely with what we mean when we speak. When I speak aloud or write down my thoughts, anyone who understands my language and hears or reads what I say has the opportunity to go to where I am or where I have been. Ideally, we are in the same place: for example, in the story of Jack and Jill that I have just told. But where exactly is this place? Where are Jack and Jill? They are no longer in the situation that the story is about—always assuming that the story is true and that this place ever existed.

Speaking and thinking, as strange as it may sound, we are neither here nor there, but somewhere else. However, we lack the words to describe where that elsewhere is. For us in this book, it is in the nowhere, that is, exactly where we have already been in our train of thought: in the discussion of *Consciousness in General* as the place where all those who communicate with each other can meet. The view from nowhere is the view from the "place" from which everyone else could also look. It is the standpoint that, in principle, anyone who speaks our language and understands the meaning of the words can take. It is an impersonal standpoint, in other words, from which we become aware of one and the same things.

But the consolation remains. Even in the impersonal nowhere, we are not alone. It is the place where people can meet as beings with the power of language, even if they want to communicate about the most personal things that moves them: their feelings, sensations, wishes, and hopes.

So much for the familiar way of distancing ourselves. But where is the philosophical distancing? This too has no other place than that of *Consciousness in General*, the view from nowhere. But what it tries to grasp are no longer individual manifestations in the *World*, but the *World* as a whole and our life as a whole. What is it that defines me? What is this whole in which I stand? Where does it come from, and what is its goal?

Only when we ask in this way do we realize that these are questions that lead nowhere. For what is this ultimate whole? Matter, the Spirit, History, or God? As we already got to know, with everything that we declare to be the *Ultimate*, the question immediately arises: Where does it come from? And in the end: Why is there anything at all and not nothing? It's again like looking across the sea: behind every horizon, another horizon opens up—and so into infinity. To where there can be no more knowledge.

Ancient myths, called *Cosmogonies*, have tried to answer the question of the origin of the world with moving images. If we generalize these answers, we end up with two basic ideas: that the *World* has always existed, or that there was a time when the *World* was created from nothing, that is, the idea of *World creation*.[5]

These mythical answers still affect us today. Because wherever we think we are in our "mental nowhere," we have already decided which myth we follow: If we assume that this nowhere is somewhere in the *World*, that it is a product of the human mind, and that the human mind is a product of this *World*, we have already taken the position that there can be nothing but this *World*, that it is—for all eternity—the end point of everything. But if we assume that our nowhere is an otherworldly place, then we must be in the nothingness from which the *World* was created. And what we think when we go into the depths would be, in multiple brokenness, the thinking of God before the creation of the *World*. Man could become a witness to the creation of the world. An absurd thought? It is not if we relate the question of the creation of the *World* to ourselves: Where do we come from? Are we a mere product of this *World* and its development?

The Kantian idea of the phenomenal nature of the *World* alone already points us to a place beyond or outside the empirical *World*. Nothing that appears of me in this *World* is my ultimate, my real self. And if I believe that I possess it in what I now call self, soul, mind, or whatever else, the mystery remains as to how I can be that something and at the same time be the I that is cognitively opposed to that something as consciousness. The more we immerse ourselves in such trains of thought, the clearer it becomes: What we are searching for is something beyond anything imaginable. We believe we are a whole and we find ourselves in this whole we call the *World*, but we do not know who we are and what we are supposed to be. The only thing we can recognize is our *Ground Situation*: born by chance and only here to fight, suffer, become guilty, and die. A fact for which there is no explanation: nothing that precedes and from which all this would necessarily follow, no *why* that we could understand. That's the way things are. Pure contingency. Yet it is inconceivable that anything could be different. Why inconceivable?

Let's take the fact that we are bound to situations as an example. Abstracting from all situations and negating them, we can try to imagine what it would be like for us not to be bound to situations. However, we fail for the same reason we fail when we try to imagine what it would be like for us if we were no longer here. This failure is not an accidental failure, not one that could be overcome with a little more imagination or better powers of thought, but lies in the nature of the matter itself: If there is no one left, there is no one left for this nonexistence to worry about. Trying to establish your nonexistence as someone who no longer exists is as absurd as being in a situation in which you are no longer in any situation. The impossibility inherent in this thought only makes us aware of the absolute limit we encounter when we try to think of our death, which is possible at any time, or even the state in which we are no longer in any situation.

However, this limit is not given to us directly; we only encounter it when we try to reach beyond the whole of our existence in our thoughts—into a being that is no longer an existence in the world, placeless and timeless at the same time. The collision with this limit throws us back to our *Ground Situation* and makes us fully aware of the prison in which we find ourselves.

What have we gained by recognizing this? From the perspective of *Consciousness in General*, we can do nothing but take note of it without illusion. And practice philosophical serenity as an observer.[6]

## Experiencing Borderline Situations Existentially

But we are not just spectators, not just *Consciousness in General*. We are finite beings, struggling for self-assertion and self-preservation. Thinking about our *Dasein* in purely theoretical contemplation is granted to us at most for certain self-forgetful moments. We care about existence, and our greatest concern is our own being. Therefore, we cannot help but see everything we encounter from the perspective of our self-centered interests and evaluate it accordingly; as good or bad, as right or wrong, as moral or immoral, as beautiful or ugly, as sinister or salutary, as divine or diabolical, or whatever. And evaluation goes hand in hand with feeling and wanting. What is *Valuable*, as a concept of all that is positive, is what we love and what we desire; what is worthless and unworthy is what we hate. What we love, we want to last and remain; what we hate, we want not to be born at all or to disappear as soon as possible.

Because of our desires, the *Ground Situation* takes on a new face. It is not about the fate of man per se, but about *myself*. I am deeply shocked when I realize that everything of value that I desire and try to realize is always connected with what is contrary to value and destructive—in short, my entire being coexists with ruin, destruction, and death.

At this point, if not before, I begin to desperately ask myself why I want to live and for what purpose. When I ask this question, I ask it not as an impersonal *Consciousness in General*—as a consciousness that could also be that of any other thinker—nor as a particular self in this or that role, but as this individual interested in itself, from which everything that previously seemed valid is slipping away, and which, sinking into the abyss, is looking for a final foothold.

The previously unquestioned purposes of life and generally comprehensible reasons for action have become null and void. What remains is either despair and sinking into nothingness or the belief that—beyond all finite purposes—there is something for which I must and will stand up—not just for this or that purpose, not just for this or that reason, but absolutely, without condition and without reservation, *unconditionally*. Where this unconditional will is present, there is no longer the division of *Consciousness in General*: here my will and there my reasons. Will and reason have become one. In other words, the will has the reason within it, it is the reason itself.[7] Only through this do I experience myself as free, moved by myself. In Jaspers's words: "because I am there as myself, who can absolutely depend on something that depends on him, I must be able to be free."[8] It is this unconditionality of the person standing in himself that speaks from the words of Luther, which Jaspers likes to quote: "Here I stand, I cannot do otherwise." It is this unconditionality that Kant's *Categorical Imperative* expects of us. Jaspers himself experienced it in his will to unlimited communication and in his love for his wife; we believe we can hear it in his work.

Where everything is on a knife edge, there is also the great either/or situation and the demand for a decision in the situation I am in right now: What is important to me here and now? Where do I really stand? Where I end up in this reflection process is where I am myself, where the real me is. But once I am where I want to be, I am also committed to the truth that holds in that place—in that *Mode of Encompassing*—and I have to face the reasons that hold in that place. If I enter fully and completely into the struggle for *Dasein*, I must also seize the means by which I can assert my *Dasein*, and if I place myself fully and completely at the service of an *Idea*, everything that makes the *Idea* real is at the top of the list.[9]

It is not *what* I do, but *how* I do what I do that is existentially decisive: the way in which I participate, the *seriousness* with which I do it. What defies justification is not what I have to do in concrete terms, but rather how I do it: that I identify fully and completely, unconditionally, with this task and immerse myself fully and completely in the I that I am in the *Mode of Existence*. In short: the *Unconditionality* with which I do what is unconditional for me is the only thing that matters.[10] Only to the extent that I want what is unconditional for me in the *Unconditionality* of being myself do I become the person who constitutes me and me alone, unique, historical, unrepeatable. But who can ever satisfy this demand? Is this not a task for "existential heroes"?

For Jaspers, the possibility of being oneself is not an exceptional experience for chosen people.[11] To search *Unconditionally* for what we want and thus to become who we are: This is the demand Jaspers makes of everyone and first and foremost of himself in his life and in his philosophizing. He expects everyone to be able to fulfill this demand. We are *Existence* in the sense of Jaspers's existential philosophy only to the extent that we try to fulfill it. *Existence* is the fourth, the transcendent mode, of the *Encompassing* that we are. But since we, as temporal beings, are never finished with our existential task, Jaspers always speaks only of *Possible Existence*.

We are not *Existence*, we only become it, and that we become it is not a necessity but a mere possibility. The possibility of every human being to bring *Unconditionality* into his life gives his life continuity and temporal duration. By constantly repeating the decision he has once made, he reaffirms his freedom over and over again. This is the only kind of truth that there is in the realm of *Existence*: that which makes *Possible Existence* real is true. The fundamental condition, however, is that the *Unconditional* exists at all. But isn't that just another chimera?

## THE UNPROVABILTY OF THE UNCONDITIONAL AND THE NECESSITY OF BELIEVING IN THE UNCONDITIONAL

There is no empirical evidence or proof of any kind that the *Unconditional* exists. It lies beyond the boundary of the cognizable, in the objectless darkness of ignorance. For what we can know is always conditional; every question about a *why* presupposes that the object whose existence or suchness we are asking about is due to something else. When we try to grasp this ultimate and *Unconditional* with the means of understanding, we run into those *Antinomies of Reason* that Kant exposed: for example, the contradiction that the spatial *World* is both finite and infinite, that it has a beginning in time and no beginning, that everything happens according to causal necessity and that, at the same time, there must be freedom as the beginning of a causal chain.

But while in the realm of cognition we are left with the modest thought that we at any rate have *Ideas* of the *Ultimate* and the *Unconditional*, of the whole of the *World* and of the whole of our being, even if these are not recognizable, the antinomies of our existentially experienced *Borderline Situations* do not reveal any reconciling perspective. In all of them, the basic contradiction remains that the reality of the *World* ruthlessly ignores all our values: whatever we want in terms of value has consequences that we do not want and cannot want. Not only the *World* as a whole, but we ourselves are antinomically divided. Those who experience this fundamental contradiction experience not only powerlessness but also despair. It throws them back on themselves—as an *Existence*. Why live if everything I want ultimately fails? Where is the *Unconditional* that is not just a possibility of thinking, but gives me the strength to orient my life toward it?

Such an *Unconditional*, which eludes all conceivability, can only exist for me as I believe it despite my inability to understand it. The psychologizing search for explanatory motives for this belief, whether conscious or unconscious, already excludes this belief. Even the terms we use when we speak of the *Unconditional*—since we cannot speak other than in terms such as freedom, decision, or choice—are meaningless because they are not terms that refer to recognizable objects that are independent of us and under which we could subsume these objects. Such concepts, therefore, have another function. They are mere signs, signposts without an inscription. Jaspers calls them *Signa of Existence* (a term we will shed more light on later). We only understand their meaning when we try to follow them: what *Unconditionality* is by trying to bring *Unconditionality* into our lives, what selfhood is by trying to get to the point where we are ourselves, what freedom is by freeing ourselves from all ambiguities, considerations, and ulterior motives, and wanting only the one thing that matters to us.

But why should we believe that there is such a thing as *Unconditionality*? What difference does it make whether I believe it or not? The possible answer is: only with this faith will the restlessness come into my life that awakens my will to be independent, which makes me ask myself in everything I think and do whether it is really what I want to think and do. It prevents me from blindly committing myself to things that my natural impulses, old habits, and traditions, social conventions, or unquestioned authorities make me take for granted as if there were no alternative.

The will to be independent, if I am honest, makes me aware of the extent to which I am trapped in dependencies. My full independence would be attained if I could know that I am being guided by the one and final Authority which, as the Absolute, transcends all instances of the world of appearances. To speak in *Chiffers*: if I knew what God wants with me, what He has planned for me as my destiny from eternity. But all this is beyond what I can know and recognize. I have no knowledge of such an Authority, nor do I know how I could turn to this Authority or how it could turn to me. Nor could I communicate what I have experienced in this way because it would apply only to me and to no one else. It would be what I alone and no one else has to do. There is no general validity as there is in intellectual knowledge. Independence therefore remains an unattainable *Idea.* It consists only of freeing myself again and again from dependencies by which I do not want to be determined. Independence is not a state but a never-ending journey.

But if I am always on the move and never at my destination, how can I ever know what the *Unconditional* is for me? To use Jaspers's terminology, how can *Possible Existence* ever become real *Existence*? Objectively, it remains forever uncertain what the *Unconditional One* has "intended" for me, what I have to grasp unconditionally: be it my love or my purpose in the world. And yet there is the experience that I can become certain in an inexplicable way of what I want and have always wanted—like an inner voice telling me that is mine and yet not my voice. As if the ultimate Authority from which I have my origin and by which I can defy all instances of this world, were speaking to me out of my judgment. How this can happen remains inexplicable. It is as if a *Leap* that changes me in my being passes through me, transforming my mere I in the immanent *Modes of Encompassing* into an *I myself* in a new sense.

The metaphor of the *Leap* makes it clear that the transition cannot be explained by what preceded it; it cannot be planned, it cannot be achieved, and it cannot be justified by any grounds.

## FREEDOM AND BEING GIVEN TO ONESELF

Jaspers touches here on the problem of free will as we know it from Augustine, who, according to Jaspers, was the first in the history of Western philosophy to have in view "the questionability of freedom and the question of the reason for its possibility."[12]

His discourse on Augustine in the *Great Philosophers* shows his closeness to Augustine, but also the point at which he can no longer follow him. Jasper's account begins with Augustine's "most exciting self-observation," that of the divided nature of his will. For him, the will was the center of existence, was life itself. "If I wanted something or did not want something, I was quite sure that not someone other than myself did want it or did not want it." And it was here, at the center of his being, that he experienced the "terrible thing": that his will did not find obedience, that he found himself divided into a willing and an unwilling. And this is not because he is dominated by two powers, one good and the other evil, but because he himself is this division.

But suddenly comes "the reversal, the *Leap*. With one blow the division was over. The light of certainty 'poured into my heart.' God helped him."[13] Augustine thus shows "the incomprehensibility of certainty, this certainty of the will, which now can do nothing else. The will becomes a necessity." It is "the tranquility of having chosen, which no longer chooses but must."[14]

Jaspers asks himself, and he asks Augustine: Where does this freedom of the will that can suddenly will come from? "What happens in the decision that brings full certainty and irrevocable certainty of the will?"[15]

In his search for an answer, Jaspers recalls the "fundamental experience" in the "freedom of our action": When I know what I want,[16] I also know that I cannot will my will.

> I experience the originality of this will within me, but I cannot produce this origin, not the ability to conclude myself. I love, but if I do not love, I cannot create love in myself. I am myself, but I can fail to be myself. I have to trust myself, but I cannot rely on myself. (. . .) Therefore, I am not absolutely free in my will, my freedom, my love. I am given to myself, and as a gift I can be free and become myself. I have not produced myself in order to produce myself. Not only the external conditions of my existence, but also myself, I do not owe to myself. Hence Augustine's sentence: What do you have that you have not received (*quid habes, quod non accepisti*)?[17]

Does Jaspers still fully agree with this last sentence of Augustine's?[18] Jaspers is indeed paraphrasing here what he has been repeating like a mantra with the same or similar words since the *Philosophy:*[19] When I succeed in "rising," it is "as if I had been given to myself." Because the opposite experience is also always possible: that I am "missing out," that I am at a loss and don't know what I really want. To be "given to me" means I am what I am and what I want to be as an *Existence*, not by myself—no more than I came into the world by myself. To the extent that I become aware of my unconditional will, I also become aware of the Other through which I am myself: *Transcendence*, but now no longer as a mere thought, but as a being that is active in me—as a reality. But now comes the big but, which is directed against Augustine: the way of speaking of "being given to oneself" is only a *Chiffer* (a sign that wants to tell us something but we do not know what it says), and this *Chiffer* is deceptive when it coagulates into a single *Chiffer*, a total *Chiffer*. But this is exactly what happens with Augustine's dogmatic hardening.

The dogma of *Predestination*—that every individual human being is destined by God from eternity to a state of freedom in grace or to a state of bondage in evil—has the consequence that God's will in its incomprehensibility is conceived as the all-encompassing will that also omnipotently determines man's freedom. Man cannot change what he is destined to do. He is "totally dependent on God's will, predetermined by him in his very being," even in his freedom.[20]

That man himself is capable of anything, that he owes anything to himself, that he can have merit, is impossible for this faith. The slightest hint that man stands on his own, even in relation to God (as the Pelagians thought against Augustine), means a violation of God's omnipotence. God alone is free.[21]

This dogmatic belief in the all-determining omnipotence of God leads to "rational contradictions": man, though totally dependent on God, is nevertheless to blame for his condition; God is supposed to be all good, but according to God's will evil is just as necessary as good, and so on.[22] But it is not these contradictions, which have been worked out by Christian dogmatists for centuries, that make the totalization of Augustine's *Chiffer* unacceptable to Jaspers. It is the opposite existential claim that speaks from the Pelagian *Chiffer*: that there is an "*innate Nobility*" of man,[23] that man has the freedom of choice and thus also the possibility of conversion and a new beginning at any time,[24] that he can make demands on himself and trust that he will be able to meet them. The significance of this shift can best be appreciated when one considers that it is only through the belief in the "nobility in man" to which Jaspers devoted himself,[25] that an (autonomous) philosophical life independent of ecclesiastical authority and the belief in revelation is possible at all.[26]

But even the Pelagian *Chiffer*, according to Jaspers, is not allowed to become a total *Chiffer*. It can become a seduction if I believe that "something is good because I am doing it," and I am allowed to "be satisfied with myself as I am because I am noble in any case."[27]

The fact that neither of these *Chiffers*, the Augustinian or the Pelagian, is allowed to become a total *Chiffer*, does not mean that these *Chiffers* lose their power and justification. Each has its truth: in the Augustinian *Chiffer* there is "the truth of the demand for conversion, which belongs to man as man, and the awareness of being given, not knowing from where and not knowing how"; in the Pelagian *Chiffer* is "the truth of the demand to be obedient to what I can actually be, to which I arrive in conversion."[28]

The tension between these two *Chiffers* thus becomes a parable whose truth can only be expressed as a paradox: We are given to ourselves, but it is up to us whether we are given to ourselves. It does not come of itself, as another, as a stranger. Just waiting is futile. What happens to us is prepared by ourselves. What happens to us as an event, as a chance, as an opportunity, becomes real in the way we make it our own.[29]

Jaspers believes that the circle in this parable cannot be broken: it is *Transcendence* that grasps me, but it grasps me only by my grasping that which grasps me. But I can never know whether that which grasps me is really *Transcendence* itself. I can only believe it. The only thing that can come to me is the inner certainty of what I want. Jaspers could be interpreted as saying that the certainty of what I really want is again eclipsed by the light of a very different reality that shines through that certainty, the reality of my freedom.[30] My inner certainty itself becomes a *Chiffer of Transcendence*. It is as if, having become homeless in the world of appearances, I have now found a new eternal home.[31] As a *Chiffer*, it gives me the courage to face my task. In the uncertainty of whether I will ever be able to fulfill my task, it gives me confidence in a "help from the ground of things that can never be accounted for."[32] And even if everything goes wrong and everything fails, the inner certainty of having decided in the spirit of eternity remains. This is the deeper meaning of the formula that runs through Jaspers's work: *no Existence without Transcendence*.

## NOTES

1. W 69, De 13.

2. In the following considerations, I also use portions of text from my article: "'Grenzsituationen erfahren und existieren ist dasselbe'—eine Meditation über einen Satz von Karl Jaspers," in *Swiss Archives of Neurology, Psychiatry and Psychotherapy,* 2020/2, 1–7.

3. Ph 2, 204.

4. On Jasper's distinction between *Ground Situation* and *Borderline Situation*, cf. PGO 318f.

5. Co-knowledge (*Mitwissenschaft*) with creation is the word most often quoted by Jaspers from Schelling. He also mentions Hegel's understanding of his *Logik* as God's thoughts before the creation of nature and the finite mind (ChT 74).

6. Another way to approach the *Borderline Situation* from a distance is to visualize tragic events through theatrical and literary means. Cf. Hans Saner, "Kunst als Antizipation der Grenzsituationen," in *Existenz und Sinn. Karl Jaspers im Kontext,* ed. Anton Hügli, Dominic Kaegi, Bernd Weidmann (Heidelberg: Winter, 2009), 23–36.

7. Jaspers distinguishes between the reasons *why* we want something and the reasons *out of which* we want something. He calls the latter the *origins* of our volition. Accordingly, there are different kinds of volition: the conditioned, "purposive" volition under the guidance of the intellect (intending, planning, and doing), and the unconditional volition awakened by *Reason*, which I cannot will myself but which is given to me, which I cannot dispose of, and of which I cannot know why I know it, in contrast to all intellectual knowledge (see VE 122f.).

8. Ph 2, 176.

9. However, the determination of what is absolutely valid for me will always have to be examined in terms of the concrete situation and consists in excluding rather than in requiring concrete actions. The reason for this is to be found in the hierarchy of the *Modes of Encompassing* that I am. They are already in a hierarchy insofar as one mode of being is the basis for others: *Dasein* is the basis for *Consciousness in*

*General*, which is the basis for *Spirit*, and *Spirit* is the basis for *Existence*. On the other hand, there is an inverse hierarchy of higher and lower: the demands of the higher Modes set the conditions for the lower ones: *Ideas* determine the direction of *Consciousness in General* and channel the impulses of life. Ultimately, it is the *Idea* of morality that sets the conditions for what is permissible in the struggle for *Dasein*. But even this is not to be applied strictly and rigidly: at the extreme limit, where I have to deal with people who behave toward me like beasts and are "in possession of lawless violence against me," my moral obligations can also fall away (see GP 492). But the affirmation of the hierarchy is part of my seriousness.

10. The textbook example of an unconditional will to the *Unconditional* is the fulfillment of the demand that Kant's *Categorical Imperative* makes of us. The *Unconditional* is the demand to check in everything I do whether the maxim of my action can become a general law, a law for all, and to refrain from any action that does not fulfill this condition. But it is not enough to act in accordance with this demand; this is mere *Legality*. What is decisive is whether I still want to follow this demand unconditionally, even when the interests of *Dasein* are at stake, no matter how great. According to Kant, it is only this *Unconditionality* that constitutes our morality; it is the *Good Will* of which we never know if it ever existed, and from which the individual is furthest removed, especially when he thinks he has it.

11. The following reflections in VuD 148f. are evidence of how Jaspers attempts to reconcile this *idea* of the equality of all with actual inequality: "Quite wrong, existentially ruinous: elite consciousness—one is not more intelligent or better, but different. Intelligence and goodness[,] humanity not the essence of the independent."

> In other words, it is the same: I am free only when the other is free,—I think independently only when the other thinks independently. In addition: I do not want to dominate others. I do not want to be dominated by others. (. . .) Everyone gets better if you assume they are better, everyone understands when the power of persuasion is not based on demagogic and violence and blackmail—they understand more than you might expect, if you are calm and patient, and if the other person realizes that he is being taken seriously and not raped and despised.

12. GP 363.

13. GP 355.

14. GP 355f.

15. GP 356.

16. For Jaspers, this is the highest I can achieve: "that I know what I want, that I know what I want to live for. Every person who succeeds in getting there is to be praised, that he knows what is worthwhile" (Prov 53).

17. GP 356f.

18. The way Jaspers deals with Augustine here is exemplary of his understanding of an existential appropriation of the thoughts of the great philosophers, which he understood as *Self-Illumination*. "Their self-illumination ignites ours when the torch passes from hand to hand. But the contact with the *Existence* of the philosophers has its concreteness only in the moment when the sense of thought becomes one with a selfhood, or in the transformation into present reality" (Ph 2, 326).

With regard to the appropriation of Augustine's thought, the guiding question for Jaspers is whether "a separation is possible" between philosophizing and the thinking of revealed faith (guaranteed by the authority of the Church), "that is, whether the truth of thinking can remain even when faith in Christ has been extinguished" (GP 354; on this problem, see Roberto Celada Ballanti, "Die Augustin-Deutung von Karl Jaspers," in *Studia Philosophica,* vol. 67/2008, 251–264).

19. Ph 2, 199.

20. GP 359.

21. PGO 352. Jaspers's discussion of Augustine in this work makes it even easier to understand what he only hints at in *Die grossen Philosophen.*

22. PGO 352.

23. PGO 365.

24. GP 358.

25. How central this *Nobility* in man is for Jaspers becomes clear already in: GSZ 191–201.

26. See GSZ 198: "The *Nobility* of being human can be called the philosophical life."–This playing off of one *Chiffer* against the other is exemplary of Jaspers' thesis that the *Chiffers* are at war with each other and that we can only prevent ourselves from falling for a single *Chiffer* with "skin and hair" by bringing it—through confrontation with the opposite *Chiffer*—into "suspension."

27. PGO 565.

28. PGO 565.

29. Karl Jaspers, "*Antwort auf die Frage: Aus welchen Kräften leben Sie?*" (1962), in *Philosophische Aufsätze* (Hamburg: Fischer, 1967), 238–247, 246. On this contradictory unity, which lies in the awareness of the *Innate Nobility* of man: to be certain of his freedom, but at the same time also of his "being given," see also Ph 3, 191f.

30. See, for example, Ph 2, 198: "By being free, I experience *Transcendence* in freedom, but only through it." However, the certainty that I am free through the certainty of the *Unconditional* is only one way to the consciousness of freedom. The opposite way is the "experience of my guilt" and the "evil in the world," the suffering of my lack of freedom and my guilty entanglement, which was the focus for Kierkegaard. (See Einleitung zur Metaphysikvorlesung, pp. 3, 5, DLA, A: Jaspers). For Jaspers, this is the way through the *Borderline Situation.*

31. Jaspers already used this metaphor in his *Einleitung zur Metaphysikvorlesung* (p. 6, DLA, A: Jaspers) in the winter semester of 1927/28 to characterize the "happiness in which I come to myself with the other": "The incomprehensible fulfillment of the certainty of what is true urges us to understand ourselves in a way that is impossible in the *World.* It is as if the individual were stepping out of homelessness into an eternal home." This formulation is probably a paraphrase of Plotin. See Tolga Ratzsch, *Karl Jaspers und Plotin. Eine Untersuchung zu den Quellen von Jaspers' Metaphysik der Transzendenz* (Baden-Baden: Alber, 2023, 156).

32. KlSch 139.

# *Chapter 4*

# Loneliness (Einsamkeit) and Communication

If it is true that in the end it is not up to me, but it is up to me again, whether I am "given to me," then what exactly can I do? To whom or what can I turn, if there is no God speaking directly to me? Nature, perhaps? But nature around me is silent, terribly silent. Sure, I can see something like a sign in this or that which happens to me, which gives me an understanding of how to decide, but everything that serves as a sign remains ambiguous and throws me back on myself, back into my *Loneliness*. It is a *Loneliness* of a very different kind than the *Loneliness* of someone abandoned in an emergency situation, than the *Loneliness* of someone excluded from his traditional community, than the *Loneliness* of a genius who has reached spiritual heights or an emeritus who has turned away from the world. I am lonely because only I can give myself the answer, and yet I can never rely on myself. It is all too easy for me to deceive myself as to whether I really want the *Unconditional* and whether I want it unconditionally. So in my *Loneliness* I push myself to where I can be heard. Toward communication with others. Just as we can only find truth in the world-immanent *Modes of Encompassing* through communication, I can only find my unconditional truth in communication with others.

But how can the other person help me if no one knows the truth? He helps me, the paradoxical answer goes, precisely by daring to stand in *Loneliness*, because he himself is also struggling for the *Unconditional* in his life. In our communication, we are separate and yet connected. We are separated because each one has to find the truth that is truth for him, and we are united because each one needs the other for this. This paradoxical relationship between *Loneliness* and communication—no *Loneliness* without communication, no communication without *Loneliness*—is a key to understanding the kind of communication that Jaspers calls *Existential Communication*. It is the communication of people who want to be themselves, and who therefore know

*Loneliness* as it can only be experienced from the bottom up in *Borderline Situations*,[1] and who nevertheless want to break out of *Loneliness* again and again.

Communication requires *Loneliness*, *Loneliness* requires communication; if one of the two poles is absent, then there are two basic forms of the lack of *Existential Communication*: the one in which the individual, because he cannot bear his *Loneliness*, allows the other to give him his truth and submits to him in obedience of faith, and the other in which the individual refuses communication and heroically wants to justify himself out of himself. He wants to be everything to himself, because others mean nothing to him.

The historical model of the first form of noncommunication is the relationship of the believer in Christ to Jesus Christ: Christ alone is the way, the truth, and the life. Those who follow Christ no longer know *Loneliness*, they are with God and God with them (Ishmael). Christ's way is the way for all; only faith in his message of peace can unite us human beings. Nietzsche's figure of the *Superman* (*Übermensch*) is an example of the second form of lack of communication: the human being who tries to elevate himself out of himself to his highest being, who creates himself out of nothing, as it were.[2] He is the lone exception who draws all his strength from himself and looks down nobly on everyone else.

## EXISTENTIAL COMMUNICATION

The model of *Existential Communication* is the Socratic dialogue, that is, communication on an equal level, from person to person, where truth is at stake, not power and submission, and not the desire to be a heroic exception. Because the search for truth always requires a new impulse, each person must be a "sting" for the other, countering with radical openness when the other wants to make things too easy for himself. Their communication, therefore, has the character of a struggle, but it is a struggle without the will to power. It is conducted "with the mutual surrender of all weapons," on an "equal footing,"[3] and with "complete openness."[4]

What sustains *Existential Communication* is love. Not love in the sense of caritas, which is ultimately based on a power relationship in which one gives and the other takes. Nor in the sense of erotic love, which forges two people together to the exclusion of all others, but love in the sense of Socratic *Eros*, which is directed to everyone and which is not directed to what people actually are, but to the best in them that they can be. Socratic *Eros* is therefore far removed from any emotional upsurge, beyond sympathy and antipathy. It is itself already of the *Unconditionality* it seeks.

For the sake of the "dignity of *Loneliness*," Socratic communication, for all its closeness to one another, preserves the hardness of distance, which throws everyone back on himself and demands his own decision. Jaspers speaks of a "*loving struggle*" *(liebender Kampf),* a formula that in its paradoxical nature best expresses what is at stake here: an "incomparable solidarity" in which people help each other to increase their strength in the struggle against each other, so that they can manifest what they are capable of being.

To find the other person who wants to enter into *Existential Communication* with me is a gift of fate, and yet depends on what we do: whether, without abandoning the "dignity of *Loneliness*," we have the will, in all our vulnerability, to remain open to the encounter with the other person, to reveal ourselves to him, and to dare to speak without considerations and reservations, without bridges and railings.[5]

But what should the dialogue be about? It is never about the other person directly, not about a mutual understanding of souls, nor about a mutual appreciation of merits and demerits, but about what is at stake in the respective situation and what are the realities within the respective *Modes of* (world-immanent) *Encompassing*.[6] More precisely, to find out what is at stake and how serious I am about it. And I am only serious if, whatever my efforts, I am always concerned with my relationship to it: what it means *to me*, what meaning and value I give it. And since it is precisely the latter that is up for examination, another relationship comes into play: my relationship to my own behavior, and thus my relationship to myself. But what does that mean? We can call the first relationship the objective relationship, and the second the subjective relationship. Objectively, everything revolves around the question of what the matter is; subjectively, however, the emphasis is on the being of that which matters, that it is or becomes real.

The most general word for interest in the being of something is love. What I love, I not only wish it to be but also want it to be. Wanting, as opposed to merely wishing, implies that where the existence of the beloved object depends on me, I will do everything I can to ensure that it can be there. I want it not only in the here and now but also forever; that is, for the greatest possible duration in the time allotted, not for this or that purpose, but as an end in itself. But if I want something to last forever, I must first and foremost make sure that my will does not evaporate tomorrow, but remains my will over time. I must want not only the object of my love but also my will. I must want myself to be a lover and to remain a lover. This is the concrete expression of my relationship to myself, that is, to be my own will and to want to be myself. This is the selfhood of which Jaspers speaks. When I find in my life what I want to love, I also know through my love who I am and who I want to be.

## INTERNAL ACTION

The expression of the will is what follows from the will: the corresponding action. Love wants reality. It wants the beloved object to become reality in *Dasein*. This is done through action in the world, which sets goals and pursues objectives under the guidance of the cognizing and planning *Consciousness in General*. In addition to this outward action in the physical world, however, there is a very different kind of action: action on myself, by which I give my will itself lasting reality. Jaspers calls this *Inner Action (innere Handlung)*. Psychologically, we are quite familiar with a certain kind of *Inner Action*, which includes any planned, reflective, and purposeful mental activity, such as the effort we make to concentrate on an object. However, the inner action involved in love is of a very different nature. The love that I give permanence to by keeping to my decision to love is already there; it does not need to be brought about in a planned way—as a purpose set by me. Nor is there any motive other than love itself that would drive me to maintain love. Love itself is the reason why I want love, and there are purposes only insofar as love itself sets purposes for me, be it for my external actions or for the psychological work on myself. But the decision to remain faithful to love is like a new beginning in time. It becomes proof of my freedom. For it is up to me, and to me alone, that my will remains constant.

Every action is connected with thinking. Both *Inner* and outer *Actions* involve the calculating and causal thinking of *Consciousness in General*. But *Inner Action*, as an act of love, revolves around the being that my love reveals to me. The object of my love does not stand alone; it stands in a *World* context, it is being only because there is *Being* at all, because there is something rather than nothing. When I love, I also love the being of this whole. That is the metaphysical reason for all love.[7] We will have to talk about this later.

*Inner Action* can never be separated from outer action. It is only the inner side of outer action, that is, how I am involved when I act outwardly. By outward, we mean that it is a matter of keeping the object I love in existence: in the struggle for *Dasein*, in the idealistic struggle, and in the struggle for clarity of *Consciousness in General*. When I love, I also love what sustains and protects the object of my love in the real world, and hate what threatens it. But is everything permissible in this struggle? Is my love beyond the question of good and evil? Am I entitled to everything just because I love?

For Jaspers, it is clear that love cannot be the sole guide to our actions. It is not enough to say, with Augustine, "Love and do whatever you want." I can only love what I understand to be good in the choice between good and evil.[8] Therefore, we cannot rely on love. It too must be examined at every moment.[9] It is only through this examination that unconditional *Existence* differs from that of a fanatic. It is the only thing that prevents me from being completely absorbed in the chosen way of my appearance, but setting limits to it in everything I do. But what is the standard for this examination? And what does it require of me?

## EXAMINING ONESELF BY THE STANDARD OF THE MORAL LAW AND THE QUESTION OF LOVE AND HATE

What is objectively required of us is to act according to generally accepted rules such as: thou shalt not lie, not kill, not steal, and so on. These rules find their validity in the *Categorical Imperative* and its universalizing command, in its various formulations. Their meaning is: "What I do should be such that I can want the world in general to be such that it should happen everywhere."[10] Recognizing the meaning of these demands is an act of *Consciousness in General*. But the objective rules of action that satisfy the *Categorical Imperative* are valid only if they are recognized as valid for the person acting. The crucial first question that this standard poses to me is, therefore, whether I am willing to submit to moral norms at all, or whether I give in to my pursuit of happiness and allow myself to be guided by my immediate inclinations, sensual drives, and vital interests. To choose the morally good, then, is to choose the side of duty in the alternative between moral duty and sensual inclination. Not to do it is the *Moral Evil*.

But then the question arises at the next level: I may recognize what my duty is, but am I willing to follow my duty even if it interferes with the undisturbed satisfaction of my sensual needs for happiness? When the disadvantages become too great, when sacrifice is required, perhaps even the sacrifice of my life? This is where the struggle against *Ethical Evil* begins, against the perversion of the will as Kant understood it, which follows moral demands only on the condition that they do not interfere with the pursuit of happiness, the pursuit of having our desires and our will fulfilled in the whole of our being.

Fighting evil on these two levels captures a significant part of what our earlier phrase "unconditionally wanting the *Unconditional*" attempts to capture. But it still lacks the essential part, the one that gives substance to our actions. Because the *Categorical Imperative* states the condition under which any action is to be taken, it only says what we must not do, not what we should do. The content of our will, what drives us to act, must come from somewhere else. And it must be of the same *Unconditionality* as the commandment itself. Only the object of love can fulfill this condition. Only through love can the *Categorical Imperative* find its content. For only love gives the living impulse to act; only love can still guide us in a conflict of duties when justified moral demands collide in ethical dilemmas. When love is absent, morality ends in *Moralism*; it no longer serves the purpose of self-examination, which is directed against one's own imperfections, but turns the judgmental verdict against the other—with the evil eye of hatred.

In this third stage begins the struggle for the ability to love and the fight against "*Metaphysical Evil*," as Jaspers calls it: the fight against the will to destruction as such, to torture, to cruelty and annihilation, to the "destruction of everything that is and has value."[11]

At the third level, the abysses of human existence open up. Seized by love, I can throw myself into my passion, ready to sacrifice everything for it and burn myself to death, not only accepting death but also seeking it. But I can also choose the second path, the one we have always talked about, doing everything I can to give the object of my love permanence in time, engaging with the reality of *Dasein*, maintaining my loyalty, and seeing death without seeking it. Jaspers describes the first way as that of *Passion for the Night (Leidenschaft zur Nacht)*, the second as following *the Law of the Day (Gesetz des Tages)*.

## THE LAW OF THE DAY AND THE PASSION FOR THE NIGHT

Why these two ways in particular? Jaspers interprets them as reactions to the experience of the *Borderline Situation* that shatters man's entire existence: that even what I love must perish, that one day everything will come to nothing, and that nothing in the world can ever stop the doom. Happiness is a vain moment in the stream of destruction.[12] Defiance and indignation will be the first reactions to this experience. How can I love this whole that makes the object of my love possible, only to destroy it again? Indignation can turn into hatred of all that is, awakening the will to push down what falls, to destroy oneself in suicide, and ultimately to drag everything down with it into the abyss. This hatred leads to the will to *Night*, the will to throw oneself into nothingness, which means the end of all Being.

On the other hand, there is another attitude: "What goes down must have been once."[13] It must have been a reality and not a mere possibility. Only through what has become real can we experience what is. This becomes imperative for each individual to give reality to what they love, to preserve in time what can only be preserved through their actions, so that it will have been for all time.

What unconditional decision means appears in a new light: to decide in the clear awareness that what I decide here and now is decided for eternity, that what is eternal is decided in time.[14] This gives the decision the greatest emphasis, for only what becomes real in this way is a fulfilled being and will endure, even if, like everything else in this *World*, it perishes. In the pain of its passing, even this loss can be endured—in the knowledge that even if we never know what the ultimate *being* is, it must be such that the beloved object could be possible. And with it everything that belongs to its reality, in which I myself live and have to participate: from family and circle of friends to society and nature in its objectivity and lawfulness, which supports all this and makes it possible.

When I have done what I had to do, perhaps I can still say, in gratitude for the reality given to me in the pain of failure: even if this reality perishes, it was not pointless that it existed. For the fact that it existed will have been true forever. That there is an eternal Being is enough.[15] With this attitude, even in the greatest pain, I can experience what is contained in the words of Job (I, 20–22): "The Lord gave, the Lord has taken away; blessed be the name of the Lord." I do not simply accept failure; I surrender to it. It is not defiance and indignation that have the last word, but surrender, the "willingness to accept life as it comes."[16] Only by surrendering is it possible not to cling desperately to the immanent *Modes of Encompassing*, to the purposes of *Dasein*, to the categories of *Consciousness in General*, or to the imperatives of the *Spirit*. Through that alone I gain full independence.[17]

But how do we acquire this attitude? It doesn't just come to us. It has to be acquired again and again. And we are never sure of it. We reach it only in rare climaxes on a never-ending path of ups and downs. At the beginning of this path is the experience of the *Borderline Situation*, the insight into the futility of everything that belongs to this *World*, and the despair that goes with this experience, the readiness to be indignant and defiant, the threat of falling into the *Passion for the Night*. The only way out, it seems, is to adopt the attitude of the Stoic, who, in order to preserve the imperturbability of the mind, allows nothing to disturb him, and who, in inner indifference, tries to save himself at least as an abstract ego. But that would mean living as if we were already dead. To have nothing left that could fulfill us, that could give substance to our lives. Only those who love will stay alive, and only those who find their substance in their love and want to make it real in accordance with their conscience, remain true human beings. On this path—perhaps—one can succeed in ascending to eternal existence. And only on this path, according to Jaspers, can one attain immortality—immortality not as a continuation of life after death, not as a return in another temporal form, but as the presence of the *Eternal in Time* (*quer zur Zeit)*.[18] This is summed up in his phrase: "We are mortal where we are unloving, immortal where we love."[19]

But instead of the upswing, there is always the threat of falling, the pull of despair, the horror of the possibility of nothingness, the tendency to choose the last resort—suicide. It is as if we are under the spell of two forces that pull us in opposite directions. Jaspers gives them mythic names. He speaks of the *Genius* and the *Demon*, each of which becomes a counterpart in our communication with ourselves, as if they were two figures of our true self that enchant or seduce us.[20]

"The *Genius* leads to the light," it is that in me that wants loyalty, realization, and permanence, that urges for law and order. "*The Demon* shows a depth that frightens me. It wants to lead me into a worldless existence, can advise destruction, makes me not only understand failure but also fulfill it straightaway." "He can ruin fidelity, law, and brightness," because for him the negative is the true positive. The *Genius*, although unrecognizable and distant by nature, can be the only God who can be close to me in this form. The *Demon* is like a "divine, counter-divine power" that tolerates no certainty in its darkness. It is not evil per se but a constant companion of the *Genius*, who wants to create certainty and finds himself exposed to "unfathomable ambiguity" through the *Demon*.[21]

At this point, if not before, the sober reader may ask what these mythologies are all about. What sphere are we in when we develop such thoughts, and what meaning do they have? And where is the communication and connection between people if we are already divided within ourselves and cannot find ourselves in any definitive form?

## NOTES

1. For this reason, the sentence applies: "Experiencing Borderline Situations and existing are the same thing" (Ph II, 204).
2. See Jaspers's description of this *idea* of the self-producing human being in N 153–169.
3. W 37.
4. Ph 2, 65.
5. Ph 2, 59.
6. Ph 2, 68f.—"What the realities are" means what is true in the sense of the corresponding concept of truth. So, for example, when it comes to a question of *Dasein*, the concept of truth within the corresponding *Mode of Dasein* also applies. Thus, Jaspers can say with regard to his attitude toward the Nazi functionaries: they were "functionaries of beasts," "who must not be treated like human beings, but, since they are in possession of power, only with cunning and deceit, just like beasts" ("Letter to Ernst Bloch," 19.4.1963, in KorrPhil 151).
7. Karl Jaspers, «Das Unbedingte und das Böse», in *Das Wagnis der Freiheit. Gesammelte Aufsätze zur Philosophie*, ed. Hans Saner, 86–96 (München; Zürich: Piper, 1996), 89.
8. WF 86.
9. WF 85.
10. Ph 2, 269.

11. Karl Jaspers, «Das Unbedingte und das Böse», in *Das Wagnis der Freiheit. Gesammelte Aufsätze zur Philosophie*, ed. Hans Saner, 86–96 (München; Zürich: Piper, 1996), 87.
12. Ph 3, 71.
13. Ph 3, 225.
14. Karl Jaspers, "Unsterblichkeit" (1957), in *Wagnis der Freiheit. Gesammelte Aufsätze zur Philosophie,* ed. Hans Saner (München; Zürich: Piper, 1996), 339.
15. Ph 3, 233; "Unsterblichkeit" (1957), in *Das Wagnis der Freiheit. Gesammelte Aufsätze zur Philosophie*, ed. Hans Saner (München; Zürich: Piper, 1996), 338.
16. Ph 3.75.
17. Cf. W 110.
18. Karl Jaspers, «Unsterblichkeit» (1957), in *Das Wagnis der Freiheit. Gesammelte Aufsätze zur Philosophie*, ed. by Hans Saner (München; Zürich: Piper, 1996), 336–341; Ph 3, 92–94.
19. Ibid. 339.
20. Ph 3, 90f.
21. Ph 3, 91.

# *Chapter 5*

# Encounters with Transcendence

## READING CHIFFERS

The Kantian idea of the phenomenal nature of the world has led us to the limit at which all knowledge ends. Given the radical division of subject and object within the cognizable world, it confronts us with the question of what kind of *Being* it could be that transcends all divisions and is neither subject nor object, but always both at the same time. It would have to be such that it encompasses everything that appears to us in the various *Modes of Encompassing* and should have nothing outside of itself by which it would again be encompassed. In a word, the *Encompassing* of all that encompasses. But we do not know what this could be. We have a name for it, we call it *Transcendence*, but with it we know no more than this: that it exists at all. Because everything that exists for us would not exist if this *Being* did not exist. So *Transcendence* can also simply mean *Being*. Our only access to it is that we can think it, must think it. However, the question of why there is something rather than nothing also shows that this *Being* could just as well be *Nothing*, for only if it also encompasses *Nothingness*, which could be in place of *Being*, would it be the truly *Encompassing*.

There is a way of "experiencing" *Transcendence* in the *Borderline Situation*. It is the reality in which we live and which is revealed to us in our failure *(Scheitern)*: as the *Being* that makes us struggle, become guilty, suffer, and die. Jaspers calls it the *Actual Reality*.

Where we believe we hear a call of conscience addressed to us, which in its *Unconditionality* differs from all the conditional imperatives that come to us from the various *Modes of Encompassing*: from *Dasein*, from *Consciousness in General*, or from the *Ideas* of the *Spirit*, we experience *Transcendence* as a demanding, otherworldly authority. In this form, it can also be called *Deity*.

Where the individual is struggling to find what is unconditional for him in his life, animated by the will to be himself, it is as if *Transcendence* is speaking to him personally, as a "You." In this situation, Transcendence can become a *Personal God* for him.

But whether *Being*, *Reality*, *Deity*, or *God*, these are not objects but names for different ways in which Transcendence can "appear" to us. But the word "appear" itself is false, for what does it mean that *Transcendence* can appear to us?[1] If it were an appearance, as objects of our knowledge appear to us, then *Transcendence* would be a thing in the *World*, and therefore not *Transcendence*. It is nothing but superstition to believe that anything in the *World* is already *Transcendence*. For us, there is no being other than the being that we ourselves are in the various forms of our appearances and the *World* as the being that encompasses us. If there is such a thing as *Transcendence* that appears—even if it can only be meant metaphorically—it is not an appearance in the *World*, but a shimmering through the *World*, just as a light background shimmers through in certain places in a picture painted over it, or as the light of the sun is reflected in a drop of dew. And just as it always remains ambiguous to our gaze whether this background really exists, or whether the shimmering light itself is just part of the picture, so it is with the appearance of *Transcendence*: the ambiguity remains as to whether I am merely dealing with a reality in the world of appearances, or whether *Transcendence* is somehow "revealed" to me through this reality. If it is the latter, then sensual appearances become a language of *Transcendence*, signs through which *Transcendence* speaks to us, so to speak. They become *Chiffers of Transcendence*, as Jaspers calls this sign-like quality of the world of appearances.

We have already encountered examples of *Chiffers of Transcendence*, for example, the Augustinian *Chiffer* that our salvation is already predetermined by the eternal counsel of God, and the Pelagian *Chiffer* that man can freely choose his own path to salvation. Whichever of these *Chiffers* becomes the voice of *Transcendence* for me, it can transform me from the ground up.

Every phenomenon in the world can become a *Chiffer*, from the "burning" thorn bush and the dewdrop in the grass to the images and ideas of mythologies and religions to the speculative thoughts of philosophers. But only the clairaudient, the *Possible Existence* that believes in guidance through *Transcendence*, can hear the voice of a *Chiffer*. It is the manifestation of *Transcendence* for him and him alone. However, what he thinks he hears from it is full of ambiguities. If *Transcendence* appears to him in concepts and images of *Being* and light, this may only touch him in a contemplative way without changing anything in his life. But if he understands the *Chiffer* as addressed to him, it may become a claim on him to place himself under the *Law of the Day*, however, he may understand this possibility of meaning described by Jaspers under this term. If, on the other hand, he sees only the darkness and the *Nothingness* that stares out at him from the *World*, he may, seized by the *Passion for the Night*, want to throw himself into this Nothingness.

## PHILOSOPHY AS PRECURSOR TO CHIFFER READING

The ability to read *Chiffers* is not a natural gift. It can be awakened and developed—because it depends on the way in which *Transcendence* becomes a question for us, the question with which philosophy begins: What is the real Being that is behind the endless beings that are found arising and passing away in the *World*? What holds it all together, underlies it all, and allows everything that is to emerge from it?[2]

This question has led to answers such as everything is water, or fire, or air, or the indeterminate, or matter, or atoms, or *Spirit*. A being that is present in the *World* has been declared to be the real and true *Being* that is at the root of all other beings. There were too many answers, and each one was wrong. They only became convincing when they produced research programs that taught us to see the *World* anew, such as atomic theory or quantum physics. But they become false as soon as they are made the sole basis for explaining the *World*.

At the latest, with Kant's insight into the phenomenal nature of the *World*, we also know the reason for this.[3] Nothing that we lift out of the whole of the *World* as the actual *Being* and make the object of our cognition can already be the whole. This is because, outside of this supposed whole, there is still the cognizing subject that carries out this objectification. *Being* as a whole can be neither object nor subject, but only that which includes both and appears in this division.[4] It is therefore necessary to separate the philosophical question of *actual Being* from the scientific question of the fundamental phenomena of our world of appearances. With this distinction—keyword: *Boundary Consciousness*—there is also the question of decision: Is the *Immanence* of the world of appearances already *Being* itself, or is there such an encompassing *Being*? Are there only scientific questions, or are there philosophical questions as well? Even for those who want to be satisfied with *Immanence*, their answer is not a scientific one but a philosophical one. For no science in the world can tell us why there should be only scientific questions. So even a non-philosophy is still a philosophy. It is the philosophy of *Positivism* and *Naturalism*.

But if we do not close ourselves to the insight that the *World* is appearance, everything changes for us. Our gaze opens to the unknown, to *Transcendence*. It prevents us from taking what is objectively tangible and recognizable in the *World* as the actual Reality. And so it awakens the ability to listen to what *Transcendence* is telling us out of what appears to us.[5] But how can this happen? What is there to listen to?

## Mysticism and Metaphysical Speculation

There is a millennia-old stream of thought that has sought to free itself from all ties to sensual objects and to connect with *Transcendence* itself: *Mysticism*. Both Eastern and Western thinkers have been driven by the idea that it is possible to transcend the *Subject-Object-Split* to a complete fusion of subject and object, to a state of consciousness in which everything objective disappears and the ego is extinguished. Those who have had this experience reported that it was like an awakening from the slumber of the body and an immediate becoming one with the Godhead itself.

There is no reason to doubt these testimonies. Behind them are experiences of the deepest inexhaustible meaning. But in order to report what they have seen, mystics must return to everyday consciousness, and thus back to the *Subject-Object-Split*, where they must experience that what they want to communicate cannot be communicated because it is not possible to say in objective language what eludes all objectivity.

The counter-movement to Mysticism is the path of Western *Metaphysics*. It does not seek to merge with *Transcendence*, but, remaining in the *Subject-Object-Split*, wants to make *Transcendence* comprehensible through speculative thinking, by developing *Cosmogonies*, proofs of God, and abstract doctrines of *Being*. This was done, at least for the dogmatic Metaphysicians, in the firm belief that this would lead to objective knowledge of what *Being* itself is. Kant dealt this belief a death blow. His question as to how knowledge is possible at all forces Metaphysics to seek a justification for what it claims, and its answer to this question shows the impossibility of its undertaking.

There is no escaping the *Subject-Object-Split*, that is, to use Kant's language, valid knowledge exists only of objects that can be experienced by the senses and that fill our concepts with content. Concepts without perception are empty, and it is in this emptiness that the speculative thoughts of Metaphysics operate. It is a way of thinking that necessarily leads to circles, contradictions, and tautologies. In the field of Metaphysics, but not in the field of knowledge of the *World*, Kant thus proves the skeptics right, who have always denied that we can have knowledge, not of the sensible and even less of the supernatural, such as God, the immortality of the soul, and other metaphysical objects.

Kant seems to prepare the ground for the nihilist who triumphantly concludes from Kant's critique of knowledge that all speculations about *Transcendence* are nothing more than illusions and fantasies. But Kant is neither a skeptic nor a nihilist. He draws a different conclusion from the failure of

Metaphysics: we may not be able to recognize *Transcendence*, but what we cannot recognize, we can at least think.[6] And not only can we think it, we must think it. Otherwise, not only our cognition but also our entire being would be meaningless and desolate. Jaspers' understanding of what it means to approach *Transcendence* through thinking is so closely tied to Kantian philosophizing that we can best follow Jaspers's way by staying with Kant himself for the remainder of this chapter. This will show us at the same time the extent to which Kant was the godfather of the basic concepts of Jaspers that we have already encountered, and will help us to see them in a different light. But it will also lead us to the point where Jaspers starts to think beyond Kant.

## Kant and the Experience of the Sublime

Unlike Jaspers, Kant does not speak of an *Upswing* (*Aufschwung*) as we ascend to *Transcendence*. But he does speak of what we experience through the ascent. He calls it the *Sublime (das Erhabene)*.

There is a famous passage at the end of the *Critique of Practical Reason* in which Kant emphatically addresses the feeling of the *Sublime*: "Two things fill the mind with ever-increasing admiration and awe, the more often and the more persistently one thinks about them: the starry sky above me and the moral law within me."[7] In the next sentence, however, comes the warning that this is not a mere surge of emotion that allows us to drift off into mystical distances: "I must not look for either of them as shrouded in darkness or in exuberance, outside the circle of my vision and merely conjecture; I see them before me and connect them directly with the consciousness of my existence." And what is this connection? The starry sky above me makes me aware of where I am: in an external sensory world connected to an endlessly expanding, "immeasurably large" *World* of "worlds upon worlds and systems of systems." The effect of the sight of this

> uncountable mass of worlds destroys, as it were, my small importance as an animal creature which, after having been supplied with life-force for a short time (one does not know how), has to return the matter of which it was made to the planet (a mere point in the universe).[8]

This "self-annihilation" is the experience of the limit set for us, which belongs to the *Sublime* (which, however, as will be shown, is not possible without at the same time transcending this limit). The sight of the moral law, on the other hand, elevates me; it increases my value, and it reveals to me "a life independent of animality and even of the world of the senses."[9] Kant's philosophy can be seen as an attempt to conceptualize the humiliation we experience through the sublimity of nature and our self-exaltation in the face of the moral law.[10] Here is an explanation. First, to the *Sublime* of nature.

## The *Sublime* of Nature

One of Kant's main messages, and we keep coming back to it, is the thesis of the phenomenal nature of the *World*, the *Subject-Object-Split*, and the absolute limit of our cognition, which throws us back on ourselves as beings bound to sensuality. But the feeling of the *Sublime*, which the sight of the starry sky awakens in us at the thought of the immeasurable dimensions of this *World* of appearances, is itself only possible and arises solely from the fact that we still measure this size and power against the idea of an all-encompassing *Absolute Greatness*, against which everything that appears in nature again seems small.

*Absolute Greatness* is a "supernatural" *Idea*, as Kant says, to which nothing that appears to us in the *World* corresponds. But where does this *Idea* come from? To give an account of it: this is the demand that is made upon us—upon each one of us—and that we can fulfill only in one way: through the aforementioned prolonged "reflection" on what the sublimity of the starry sky asks us to think about. And the more we become aware of the *Idea* of the *Absolute Great* that it evokes, the clearer it becomes to us that this *Idea* must have a completely different *Origin* than anything we can know from the world of appearances and what intellectual knowledge can ever convey to us. And we soon become aware that there are other such "supernatural" *Ideas* that we carry within us.

The *Idea* of the *One World*, which encompasses all of nature as it appears to us in a single unity, is the most familiar of these "supernatural" *Ideas*. That we ourselves are such a unity, encompassing everything that appears in us, is a second such *Idea*. And finally, the third is the idea of a unity that includes all these entities in itself, the *Idea* of God as the *Absolute Great*. The *World*, *Man*, and God, the three great objects of Metaphysics, which Metaphysics has mistaken for objects of knowledge, are nothing but such supernatural *Ideas*. The fact that we can think them at all shows that we are more than mere *Understanding (Verstand)*. We are only able to form this *Idea* because we have within us the capacity to leave behind all sense experiences and all categories of *Understanding* and to think the *Absolute*, which can never be the object of our cognition. Kant calls this ability to form *Ideas* of the *Supernatural* (*Übersinnliche*) the faculty of *Reason*.

Thanks to *Reason*, we are not only physical beings but also reasonable beings. It is the discrepancy between these two ways of being that makes the experience of the *Sublime* possible. For what allows us to experience the *Sublime* in nature is not nature in its greatness and power—which frightens us as sensual beings—but the awareness that, thanks to *Reason*, we are free from the influences of (sensual) nature. The only judgment that the *Sublime* expresses itself in is this: none of the images and concepts that our imagination presents to us will ever correspond to the *Ideas* of *Reason*. Any representation of the *Sublime* can therefore only be negative—a judgment of what the *Idea* is not. And the effect of the *Sublime* on our minds is based solely on this. Kant illustrates this with the example of the *Idea* of God.

> Perhaps there is no more sublime passage in the Jewish law book than the commandment: "You shall not make for yourself any graven image or any likeness of anything that is in heaven or on earth or under the earth, etc." This commandment alone can explain the enthusiasm that the Jewish people felt for their religion in their civilized era, when they compared themselves with other peoples.[11]

But back to the *Idea* of *Absolute Greatness*, beyond which nothing greater can be thought! What does it mean to think this *Idea*? Many things can be thought, and as long as they are thought without contradiction, what is thought is nothing more than a possibility—a possibility of thought. Our deepest need—the need of *Reason*, as Kant would say—is therefore to make sure that what can be thought is real. How can this happen? If there are any clues at all, they should be found in the phenomena of the senses, which are the only ones accessible to us. But how can that which—as the *Supernatural*—cannot be an appearance, show itself in the world of appearances? At least one thing is certain: The *Absolute* that we conceive must be present in all phenomena of nature, both external and internal, since everything that exists is encompassed by this *One*, both subjectively—in what we ourselves are—and objectively, in what we are not.

But how can the presence of this *Idea* be "experienced"? It is never experienced in the literal sense, but it is indirectly present in its work, both subjectively and objectively. The power of the *Idea* manifests itself subjectively in the desire to find the unity of the *World* that we think we can grasp in the world of appearances. Therefore, the idea of the unity of the *World* constantly drives our mind to search for the hidden unity.[12] Therein lies its function of regulating our cognition, its *regulative* power. It gives us the reason why, whenever we set out to find an explanation for something that seems puzzling to us, we assume a priori that there is nothing that is not causally connected to something else. And when we search for such connections, it is—here the idea is revealed in its objectivity—as if the world of appearances were coming to us: The connections turn out to be lawful connections and strengthen our belief that all of nature must be subject to laws. It is as if the *Idea* that creates unity appears in the lawfulness of nature. The longer we think about it, the more amazed we are that the world is set up this way. This amazement leads us to search for the "middle ground," that is, the unifying element that holds everything together and in which everything comes together. The ground of this unity is hidden from us in the traditional *Idea* of God as the lawgiver of nature and the "intelligent cause of the *World*."

So much for the Sublime as it reveals itself to us in "contemplation," in wonder at what is. It is different, however, when we ask not what is, but what ought to be. This brings us to the second *Sublime* mentioned by Kant: the moral law in me.

## The Sublime of the Moral Law in Me

Just as everything we can perceive is subject to laws, so we are subject to laws when we act. But not to laws that tell us what necessarily happens and will happen, but to laws that *prescribe* what should happen through us (even though it may never happen). These are *normative* laws. Unlike the laws of nature to which we are subject as natural beings (and which govern us even if we know nothing about them), the laws that should govern our actions are laws that we impose on ourselves. But how do we arrive at these laws? Again, it is *Reason* that reveals to us, not in theoretical but in practical terms, the constructive principle of such self-legislation—with the *Categorical Imperative* in its various versions, for example, that which makes us the legislators of the world we have created: "act as if the maxim of your action should become a general law of nature through your will."[13] This (and the other formulas) of the imperative do not tell us what we should want in terms of content, but they do set the conditions under which we must act: Not to commit any act that follows a maxim that could not become a general law to be followed by all. Like Socrates's *daimonion*, then, the imperative has a purely negative function; it warns us against doing wrong. But *Reason*, which speaks to us in this warning, does not guide us only indirectly, like the *Ideas* of theoretical *Reason*. We should not only seek unity in the world but also create unity. This demand is direct and unequivocal; it not only commands us to produce reality, but we ourselves experience it as reality—as a fact of pure *Reason*.[14]

But what is the *Sublime* about the moral law expressed in the *Imperative*? For one thing, it throws us back upon ourselves, this time upon our inner nature and our natural aspirations. The striving of the inner nature is directed toward happiness, which, according to Kant's definition of happiness, is the satisfaction of all our inclinations, both in their variety and in their degree and duration.[15] Our inclinations are determined by the laws of our (inner) nature. But how can we obey the moral law if nature sets the ends in us, which we must necessarily follow, and which—in the absence of natural instinct—we try to achieve by the means of our intellect?

The moral law within us makes us aware that in our actions we are subject to an entirely different order of things; we are members of a *Moral World*. Even if we think that we cannot do anything other than what our sensual nature compels us to do, the voice of *Reason* within us says the opposite: if the moral law is to manifest itself in the *World*—and this is the categorical requirement—then we can also do what we are supposed to do. We must have the capacity to initiate a state of our own—the capacity for freedom. There is no proof of this, no trace of freedom, when we explore our empirical being. There is no proof even if our actual actions are in accordance with the moral law. This could be an accidental consequence of natural inclinations.

Acting in accordance with the moral law is merely *Legality*, as Kant would say. Only an action that is in accordance with the moral law and is done for the sake of the law would be *Morality*. And only Morality can be an expression of freedom. The true "proof of freedom" can therefore only be provided by each individual for himself: by his own actions—by trying to follow the moral law for its own sake, even when his conflicting inclinations are at their greatest. But even then he cannot believe himself to be moral: whether his true motivation was really the will to obey the law for its own sake, and not a motive arising from hidden dispositions, he will never be able to say for certain, even after the most serious examination of his conscience—and an outside observer will not be able to do so anyway. But whenever he tries again, the belief in his freedom remains. To feel the power that comes with this belief in the possibility of my freedom: this is the true elevation of the mind by the moral law of which Kant speaks. Through my "personality" I know that I am bound to the moral law within me, which "reveals to me a life independent of animality and even of the whole world of the senses."[16] The possibility of being a *Person*, a member of the moral order, is what gives me, and every other human being, infinite value. What deserves our esteem and respect is therefore not man in his factuality, in his mere being, but the *possible* man in him: that he can, if he only wants to, make a beginning of his own.

According to Kant, it is only from this highest point, our Morality, that our admiration for the beauty of nature can be explained. Only those who have "already developed the way of thinking either toward the good or are particularly receptive to this development" can be interested in the beautiful forms of nature, in which nature "shows itself, as it were, intentionally, according to lawful order, and as purposefulness without purpose." This purpose, which we "do not encounter externally," we therefore "naturally seek within ourselves, namely in that which constitutes the ultimate purpose of our existence, namely our moral destiny."[17] Kant called this aesthetic experience the *Chiffer of Nature*, "through which nature speaks to us figuratively in its beautiful forms."[18] The beauty of nature reveals to us that, although inexplicable to us, there must be a connection between the natural and moral order of things in that transcendent *One* who transcends both orders. As *Chiffer* again: in the one God as the lawgiver of morality and the lawgiver of nature.

## What Jaspers Owes to Kant

This excursus on the beautiful and the *Sublime* in Kant shows the extent to which Jaspers' philosophizing is indebted to Kant's philosophy and can be made even more comprehensible from Kant's perspective. For Jaspers, the *Ideas of Reason* become the *Modes of the Encompassing*. The *Sublime* is the *Upsurge* that takes hold of us in the consciousness of the eternal *Origin of Ideas*. The thought of the unity of subject and object in the *Idea*, that is, in the *Encompassing*, is the basis of that other consciousness of *Being* that Kant seeks to awaken with his philosophizing and in which he sees the meaning of philosophy in general. For Jaspers, as for Kant, the idea of freedom is the fulcrum around which their entire philosophizing revolves and the only place where *Transcendence* can become tangible for us. What Kant suggests about the *Chiffer*-like character of the beautiful in nature, which reminds us of our eternal destiny as moral beings, is a core for Jaspers's *Chiffer* thinking. Finally, Kant's concept of *Reason* gave Jaspers the impetus to think further about the nature of this thinking, which rises above all intellectual cognition to *Transcendence*. He hoped that this further reflection on what Kant intended would lead to even greater methodological clarity about what constitutes the thinking of *Reason*, which, as he critically notes, Kant was not always fully aware of.

Confronted with the counter-reason and hostility to *Reason* of National Socialism, this task became a contemporary historical necessity for Jaspers. *Reason* thus became, along with *Existence*, the second key concept in Jaspers's philosophizing. The concept of *Reason* shaped his late work and led him to say that he now preferred to call his philosophy—which he believed to be identical to what philosophy had always been—the "*Philosophy of Reason*" rather than *Existential Philosophy*, because it was urgent "to emphasize this ancient essence of philosophy. When reason is lost, philosophy itself is lost. From the beginning, its task was and is to regain reason, to restore itself as reason."[19] If we follow what Jaspers says about *Reason*, we will also better understand what that thinking is supposed to consist of, of which we only know that it begins where all scientific knowledge and all "planning" and "doing" oriented toward the interests of *Dasein* and predetermined purposes end, in short, where there is nothing more to know in the sense of *Understanding*.

## NOTES

1. Cf. W 111.
2. Einf 28.
3. The de facto separation of philosophical and scientific questions began with the development of modern scientific thought, which, even if it still ran under the

title of *Natural Philosophy*, paved the way for the methodically assured course of scientific knowledge. For Jaspers, this "purification" of philosophical and scientific thought is the decisive further step in human thought since the *Axis Period.*

4. Einf 30.

5. Einf 31.

6. "With this sentence," writes Jaspers, "Kant has in fact opened up the field whose access seemed completely blocked by him. What we think but cannot recognize has an immeasurably broad content" (GP 465).

7. «Kritik der praktischen Vernunft», in: *Akademie Ausgabe*, (Kants gesammelte Schriften, ed. Königlich Preussische Akademie der Wissenschaften) vol. 5, 1–164 (Berlin, 1908, reprint 1968), 161.

8. «Kritik der praktischen Vernunft», in: *Akademie Ausgabe*, vol. 5, 1–164 (Berlin, 1908, reprint 1968),161f.

9. Ibid.

10. The difference between these two kinds of the *Sublime* corresponds to the distinction that Kant will make in his *Kritik der Urteilskraft*: in the case of the *Sublime of Nature*, we are dealing with the *Mathematical Sublime* (the *Sublime* that transcends all orders of magnitude); in the second case, with the *Dynamic Sublime* (the *Sublime* that moves our will) ("Kritik der Urteilskraft," in: *Akademie Ausgabe,* vol. 5, 185–125 (Berlin, 1908, reprint 1968), 248–264).

11. «Kritik der Urteilskraft», in: *Akademie Ausgabe*, ed. Königlich Preussische Akademie der Wissenschaften, vol. 5, 165–486 (Berlin, 1908, reprint 1968), 274.

12. Cf., for example, Kant's astonishment at "the possibility of an experience of nature" according to empirical laws, "as if nature were deliberately arranged for our powers of understanding" («Über eine Entdeckung, nach der alle neue Kritik der reinen Vernunft durch ein ältere entbehrlich gemacht werden soll», in: *Akademie Ausgabe*, ed. Königlich Preussische Akademie der Wissenschaften, Bd. 8 (Berlin, 1912, reprint 1968), 185–251, 250).

13. «Grundlegung zur Metaphysik der Sitten», in: *Akademie Ausgabe*, ed. Königlich Preussische Akademie der Wissenschaften, vol. 4 (Berlin, 1903, reprint 1968), 385–464, 421.

14. «Kritik der praktischen Vernunft», in: *Akademie Ausgabe*, ed. Königlich Preussische Akademie der Wissenschaften, vol. 5 (Berlin, 1908, reprint 1968), 1–164, 31

15. *Kritik der reinen Vernunft*, ed. Raymund Schmidt, 2nd ed. (Hamburg: Meiner, 1930, reprint Hamburg, 1956), A 806.

16. «Kritik der praktischen Vernunft», in: *Akademie Ausgabe*, ed. Königlich Preussische Akademie der Wissenschaften, vol. 5 (Berlin, 1908, reprint 1968), 1–164, 162.

17. Kant, Immanuel, "Kritik der Urteilskraft," in: *Akademie Ausgabe,* ed. Königlich Preussische Akademie der Wissenschaften, Bd. 5 (Berlin: de Gruyter, 1908/13, reprint 1968), 165–486, 170.

18. Ibid. For Kant, this is "the true interpretation of the *Chiffer* script" of nature.— This passage is a kernel of what Jaspers developed with his theory of *Chiffers* as one of the ways to *Transcendence.* (cf. Jaspers's conversation with Xavier Tilliette: «Begegnung mit Karl Jaspers», in: *Erinnerungen an Karl Jaspers*, ed. Klaus Piper

and Hans Saner (München: Piper, 1974), 269–280, 277. See also: Dirk Fonfara, «Einleitung des Herausgebers», in *Karl Jaspers Gesamtausgabe* (Basel: Schwabe, 2022) I/15.1, XXVIII, note 123).

19. VWZ 50. Jaspers comments on the significance of the role of *Reason* in his work as follows: It is true "that the concept of *Reason* is only explicitly emphasized in my work after 1933." However, it is "not correct" to see in this "something like a conversion" (i.e., a turning away from his earlier philosophy with the concept of *Existence* at its center): "The matter is present in all my earlier writings and has always been their vital force. But I was prompted to elaborate it by the realities of National Socialism in Germany." The "elaboration, yes, the glorification of *Reason*" in my later writings, "the formulation of *Reason* on the basis of Kantian thought, perhaps in a new form, meant for me at the same time the clear separation from philosophical movements that could be brought together with my attempts and from which I had not distanced myself inwardly until then" (Ant 829f.). The decisive first attempt to "elaborate *Reason*" was Jaspers's 1935 book *Vernunft und Existenz,* but his thinking on *Reason* is fully developed in the monumental work *Von der Wahrheit,* written in the last years of the war.

# Chapter 6

# Jaspers's Notion of Illumination of Reason

## REASON AND UNDERSTANDING

In everyday language, no distinction is made between *Understanding (Verstand)* and *Reason (Vernunft)*. This makes sense in at least one respect: there is no *Reason* without *Understanding*. The thinking of *Reason*, however, goes beyond *Understanding*, but without losing *Understanding*. Thus, it is not thinking that indulges in feelings, evaporates into the mystical, or surrenders to the irrational, but it uses the means of *Understanding*, that is, logic and argumentation, at every step, knowing that these are the only means we have, even if they never lead to objective results that can be seen by anyone but rather repeatedly disintegrate all these objectivities.

The driving force of *Reason* is the will to unity, the will not to accept any unity that claims to be the ultimate unity. It wants the *One* that encompasses all.

Everything that exists and can be considered possible must be taken into account; nothing may be excluded. *Reason* therefore demands boundless openness. It leads into the infinite space of the possible, wanting to understand and comprehend everything—even the unreasonable, even the incomprehensible. It does not stop at any question; it questions even the seemingly final answer. It is not satisfied with the information that God is the supreme authority but asks: And where does God come from? It is not satisfied with the fact that there is *Being,* but asks the metaphysical question that moved Leibniz and Kant and found its most succinct formulation in Schelling: Why is there anything at all, why is there not nothing?[1]

*Reason* thus opens up the realm of possibility to the point where it seems conceivable that there could have been nothing of all that there is, no *Being*, just *Nothing*. It poses the existentially disturbing question of the origin of moral evil and the evil in the *World*, which goes even deeper than the question of God's justification in the face of the terrible evils in the *World* (the so-called *Theodicy question*), which drives all religions that believe in a personal God. It goes deeper because it also asks this personal, omnipotent, omniscient God about the possibility of evil in Himself. It does not accept the *World* as it is but contrasts it with the possibility of another *World* free of all evil.

*Reason* not only continues to ask questions but also questions itself: What is it actually doing when it asks and thinks in this way, what empowers it to do so, and where does it find its own limits and adversaries? Not only to understand everything that exists and could exist, but also to understand itself, is the paramount motto of *Reason*. Jaspers followed this motto in his monumental work on *Philosophical Logic*, of which only the first volume, which itself already exceeds all dimensions, has been published. His work *Von der Wahrheit was* written in the last years of the war and published in 1947. We follow this motto here with this condensed visualization of the essence of *Reason*.

*Reason* wants to understand everything, we said, but as humans, as temporal thinkers, we will never be able to think and understand everything at once, in one fell swoop, so to speak. *Reason* is the counter-model to the type of Divine Mind that is conceived as an alternative possibility by being intuitively able to see through everything at once and to think as one thing what we can only think separately.[2] *Reason*, therefore, can approach the Absolute it seeks only in one way: by not stopping at any point, but by remaining in constant motion, filled with eternal restlessness, moving discursively from one to the other.

But what keeps it moving? Precisely the fact that in its search for unity, no point of view, no position is sufficient as an answer. It always uses its *Understanding*—without which it cannot take a single step—in such a way that it destroys all positions that become absolute and fixed.

The disruptive power of *Reason* comes into play where inherent contradictions and apparent certainties need to be exposed, where unconsidered premises need to be emphasized, and what has been omitted or not considered needs to be brought to light. Those who are too quick to reassure themselves, to settle into their prejudices, and to follow the "natural inclination" to "free themselves from further thinking by definitively fixed thoughts"[3] must therefore see *Reason* as the great enemy and troublemaker that must be silenced. Those who entrust themselves to the movement of Reason, on the other hand, will find themselves in that strange state that Jaspers calls *Limbo (Schwebe)*, the state in which one swings from one thought possibility to another, only to leave each one behind.

But where do these thought possibilities come from which we can use to work our way up to? Is it a lonely game with the products of our own imagination? It is through *Reason* that what Jaspers says about the path to truth in all of its forms is brought to full fruition: no truth without communication. Possibilities of thought are possibilities that have been considered long before us in the history of mankind. The will to self-criticism pushes *Reason* toward the other, the foreign, the not yet understood, in order to give it a language and allow it to come into its own. For Jaspers, then, *Reason* is nothing other than the "boundless will to communicate"[4] that seeks to understand, examine, and appropriate everything that has already been thought and said. In the words of one of his metaphors, it is nothing more than the stretching out of one's hands.

## REASON AS AN *OUTSTRETCHING OF THE HANDS*: KANT'S MAXIMS OF *COMMON SENSE*

What this outstretching of hands requires of us can be well visualized by means of Kant's maxims of "common sense," that is, the "human Reason" common to, and uniting, all human beings, which Jaspers always tacitly took into account in his *Illumination* of *Reason*.[5] According to Kant, there are three principles to which the individual who embarks on the path of *Reason* must commit himself: (1) to think for himself, (2) to think (in community with others) in the place of others, (3) to think at all times in harmony with himself. Kant calls the first maxim "the unprejudiced way of thinking," the second "the extended way of thinking," and the third "the consistent way of thinking."[6] These three maxims are briefly explained as follows.

### The Maxim of Self-Thinking

A good illustration of the maxim of self-thinking is Seneca's admonition to his pupil Lucilius. For "a steadily progressing man," he writes, "it is a disgrace to take his wisdom out of the college notebook, as it were: This is what Zeno said. And what do you say? This is what Cleanthes said. And you? How long shall another inspire you?"[7] The meaning of this admonition is seemingly simple: Take responsibility for what you claim or demand to be true. Be prepared to give reasons for what you believe and do. But also hold yourself accountable for the soundness of your reasons by asking yourself, as Kant advises, whether you think it "advisable" to "make the reason why one assumes something, or the rule which follows from what one assumes, the general principle of one's use of reason."[8]

Thinking for oneself, using one's *Reason*, according to Kant's basic idea in formulating this test, is always connected with the use of rules. Even the use of concepts is an observance of rules. A concept specifies how something should be done according to a rule; for example, the concept "red" is the rule to refer to red things whenever you want to use it correctly. And since thinking is nothing more than using concepts in judgments and combining judgments into conclusions, all thinking is subject to rules: epistemic rules when it comes to saying what is true, and moral or ethical rules when it comes to making things true. Rules I want to be governed by are valid for me, but they are only valid for me to the extent that I give them this validity, that is, that I commit myself to them, make them my rules, the "general principles" of my "use of *Reason*." Thinking for myself therefore means constantly checking which rules I commit myself to and being prepared to stand by my commitments, my principles, over time. To the extent that I can do this without contradicting myself, I am asserting myself as a rational being. Kant's maxim of self-thinking can therefore rightly be called the *Maxim of self-preservation of Reason*.[9]

But why does Kant refer to this maxim as that of the "unprejudiced way of thinking"? "Prejudice" has a special meaning here. Prejudices are judgments that I have had (unchecked) given to me by others, judgments that I already have before I have ever judged. I believe what I have been taught to believe to be true. The maxim of self-thinking calls on me not to let others dictate the rules of my thinking, but to give them to myself. In a word, it is about the choice between *Heteronomy* and *Autonomy*. *Reason* is therefore not a passive faculty; it begins with the will to *Autonomy*, the will to make use of one's freedom and not to hand over one's freedom to others.

But what does it mean to give yourself the rules of your own thinking? Does it mean that I can arbitrarily determine what should be my rule or reason? A clear distinction must be made here, that is, between the validity that I give to a rule—through self-commitment—and the objective validity that this rule has. The criterion for whether a rule has objective validity is—and this already refers to maxim two—whether it can be made a general rule of *Reason* not only for me but also for everyone else. Therefore, it is always necessary to check whether the rule to which I want to commit myself, or to which I have already committed myself, is actually valid. If it turns out to be invalid, then any commitment also lapses. This negative formulation is of some importance: the maxim to think for myself says nothing about how I arrive at new truth, but only that I should avoid untruths (prejudices, errors, thoughtlessness, raptures, etc.).[10]

Self-thinking, that is, autonomous thinking, is therefore only a necessary condition for the general search for truth but not a sufficient one. Whether I can think for myself is not shown by the extent of my knowledge, but by my inner attitude: whether I can justifiably, with good reason, stand by what I think I know. This reflective attitude—the will to be clear about oneself, one's own opinions, and especially one's own final opinions—is the attitude that characterized Socrates and which he tried to instill in his interlocutors with his demand of *logon didonai*, of giving a good account of oneself and one's actions.[11] There are various names for this attitude. Kant calls it *Enlightenment*,[12] Nietzsche speaks of "our" (the "free spirits") *Honesty* (*Redlichkeit*)[13] and Max Weber calls it *Intellectual Honesty*.[14] It is this demand for *Honesty* that also culminates in Jaspers's thinking.

## The Maxim of the Extended Way of Thinking

The maxim of the extended way of thinking is the guide to the self-examination required of every self-thinker. It demands the truth test of communicability, that is, to see if you find any contradiction in what you assert to be true or demand to make true from others who also seek truth. This way of thinking is called "extended" because, as Kant explains, the thinker "leaves aside the subjective private conditions of judgment, between which so many others are bracketed, and reflects on his own judgment from a general standpoint (which he can determine only by putting himself in the standpoint of others)."[15] Kant himself has provided a good illustration of what he means here with his very personal account of his own "struggle against the prejudices within himself." "I have," he writes,

> purged my soul of prejudices, I have destroyed every blind devotion that ever crept in to give me access to some imaginary knowledge. Now I care for nothing, for nothing worthy of honor, but for what takes place by the path of sincerity, in a calm mind open to all reason: it may confirm or annul, decide or leave undecided my previous judgment. The judgment of him who refutes my reasons is my judgment, after I have weighed it first against the shell of self-love, and then in it against my supposed reasons, and found in it a greater substance.[16]

Putting oneself "in the shoes of others": this maxim ultimately encompasses everything that schools can do in terms of teaching. It begins with the creation of opportunities for children to develop empathy; it continues with guidance toward a deeper understanding of how people have lived in other times and, more recently, in other living conditions, other cultures, and other countries; it culminates in seeing others, and thus oneself, not just as a member of a local group or a particular society, but as a human being with equal rights, equal needs, and equal claims to respect, and as a citizen of the *World*. This practice of empathy goes hand in hand with the cultivation of narrative imagination:[17] the ability to put oneself in the shoes of literary worlds and characters, to see the world through their eyes, to penetrate their way of judging and understanding, and to understand their language.

We are called to take a common stand not only when it comes to understanding the *World* but also when it comes to questions of our coexistence, to morality. The basic question of morality: What are the demands on our behavior that we can justifiably make on each other, because their fulfillment is good for everyone, requires that impartial standpoint that is at the same distance from all individual interests. It is the standpoint to which the *Categorical Imperative* elevates us, and it is probably only possible to reach it as the final stage in the development of moral judgment, as exemplified by Kohlberg's theory of moral development, which postulates a gradual development from the pre-conventional (egocentric) to the conventional (group-centric) to the universal standpoint.

## The Maxim of the Consistent Way of Thinking

Always think in harmony with yourself: According to Kant, this is the maxim that is "most difficult to achieve."[18] In terms of its definition, however, it is easy to determine: unanimity with myself means standing by the commitments I have made and drawing only those conclusions to which I am entitled. This is true both logically and epistemically, with respect to the truth of my statements, and prescriptively, with respect to what is to be made true.

But to what extent does the pursuit of unanimity go beyond what the first and second maxims already tell me to do? Without practicing the first and second maxims, we will never reach the third. The third maxim "can only be attained by combining the first two and following them more often after they have become a skill."[19] But this is only a necessary condition. The ability to conclude—and the third maxim is about practicing this—requires something additional. It requires not only that I connect knowledge by reasoning from one conditional to another conditional but also that I do not stop there, and continue in the series until I have reached the conclusion from the conditional, which I know, to the *Unconditional*, through which everything conditional first acquires its validity. It is such conclusions that lead to the three *Ideas of Reason*: the conclusion from the empirical fact that I experience myself as a self-conscious subject in every act of thinking to the transcendental *Idea* of a unity of this subject, the conclusion from the phenomena in the world given in experience to the *Idea* of a *World* unity, and the conclusion from these two *Ideas* to the *Idea* of a transcendental *Being* of all beings that contains these two unities in itself.

But the *Illumination* of *Reason* itself also includes the insight into the dubiousness (in the form of never-ending disputes) of all further conclusions by which the reality of these *Ideas* is inferred from the necessary possibility of thinking them. According to Kant, the ability to deduce, which constitutes the "logical form of knowledge" of *Reason* and whose exercise is at issue in the third maxim, can be legitimately exercised only in one way—in the way in which it simultaneously becomes the maxim of philosophy in general,[20] philosophy as a worldview, which concerns all human beings and not only school philosophers. This only legitimate way consists in the "practical" (action-related) use of *Reason*, that is, in combining all our "knowledge and faculties" into a unity and in examining whether they can agree "with the highest ends of human *Reason.*"[21] For Kant, there is no doubt as to what these ends consist of: in the "highest possible good in the *World*,"[22] the promotion of *Morality* combined with the hope of being able to prove oneself worthy of a happiness in accordance with this Morality.

For Jaspers, however, it is not this Kantian doctrine of the connection between happiness and *Morality* that is decisive, but the way in which Kant's third maxim of the consistent way of thinking connects *Reason* with one's own *Existence*: Only when I want unconditionally the one thing that I love and that is important to me can I become one with myself, and only when I am one with myself can I also seek the unity of everything. Jaspers reminds us of Plato. Plato

> saw man as himself only when he was at one with himself, when he did not contradict himself—and saw the greatest disaster for him in the fact that he would fall apart in himself, meaning one thing and then another, and being, without reference to each other, in the whirl of chance.

Kant, continues Jaspers, repeated this, and one could rightly say of his Ethics that it is "the only one that does not try to obscure the harsh and severe inner voice of the *One* with the noise of the many."[23] Let us clarify this connection between *Reason* and *Existence*.

## ON REASON AND EXISTENCE

Kant's three maxims of *Common Sense* are concretizations of a way of thinking that must permeate all forms of thinking, including general and scientific thinking, because the will to self-thinking, to being autonomous, knows no dispensation; it is either present in all thinking or not present at all. In other words, it is an unconditional will. But where does this *Unconditionality* come from? What makes me want *Autonomy*?

The will to *Autonomy* can't be justified by autonomous reasoning because autonomous reasoning can only determine me if and to the extent that I have already decided to let it determine me. And having someone else tell me that I should be autonomous sounds rather paradoxical. The peculiar thing about the will to *Autonomy* is that this will presupposes itself: Only those who have decided to be autonomous can ask why they should be autonomous in the first place. But if it is not the reasons, what is it that makes me want it? The answer of today's prevailing *Naturalism* to this question is clear: if we do not want to seek refuge in a mysterious, uncaused beginning from within ourselves, we would have to admit to ourselves: This ultimate will must have its origin in some biological, physiological, psychological, social, or educational conditions.[24] The argument that we could do otherwise if we only wanted to is not wrong, but it does not take into account the crucial fact that we do not have the freedom to want anything other than what we want.

So, is our will really just the outcome, the sum of all these causalities? The awareness that such decisions must have a special meaning has not been completely lost. Harry Frankfurt's concept of volitional necessity is an example of this within today's dominant analytic philosophy.[25] As Frankfurt emphasizes, there are things we can become aware of that we cannot help but want—our love for a person, for example, or for an institution or tradition, or for a moral or nonmoral ideal (which could therefore also be the ideal of *Autonomy*). This will, or more precisely the will to have this will, is what gives us identity and comes to us with the same necessity as the triangle with the angle sum of 180 degrees.

To ensure that nothing else becomes more important to us than this unconditional will, even in the long run, is the imperative that speaks from this will. Not following it would be to abandon ourselves and, as a result, to despise ourselves. Our true freedom consists only in doing what our necessity of will dictates. And, according to Frankfurt, one of the ways in which this is true freedom is that it is not the value of the object of our love that is the reason why we love it, but, conversely, that the object derives its value from the fact that we love it. Our love, then, as Frankfurt notes in passing, must have its source (and that probably means its *Origin*) in something other than the possible effect that the object of our love has on us. The question of what this other *Origin* might be, however, seems of little interest to Frankfurt.[26] He is content with conceptual analysis and description of phenomena. But exactly this question would be a good bridge to get to where Jaspers wants to lead us with his concept of *Existence*: to the transcendent *Origin* that breaks through all causalities of the world of appearances, to the *Unconditional*, to the freedom in which I am myself and in which I know that I am given by an Other, by *Transcendence*—also in my will to autonomy and to *Reason*. But here, too, the circularity of transcending thought becomes apparent: the will to *Reason* that arises from *Existence* makes *Reason* possible in the first place, but it is only through *Reason* that what this will wants can become clear. Jaspers speaks of a polarity: *Reason* and *Existence* are the two poles that pass through all ways of grasping. "They are inseparable. Each is lost when the other is lost." "*Existence* without *Reason* would be like a defiant closing that wants no openness and no *Illumination* of itself; *Reason* without *Existence* would be a blown-out thinking that can take root nowhere."[27]

This insight into the polarity of *Reason* and *Existence* also provides an answer to a question that the previous characterization of *Reason* may have raised: If it is about absolute openness, about the greatest possible breadth of thought possibilities, about "hovering" above all positions, is this not ultimately a praise of absolute placelessness? A playground for all those who can't stand themselves and want to evaporate into intellectual gimmicks and beautiful thought patterns? If it were, it would be exactly the kind of dizziness that is opposed to being grounded in *Existence*. It is not about self-exile but about distancing oneself from oneself in order to return to the here and now with a keen eye for the "hierarchy of things,"[28] and a sense for the essentials.

This process of turning to *Reason* and returning to my situation in the *World* is the basic form of what Jaspers understands by *Conversion* (*Umkehr*)—the very *Conversion* that, according to his interpretation, constitutes philosophy par excellence.[29] The process begins with a "decision," a "leap"—because it is not a natural event, but an act of freedom[30]—by which we free ourselves from the illusion that we can know, plan, and do everything with the help of *Understanding*, and entrust ourselves to the flight of *Reason* in its vastness and openness, in order to return from there to the world of knowledge and planning.

What we gain from the flight of *Reason* is not a "teachable doctrine," a concrete knowledge of what to do now, but only this: "the recognition, practice, and consolidation of an inner philosophical attitude from which our power of judgment in concrete situations arises, not as a calculable consequence, but as the proof of a *Possible Existence* that has made itself certain."[31] And of what is *Existence* supposed to have assured itself? Of the limits that are set for us, of the vastness of the *Encompassing* in which we find ourselves, of the guidance by the *Encompassing* that can come to us in our unconditional decisions and in what we believe.

Because *Reason* is anchored in the pole of *Existence*, thinking according to *Reason* is always historical and individual, bound to place and time, and at the same time a reflexive knowledge of this boundedness. For this reason, *Reason* is always both broad and narrow, bound to time and yet supra-historical, directed toward the eternal, but only tangible in individual people who are part of a historical movement and can themselves influence further historical movements. It is only in the encounter with these individuals that we ourselves can participate in the movements of *Reason*, because "the matter" that philosophizing is about is inseparable from the person who thinks it.[32]

## *ILLUMINATION* AS A WAY OF THINKING ACCORDING TO *REASON*

*Reason*, as we have established, begins with a *Conversion*, with a new awareness of *Being*,[33] the conviction that everything that appears to me in the *World* cannot be the ultimate, or the actual *Being*. The actual *Being*, however, is not an object of our cognition; it is the ultimate non-object. If we nevertheless try to think about it, we have already objectified it, making the indeterminate *Being* into a definite one.[34] From an epistemological point of view, therefore, any statement about the *Encompassing* is "absurd." One enters the "vast space of the *Possible*," "out of which everything we can know approaches us, announcing *Being* without being it."[35] We are talking about something we cannot talk about. In this respect, skepticism seems to be the final answer.

Like Kant, however, Jaspers does not regard skepticism as the last word. Even if there is no longer any cognition here, we can at least *illuminate (erhellen)* the *Encompassing*, by gaining a language that allows us to express the way in which we "find ourselves in the *Encompassing*." It is as if in this way we could shine beyond the boundary into the darkness of the unknown and the space of the *Encompassing* could become bright—at least for a moment. *Illumination* in this sense is the task of that part of philosophy that Jaspers calls *Periechontology* (the doctrine of the *Encompassing*).[36] But the concept of *Illumination* is also of central methodological importance for the rest of his work.

### The Periechontological Relevance of *Illumination*

The results of illuminating thought are the *Modes of Encompassing* that we have already encountered. Following the striving for unity of *Reason*, it became clear that although we are looking for the one *Encompassing*, it is divided into different, mutually dependent *Modes of Encompassing*,[37] each with a different objectivity and a different understanding of truth and reality—on the one hand, the *World* as the epitome of what we can recognize, but which as a whole can never be the object of our cognition, and on the other hand, the *Encompassing* that we ourselves are: as *Consciousness in General*, which is carried by *Dasein* and is surmounted by the *Spirit* with its ideal wholes. But all this is still in the realm of *Immanence*. It is different, however, when we dare to make the leap beyond *Immanence*—from *Dasein* as a conscious mind to *Existence* (as the *Origin* of ourselves) and through it to *Transcendence* as the *Origin* of everything. Transcendental thought begins with this leap.

Jaspers identifies three possible ways in which we can—*transcending*, as he says—go at least a little beyond the boundary of *Immanence*, in order to make sure of what we can at least believe in, even if there is nothing to recognize here.

The three paths follow the directions that Kant's three fundamental questions of philosophy point us in. When I ask, "What can I know?" I must take the path of philosophical *World* Orientation and illuminate the boundaries "beyond which there need be no further *World* and yet no nothing."[38] The question, "What should I do?" finds a possible answer in the existential relationship to *Transcendence* as the *All-Encompassing* per se, and the question, "What can I hope for—if I do what I am supposed to?" comes to rest for a moment when I am able to read the *Chiffers of Transcendence.*

It is these three paths that Jaspers explored in his three-volume *Philosophy* of 1932: the *Illumination* of the World under the title *Weltorientierung,* the *Illumination of Existence* under the title *Existenzerhellung,* and the *Illumination of Transcendence* under the title *Metaphysik.* In his efforts to illuminate Reason in *Von der Wahrheit,* he characterizes these three ways more precisely by distinguishing between (1) "the *Formal Transcending*, which assures itself of the nature of *Transcendence* by means of conceptual and methodological peculiar, failing movements of thought"; (2) "the *Existential Relations*, which make the reality of *Transcendence* present through a transformation of *Existence* in defiance and devotion, in the fall and rise of our being, in obedience to the *Law of the Day* and in the *Passion for the Night*"; (3) "the *Reading of the Chiffer script* in everything that becomes objective for us and that we can experience, i.e. the experience of the *Transparency* of things by the fact that they become comprehensible to us like a language of *Transcendence* to the extent and power that we become existential."[39]

Each of these three ways is *Illumination* in its own way. But what exactly are we doing when we are illuminating? To clarify this, we need to look at the whole field in which illuminating takes place.

## How *Illumination* Works

If we want to better understand the method of *Illumination*, we must also take into account that it is applied not only *periechontologically*, in relation to the *Modes of Encompassing*, but also world-immanently. For it is also valid for every (world-immanent) *wholeness* in which we live and therefore cannot overlook in its entirety: every (spiritual, political, historical) situation and tradition in which we stand, the social practice we follow, our own position in the struggle of the "powers."[40]

These wholes, too, can never become objective objects of our knowledge; here, too, only *Illumination* remains. In this respect, all of Jaspers's philosophical writings serve the purpose of *Illumination*: be it the *Idea* of the university or the *Idea* of the doctor, the intellectual situation at the beginning of the 1930s, the political situation in Germany after the World War II and then again in the 1960s, or, more generally, our place in the history of mankind or in view of today's global situation in the face of the threat of nuclear self-destruction on the one hand and the various forms of totalitarianism on the other. *Illumination* is not least the epitome of what Jaspers does when he attempts to penetrate the entire thought of a philosopher or the comprehensive whole of philosophical thought in general, as in his project of a *World History of Philosophy*. In this sense, all of Jaspers's philosophizing is *Illumination*.[41]

The starting point for *Illumination* is always the individual being, the individual in the here and now. Ultimately, it is about determining my place in an encompassing whole. Any encompassing whole in which I find myself is as unique as I am, a concrete and not an abstract entity, an immanent totality with a beginning and an end in time. The state of which I am a citizen, the school I attended, the university to which I belong, all have their historical place in an all-encompassing whole, the whole of Europe, the whole of *Humanity*. But a paradox arises from this: if I—reflecting on myself—try to grasp what the respective totality consists of, I have to conceptualize this totality, that is, say something general about it, which could apply not only to this totality but also to any other totality that could be subsumed under this concept. This can already be seen in the totality that connects me to another person. My father, whom I love and who, as my father, can be one and only one person, becomes, if I subsume him under the term "father," one example among countless other fathers.

Therefore, whatever I say about the totality that encompasses me, no concept or sum of concepts can capture what it constitutes as a whole. And yet these concepts have a crucial function: they allow aspects of this totality to emerge that I would be unable to see without them. A concept such as *Democracy* or *Totalitarianism* helps me to illuminate the nature of the state in which I find myself. This is the *Illumination* of which Jaspers speaks.[42]

But what does it mean for us to be an individual and at the same time to have to be a *General* (as a member of a whole, as a specimen of a species, etc.)?[43]

To clarify this relationship, Jaspers draws on a thought of Kierkegaard's, which his pseudonyms have expressed in formulas such as: Man is always himself and gender; he is the contradiction that the *General* is posed as the *Individual*. The last formula in particular—it comes from Kierkegaard's pseudonym Anti-Climacus[44]—became central for Jaspers. He subjected it to a lengthy interpretation in *Die Psychologie der Weltanschauungen*: It is part of the "basic situation of man" that he "exists as a single, finite being" who is "at the same time conscious of a General" and who therefore has to solve in his life the task of becoming that "form of the self" which "as an *Individual* is at the same time the *General*."[45]

Jaspers has in mind, first of all, the individual wholes "in which man stands as an individual member," and which he calls the *Concrete General*, meaning, for example, the "sociological wholes (family, nation, state)." But he thinks also of the *Abstract General*, which is of a purely conceptual nature, such as the *Universal* ("the imperatives, the objective truth, the valid values").[46]

Each of these forms of the *General* confronts the *Individual* with the question of what is important to him: to merge with the *General* in obedience and submission (at the expense of his individual self), to oppose it in rejection and defiance (at the expense of the *General*), or, alternatively, in a process of constant becoming, to expand toward the *General*, to become an *Individual* through the *General* (as one becomes a personality by making a *General* one's cause—always in danger of absolutizing oneself or absolutizing the *General*).[47]

If this task is understood as a mental task, as if it were a matter of deciding *abstractly*, from the perspective of the *Observer*—once and for all, as it were—in favor of one of these alternatives, they petrify into worldviews such as *Universalism* or *Individualism*, that is, into one-sided *Housings* (*Gehäuse*) that may satisfy the rational attitude because of their consistency and rational unambiguity, but are never able to grasp the life of the "living human being seeking a foothold in the infinite." The "either/or of the living personality" is always only "concrete, individual, single, and absolute."[48]

Becoming aware of this problem is part of the maturation process. We find ourselves unquestioningly absorbed in certain totalities into which we were born and in which we grew up. These are reflected in our habits; they shape what I am "even before I have asked what I want to be."[49] However, as soon as my consciousness awakens and I try to grasp conceptually what this totality consists of, there is a contradiction between me as an *Individual* and this *General* in which I have been absorbed. As soon as I become aware of this contradiction, every concept I use to try to grasp the totality that encompasses me becomes a question: Can I continue to identify with a totality that has these characteristics? Am I nothing but that very totality? With this question, the totality that held me firmly in the grip of habit begins to lose its authority over me. A window of freedom opens. I now have the opportunity to make a conscious choice. This is the choice that every *Illumination* demands of me.

How does such a choice come about? While the recognition of the objective aims at universally valid truth, which I as *Consciousness in General*—as the consciousness identical with the consciousness of all others—cannot consider to be anything other than true, I am challenged to take a stand in my unique historical situation when it comes to *Illumination*. The will in me that affirms and denies is challenged. "As freedom, I examine through myself what I not only am but can be, and what I want to be." Every illumination is therefore already "an expression of the will of freedom."[50] For this reason, the general terms I use do not merely have a descriptive function like terms in a scientific context; they contain value judgments that evaluate the reality that appears in terms of true and false, good and evil, and thus place it under conditions that are unconditionally valid.

This process of becoming self-aware reveals the meaning of *Illuminating* thought: it "does not convey knowledge of things that were previously foreign to me, but makes clear what I really mean, really want, really believe; it creates the bright space of my self-consciousness."[51] Since everything I illuminate in this way confronts me with the choice of appropriating or rejecting it, *Illumination* goes hand in hand with what Jaspers calls *Inner Action,* an action by which I transform myself by deciding what or who I want to be.

To be more precise, the *Will* is not only involved in the final step of *Illumination*, it is always present throughout the process. For *Illumination* is by no means directionless. Every illumination is carried by the will to penetrate into the essence of a whole, to go to the totality of its appearance. But this goal is never reached. The concepts with which we try to grasp the whole always fall short of this whole; they are mere schemes, steps, or means of its realization along the way. The never-exhausted essence of a totality is what Jaspers calls an *Idea*.[52]

An *Idea* is not an object in the world, but neither is it a mere thought. It is subjective and objective at the same time, both that which drives us inwardly—and in this respect, the object of our will—and objectively the never completed goal of our striving. Since the whole is always present in every part that we can grasp in this way, the parts of an *Idea* cannot be broken down conceptually and unfolded deductively like objects of knowledge; we can only illuminate them through a "circular lingering" (a lingering that circles within itself).[53]

What is completely unclear, however, is how we arrive at these general *Schemata*, with the help of which we attempt to illuminate the *Idea* that cannot be exhausted in individual steps. What leads us to say of such a *Schema* that it is a part or aspect of the Idea? Obviously, our judgment is required here. But this is a word rather than a concept. If we want to understand more, we need to go even deeper.

## ILLUMINATION AS A MATTER OF REFLECTING POWER OF JUDGMENT

What, in Jaspers's view, is the crucial difference between cognition by *Understanding* and *Illumination* by *Reason*? The difference shows itself most clearly in the different ways in which we use our power of judgment. Again, it was Kant who drew attention to this difference, with his distinction between *determining* and *reflecting* power of judgment (whereby judgment is understood as the ability to relate the *Particular* to the *General*, *Understanding* to *Reason*). He says either we are in possession of the *General* (the rule, the principle, the law) and can now subsume a case that occurs to us under it, or we have the experience of a particular case and first look for the *General* through which it can be understood. Kant calls the first procedure the *determining*, the second the *reflecting* power of judgment (*bestimmende und reflektierende Urteilskraft*).

An example may serve to illustrate this distinction. Every law of nature takes the form of an *if-then* relation; it states the conditions under which an event must occur. If these conditions are met, we can conclude that the event will occur. This is a deductive conclusion according to the rules of determining judgment. However, it is different when an event occurs for which we have no explanation. In this case, it is necessary to try to formulate the law that would allow a subsumption of the event. This search for and construction of possible laws is the work of the *reflecting* power of judgment. Its hypotheses become a guide for further research. And it is aimed at reconciling what we experience in dealing with Nature with our hypotheses. If we succeed, we have made progress in our knowledge.

But the scope of *reflecting* power of judgment is not yet exhausted. It is also at work in our hope that the progress of knowledge will never come to an end. Scientific progress in the discovery of more and more laws forces us to assume that there must be a correspondence between the subjective conditions that enable us to have experiences and the objective conditions of nature. When we know the law, the events that fall under that law prove to be *necessary*.

*Necessity*, however, extends only as far as we have already come to know the world. When things happen whose *Necessity* we do not (yet) know, we speak of *Coincidence*. As our knowledge progresses, however, we hope to be able to prove that even the accidental is necessary. But why should this be the case? Is it necessarily the case that the *World* is set up in such a way that we can recognize it? Might we not one day reach the point where all cognition ceases? We do not know what the law might be that would preclude such an end to cognition. The fact that it has not yet been found can only be seen as a *Coincidence*. And yet confidence remains. But why? Because, when we think about this *Coincidence*, we assume a purposefulness that aligns nature and our cognitive faculty in such a way that our cognition never reaches a limit. As if this had been the intention of a *higher* mind in the creation of the *World*, and we could see into the common ground of cognition and things in the *World* (quasi reflecting the thoughts of God before the creation of the world).

The assumption of a purposefulness of the *World* is the general principle with which the *reflecting* power of judgment tries to make *Coincidence* comprehensible, which should astonish us with every new advance of knowledge. The lawfulness that would make this *Coincidence* no longer appear as *Coincidence* but as *Necessity*, albeit a *Necessity* of a completely different kind, would be a principle such as: nothing happens by chance, that is, there is no such thing as *Coincidence*. But such a principle is beyond anything we can ever know. So it says nothing about the *World*, even though it seems to. Then what is its purpose? Its only function is *to guide* us, to encourage us to progress in our cognition, in the firm belief that there can be no end to cognition. But we have not yet discovered anything by this principle. In order to gain new knowledge, we must first do what it tells us to do. It is a *regulative* principle of our cognitive faculty, a principle that is not given to us from somewhere, but a principle that we give to ourselves.[54]

Self-legislation or *Autonomy*, which we have so far only found as an example in the *Categorical Imperative* as the principle of practical Reason, already exists, as we can see here, in the theoretical realm.[55] But not only there, also in *Aesthetics*, in the perception of beauty. When I say of an object that it is beautiful, I am indeed expressing an individual judgment that seems to be on the same level as the judgment that this object gives me pleasure. But the crucial point of an aesthetic judgment is that the person making the judgment is not merely expressing his singular emotional state (which is only coincidentally shared by another person), but is claiming to say something *General* and universally valid about this object.

To say something *General* means that this object has a property (a regularity) that it shares with all objects that we also find beautiful, and to be universal means that the object causes pleasure that is shared by all, regardless of all subjective and random feelings of pleasure and displeasure, according to the Kantian definition of beauty as that which pleases universally and without interest. But what is this generality, this regularity, of which the individual object would be an example? We know of no such regularity. Nor would we know how to justify or prove it. It is, as Kant says, "a regularity without law." The *reflecting* power of judgment, however, imagines such a law, which gives beauty to all that is beautiful. This imagined law is nothing other than the *Idea* of beauty, which is one of the *Ideas* of reason. The *Idea* inspires us to seek beauty, to dwell on it, and to immerse ourselves in the pleasure it arouses wherever it appears. Therein lies its regulative function, which guides our judgment (our "taste").[56]

In the nature of this search, however, the difference between *determining* and *reflecting* power of judgment becomes apparent once again: If I know what the term "gold" means, I know what to look for when I look for gold—it is a case of *determining* power of judgment—but if I look for beauty beyond the examples of beauty I have already encountered, I do not know what new objects I should look for. Only when I encounter something new and beautiful in its uniqueness do I immediately judge it as beautiful (with the help of *reflecting* power of judgment). That's why we can't really look for beauty deliberately, but only keep an eye out for it and be open to all sides, ready to see it where and how it shows itself to us.

If we return to Jaspers and his method of *Illumination* after this excursion to Kant, we can also see here how much he was inspired by Kant, this time by Kant's concept of the *reflecting* power of judgment. For Kant, as for Jaspers, thinking about *Ideas* is a faculty of Reason. Both share the insight that through the *reflecting* power of judgment, we can make accessible *Ideas* that are in themselves unknowable. And that the general rules we establish in the process of this reflection are not laws, but principles that guide our actions; they do not give us something to know, but appeal to our will to be guided by them as we walk through the *World*, starting from where we are and trying to move out into the open.

To be a guide for our own possible path is the *heuristic* or *methodological* aspect of *Ideas*, the third aspect besides the already mentioned subjective aspect that drives us to seek unity, and the objective, goal-setting aspect that we have to assume unity.[57] It is only by following and trusting the principles found through reflective judgment that we find out where they are leading us. What principles we want to follow is the question posed to us. It appeals not so much to our *Understanding* as to our will.

The range of possibilities when we rely on the reflecting power of judgment is infinite. This becomes clear when we consider the extremes. On the one hand, there is the danger of a complete atomization of the totality: we see only the details, the infinite differentiations. On the other hand, there is the danger of forcing the totality into a single *Scheme* by absolutizing a moment that is apparently common to all individual phenomena. Both extremes may allow us to see something we would not otherwise see. But when absolutized, they both lead us astray.[58]

Jaspers's reflections on the unity of history are exemplary.

The *idea* that human history must be a unity is indispensable. But where does this unity manifest itself? In the fact that we live on this one planet? That we are part of a common timeline? Yet we share this with everything else on Earth, with everything organic and inorganic. Is there one human history because it has a single beginning and a single end? But we know neither the beginning nor the end. Is there unity in history itself? There are individual lines, but they always break off again; there is no continuous line that would include everything in itself. History disintegrates "into the scatteredness of chance, into the coming and going without direction, into the pathlessness of many illusory paths."[59]

But if unity is not a fact and cannot be grasped as a recognizable goal, could we not nevertheless try to determine such a goal together? Could not the unity of history, Jaspers asks, perhaps grow out of the fact that people can understand each other in the *Idea* of the *One*, in the one truth in which everything has a meaningful relationship to everything else? That is, a meaning that gives meaning to what happens? A meaning that no one meant, but which one can try to interpret as an observer of history, and which can also become a task to live up to in the here and now? A goal that can be won or lost at any moment? But what could this one meaningful goal be? Such a goal has been named and can be named:

- The humanization of man through a legal world order, through a unity of law that gives space to the creative powers of man.
- To achieve freedom for all and to create the consciousness of freedom.
- To make possible the creations of the *Spirit*, to raise humanity to its highest heights.
- To reveal in man that which is in the depths of *Being* and up to the height of the Godhead.

But the unity of purpose is not contained in any of these formulations. Each remains with a goal that is not the all-encompassing one. These goals can be factors in history if people believe in them and are gripped by them, but without the hope that their goal could become the goal that encompasses all people. That is why it is important for each person to have a goal in mind that can be meaningful to his or her own actions.

To confuse the possibilities of meaning that serve to illuminate an encompassing whole with insights into reality is disastrous for knowledge and for action. For knowledge, because we take for knowledge what is not knowledge, and for action, because we do not allow ourselves to be addressed by what they really are: orientations, principles that are always linked to the question of whether we want to understand and pursue the *Idea* of the totality that encompasses us in this sense.

The difference between *reflecting* and *determining* judgment thus comes to a head again in the fundamental alternative that opens up here. An illustrative example is any *Illumination* of a situation. When we ask ourselves what situation (individual, political, or world-historical) we are in, this can mean either

> Where do we stand now in the whole of a recognizable, necessary historical process? Or: Where do we stand in the impenetrable horizon of events whose course eludes our view? The first question wants to know our position on the path to be recognized; the second question wants to shed light on the situation in which we find ourselves, without knowing its origin and destination as a whole, and without knowing the path.[60]

Which of these questions I choose has consequences for my actions. If I believe that I already know the way, "then I want to follow this only possible and real way with my actions," obediently in the service of the supposedly recognized whole. But if I know that the whole is not recognizable, and I only want to "shed light on the situation, then I know that I am still partly responsible for events that are by no means predetermined as necessary; it is also up to me what will become of the *World*."[61]

The question of whether we want to continue to recognize or merely to illuminate, where the whole of human history is at stake, determines which side we take: whether we are on the side of totalizing worldviews of the Marxist kind, or on the side of the freedom and responsibility of the individual on the way into an uncertain future. However, if we stick to *Reason* and have made sure that we can only take the second path, we are not without a compass and orientation. We can be guided by the principles of the reflecting power of judgment that have become our own.

## The Truth Criteria in Every Illumination

What am I supposed to work for concretely in my particular situation, if—without knowing the final goal—I take the path of *Illumination* and thus of *Inner Action*? Jaspers's answer: I work "for what I understand to be good from my own constantly testing insight that matures in communication with my friends."[62] Yet what are the standards and criteria by which this testing is possible? These can only be gained by looking at the *Idea* and the spiritual power on whose side I have placed myself and find myself. But why am I following this one power in particular? Again, the answer can only be found if, following the impulse of *Reason*, I also examine my seemingly last point of view to see if it can still connect me with the most distant one—guided by Reason's supreme criterion of truth: what connects us is true. Only from this *Encompassing of Reason* does that in which I find myself reveal itself in its full truth.

Here is an example: Only when I become aware that there is a way of thinking that is more than science and that gives it its meaning (e.g., by insisting on unity and coherence and not being satisfied with disparate and indifferent results) do I understand what science is. Only now is it no longer possible to confuse the realm of science with the space of being illuminated by the thought of *Reason*, which complements and supports it. Only now is there an awareness that science, as much as it can guide us in our lives, is itself in need of guidance.[63]

The apparently abstract criterion—that what connects us (even with the most remote) is true—can have direct political significance. Jaspers was German and thought of himself as German. But what does it mean to be German?

Jaspers could never identify with political Germany, not with the Nazi state, certainly not with the Wilhelmine state, and even less with the Bismarckian empire. For him, German was a term for a cultural area "held together only by the German language and the intellectual life manifested in it."[64] But being German in this comprehensive sense was no legitimation for him either.

> To be a human being first and then to belong to a people of this origin, that seemed to me to be the essential. How longingly I looked for an authority above the peoples, a law above the states, that could legally help the individual who was being raped without rights by his state! [. . .] Only the solidarity of all states could be this superior authority.[65]

## Illuminating the Space of Transcendence, Exemplified by the Theodicy Question

The last chapter dealt with the *Illumination* of totalities that appear in the *World*, even if the value judgments that illuminate them have their origin in the *supra-natural* realm of *Reason*. However, when it comes to the transcendent realm itself, to the *Illumination* of *Existence* and the *Illumination* of *Transcendence*, our concepts fall into a bottomless pit. They are all concepts that we do not know what they refer to, because what they refer to are not objects. Words like *the Actual Being*, *Transcendence*, *God*, *the One* have the character of proper names and seem to stand for individual objects, but we have not the slightest idea what these "objects" might be. Therefore, there are no concepts under which they could be subsumed, let alone exploited. This is also true of the concepts with which we try to grasp the totalities immanent in the world. They will never be adequate either, because no totality is absorbed in a concept, but the concepts used at least allow access to verifiable and nameable phenomena of the phenomenal world.

Terms used in a transcendental way, however, reach into the void of our ignorance. When we think we have grasped something, it dissolves into itself with the next thought. For example, if we speak of God as the cause of everything, then logically He must also be the cause of Himself. But *cause of itself* (*causa sui*) is a nonsensical concept; the category of cause only applies if we can distinguish between that which causes and that which is caused. But if we make that distinction, God would not be one, but two, the causing God and the caused God.[66]

If, on the other hand, we say that God's existence has no cause, we are faced with the puzzle of how a being can come out of nothing. We also end up with such aporias when it comes to the *existential Relation* to *Transcendence*. For example, when we ask, in view of the many terrible things that happen and can happen to us human beings, where evil comes from, the evil that happens to us from the nonhuman side of the world, the evil that people do to each other.

We can, of course, ask this question in a world-immanent way, stopping at the recognizable causes, at the necessities of natural law that lead to the catastrophic events, at the possible motives that drive people to torture, rape, and kill other people. When we ask in this way, the *World* and human beings are the last thing on our minds. But if the origin of evil and wickedness lies before man and before the *World*, then the questions that have moved and not only moved but also outraged people for thousands of years come to the fore, most magnificently in the *Old Testament.*

The first question is: Who or what is to blame for the evil in the world and for the fact that I am evil, that I can become guilty? I become guilty through myself, but since I did not create myself, the question remains: Who or what is to blame for the fact that I can become guilty? And the second question is for those who see the reason for the catastrophes in the *World* as a just punishment for the evil that people do. How is it possible that things are so unjust in the *World* that the wicked do well and the good do badly? That there seems to be no connection between happiness in the world and good deeds? These questions are meaningless if there is nothing but the world and human beings. Who or what is to blame for the *World* and people being the way they are?

Only when there is a God as Creator, a *personal God*, a You, and not an anonymous *Being*, can one also make accusations against this God. And only then does the seriousness of man's questioning and wrestling with this God begin, in a way that can only be found in the Psalmists and in the Book of Job in the *Old Testament.*[67] This is the beginning of what was later called *Theodicy*, the justification of God in relation to evil and the evils of the *World.* The Manichaeans thought they could avoid this debate by believing that there were not one but two divine powers, the power of good and the power of evil, at war with each other, and that man was called upon to decide which side he would be on. But if there is only one God, and if this one God is ascribed the attributes that have been ascribed to the Judeo-Christian Creator God: that He is omnipotent, benevolent, and omniscient, then the difficulties of reconciling these attributes with the fact of evil and wickedness in the *World* begin with these presuppositions. Where is the benevolent God? Where is His omnipotence? Where is His omniscience?

The hopelessness of these questions is impressively conveyed to us in the book of Job:[68] For Job, the personal God, whom the Jews believe in without question, becomes the great You, to whom he can attribute all the bad things that have happened to him—the truly just one. He thus challenges the opposition of his theologian friends, to whom it seems impossible that God could be unjust. In the end, God himself intervenes in this dispute. He turns against the theologians, but he does not agree with Job either, and asks the counterquestion: Where were you, Job, when I founded the Earth? On the surface, this story seems to be about the dispute between Job and his theologian friends, a dispute in which each side is concerned with being right and being proved right. But in fact, it is a struggle for the true understanding of God, pitting one image of God against another: the image of a personal, accountable God against the image of a God beyond the human category of personality, whose unknowability and unfathomability must be accepted.

This ending to the story of Job reads like a call to submit in humility and self-restraint to the inexplicable. But would this also mean blindly submitting to the incomprehensible, hidden counsel of the Deity, as Calvin's doctrine of *Predestination*, derived from Paul and Augustine, suggests? What I am, I am only by God's grace or disgrace; I may live morally as I please, but it does me no good if the eternal counsel of God has predestined me to disgrace. But if I continue to believe in a personal God, is it possible to make this submission without becoming indignant again? This struggle goes on without ever coming to an end. If we are honest, we must admit to ourselves: "There is no solution for man. He must be stranded by that which is unbearable, utterly impossible for *Reason*, justice, morality and love."[69]

In the end, the insight remains: we have not the slightest reason to assume "that the Reason of things is reasonable in the sense that we are capable of understanding Reason."[70] Even if many things in the world appear to be purposeful and beautiful, we cannot conclude from this that the whole is a glorious harmony in which everything has its place and its meaning in the whole. For on the other side is the unreasonable, the terrible, and the disturbing, which drives us to outrage, as Dostoevsky's Ivan Karamazov, for example, puts it in a shocking way.[71]

## Final Decisions and What Unites Us across All Differences

If neither belief in harmony nor indignation can have the last word, what are we left with? The only thing we can hold on to is that which makes this insight possible in the first place: namely *Reason*. Even if we don't know whether the world is rational or not, we at least have the option of wanting to be reasonable ourselves. Even if there is no discernible meaning in the whole, no God to which we can adhere, no single correct *World* Order, we can at least decide for ourselves what we want to live for. And if we ask what these ultimate possibilities of meaning are that we always end up with, we see that they are the great alternatives that we have already encountered in this study:

(1) *Immanence* of the *World* as ultimate or belief in *Transcendence*.
(2) To be guided by the *Law of the Day* or to plunge into the *Passion of the Night*.

(3) To seek the brightness of *Reason* or to submit to an absolute authority that appears in the *World.*
(4) To dare to communicate without boundaries, or to break off communication and wall yourself in with dogmatic opinions.
(5) Wanting to be yourself or wanting to live the way people live.
(6) Taking the risk of independent thinking or clinging to objective certainties.
(7) Being open to the ultimate possibilities or being comforted by the deceptive hopes of this *World.*[72]

Alternatives like these are always only constructions of our *Reason*, of which we never know if they are really the last ones, but with them, we begin to catch our breath. They confront us with choices that determine our thinking and our practice in life. But they are frightening because they open rifts between people who choose opposing paths and turn the struggle within me into a struggle between me and others. What's left to connect us? Is there a bond that transcends all these differences? Is it something to give us pause when the spiritual battle threatens to turn into a battle of violence? That allows us to approach the other, even in battle, in our struggle for a decision? Because we secretly know that every decision is always provisional, a decision in time and in our historical moment? Because the last alternatives are not the last?

These questions make it clear that we are not dealing with bloodless constructions, but that these ultimate possibilities of meaning have an inherent power that takes hold of us. When we decide, we always find ourselves already decided. Here we again encounter the paradox that we have already encountered in the *Illumination* of unconditional decision: with the intertwining of decision and—according to Jaspers's formula—being given to oneself. For here too there is an *Unconditionality* in these final decisions, except that they do not concern the content, the concrete task in our life, but the auspices under which we live our life. They set the conditions under which everything we do is to be done, as we have seen in the example of the *Categorical Imperative*, which also sets the condition for our love.

To illustrate what happens in the confrontation with such ultimate alternatives, Jaspers, following Max Weber,[73] speaks of a struggle of powers that, like the gods of antiquity, try to draw us into their battles. This struggle takes place in a space that we can never overlook. There is no vantage point from which we can look down on what is happening here. For we ourselves are always already part of the forces that are fighting each other. The divide runs between us and through us. Our task is to become aware of this and to decide which side we want to be on. To do this, we need the rational construction of final alternatives from which our actions and the actions of others follow.

The way in which these are formulated, however, always anticipates the answer and the decision:[74] the construction takes place from the place where I myself stand.[75] The opponent will therefore always find himself "misunderstood" in these formulations.[76] Nevertheless, it is precisely this antagonism that binds us together and allows us to feel the kinship in our humanity even in the fiercest struggle—through our common reference to *Transcendence*.[77]

Jaspers's conviction that there must be an ultimate solidarity of all people in relation to their humanity alone shows how deeply rooted the *Idea* of *Humanity* is in him. Faced with the same limits and the same *Borderline Situations*, all people become fellow human beings. This solidarity also goes beyond the solidarity among the *Reasonable*,[78] because they in turn, are in a struggle with all those who have sided with the unreasonable and irrational.

The struggle of the powers is what surrounds us in the spiritual space; the final alternatives, in turn, are examples of the constructions arising from the *reflecting* power of judgment with which we illuminate this space. They have the same character as the concepts and constructions with which we try to make *Transcendence* or our *Existential Relationship* to *Transcendence* comprehensible. But what is the point of communicating such constructions? What is the point of communication if the essential cannot be communicated?

## NOTES

1. VWZ 37.

2. Cf. Jaspers's interpretation of Kant's juxtaposition of *intellectus archetypus* and *intellectus ectypus* (GP 479f.).

3. VWZ 33.

4. VWZ 36.

5. VWZ 36. The German expression "gemein" is to be understood here as common to all. See Kant's sentence in: "Über eine Entdeckung, nach der alle neue Kritik der reinen Vernunft durch eine ältere entbehrlich gemacht werden soll," in *Akademie Ausgabe*, ed. Königlich Preussische Akademie der Wissenschaften, vol. 8 (Berlin, 1912, reprint 1968), 185–251, cited 218 (note): "For what is philosophically correct, no one can and must learn from Leibniz, but the test stone that is as close to the one as to the other is the common human *Reason*, and there is no classical author of philosophy."—Jaspers refers explicitly to the three maxims in: Einf 143f.

6. Immanuel Kant, "Kritik der Urteilskraft," in *Akademie Ausgabe*, ed. Königlich Preussische Akademie der Wissenschaften, vol. 5 (Berlin, 1908, reprint 1968), 165–486, §40, 145.

7. Seneca, "Letter 33," in *Letters to Lucilius*, ed. and transl. by Ernst Glaser-Gerhard, vol. I (Reinbek: Rowohlt, 1965), 80.

8. Immanuel Kant, "Was heißt: sich im Denken orientieren?," in *Akademie Ausgabe*, ed. Königlich Preussische Akademie der Wissenschaften, vol. 8, (Berlin, 1912, reprint 1968, 131–148, 146 (note).

9. Immanuel Kant, "Was heißt: sich im Denken orientieren?," in *Akademie Ausgabe*, ed. Königlich Preussische Akademie der Wissenschaften, vol. 8, Berlin, 1912, reprint 1968, 131–148, 146 (note).

10. Kant therefore occasionally calls his maxims "General rules and conditions for the avoidance of error in general" ("Logik," in *Akademie Ausgabe,* ed. Königlich Preussische Akademie der Wissenschaften, vol. 9 (Berlin, 1923, reprint 1968), 1–150, 57).

11. See, for example Plato, *Laches,* in Werke, ed. Gunther Eigler, vol. 1 (Darmstadt: WBG, 1990), 219–286, 187e–188c; *Apologie*, Werke, ed. Gunther Eigler, vol. 2 (Darmstadt: WBG, 1990), 1–70, 29d/e.

12. This is why Kant also calls the maxim of self-thinking the "enlightened" one ("Logik," in *Akademie Ausgabe*, ed. Königlich Preussische Akademie der Wissenschaften, Bd. 9 (Berlin, 1923, reprint 1968), 1–150, 57).

13. Friedrich Nietzsche: «Jenseits von Gut und Böse», in *Kritische Studienausgabe*, ed. Giorgio Colli and Mazzino Montinari, vol. 5 (München: de Gruyter, 1999), 9–244, §227, 162. See also Nietzsche's question about the origin of our "unconditional will to truth": whether this is the will "not to be deceived" or "the will not to deceive" (Friedrich Nietzsche, "Die fröhliche Wissenschaft," in *Kritische Studienausgabe*, ed. Giorgio Colli and Mazzino Montinari, vol. 3 (München: de Gruyter, 1999), 343–652, §344, 575).

14. Max Weber: "Wissenschaft als Beruf," in *Gesammelte Aufsätze zur Wissenschaftslehre,* ed. Johannes Winckelmann, (Tübingen: J. C. B. Mohr, 1988), 582–613.—The repeated attempts by Ernst Tugendhat to define the nature of *Intellectual Honesty* and, in particular its underlying motives in more detail are illuminating in this regard (thus most recently: "Retraktionen zur intellektuellen Redlichkeit," in ders.: *Anthropologie statt Metaphysik* (München: Beck, 2007), 85–113).

15. Immanuel Kant, "Kritik der Urteilskraft," in *Akademie Ausgabe*, ed. Königlich Preussische Akademie der Wissenschaften, vol. 5 (Berlin, 1908, reprinted 1968), 165–486, 295.

16. Immanuel Kant, "Träume eines Geistersehers," in *Akademie Ausgabe*, ed. Königlich Preussische Akademie der Wissenschaften, vol. 2 (Berlin, 1905, reprint 1968), 315–384, 349.

17. This is a point that Martha Nussbaum particularly emphasizes in her definition of the nature of *Liberal Education* (*Cultivating Humanity*, (Cambridge, MA; London: Harvard University Press, 1997), 85–112).

18. Kant, Immanuel, "Kritik der Urteilskraft," in *Akademie Ausgabe*, ed. Königlich Preussische Akademie der Wissenschaften, vol. 5 (Berlin, 1908, reprint 1968), 165–486, 295.

19. Ibid.

20. For this reason, Kant can equate philosophizing with "exercise in self-thinking" ("Logik," in *Akademie Ausgabe*, ed. Königlich Preussische Akademie der Wissenschaften, vol. 9 (Berlin, 1923, reprint 1968), 1–150, 26).

21. Immanuel Kant, "Logik," in *Akademie Ausgabe*, ed. Königlich Preussische Akademie der Wissenschaften, vol. 9 (Berlin, 1923, reprint 1968), 1–150, 24–25.

22. Immanuel Kant, „Über den Gemeinspruch: Das mag in der Theorie richtig sein, taugt aber nicht für die Praxis," in *Akademie Ausgabe*, ed. Königlich Preussische Akademie der Wissenschaften, vol. 8, (Berlin, 1912, reprint 1968), 273–314, 279.

23. VWZ 35 (Jaspers quotes here a sentence by Otto Weininger (1880–1903)).

24. And they will rightly point out that this does not necessarily mean that we are at the mercy of irrational forces, for good or ill: the will to reflect does not suddenly flare up in us unmotivated as the result of some fermentation process, but always has causes that may have already become the first causes of reflection in the sense of evolutionary biology. These triggers are present wherever our immediate, instinctive will encounters an (internal or external) obstacle and can no longer be directly translated into action. The impending obstacle can stop or even paralyze our impulse to act and thus become an occasion to pause for thought in order to restart the disturbed course of action by considering all the reasons and looking for an alternative course of action that we could take instead of the original action. In any case, this is how pragmatists would explain the development of thinking. This explanation is attractive because it seems to satisfy our need for a unified, natural explanation of human will.

25. Harry Frankfurt, "Über die Bedeutsamkeit des Sich-Sorgens," in *Freiheit und Selbstbestimmung*, ed. Monika Betzler and Barbara Guckes (Berlin: Akademie Verlag, 2001), 98–115, 105.

26. Where he mentions it at all, Frankfurt shows little inclination to abandon the naturalistic view. He states: "My own observation is that certain people tend by nature to be wholehearted, while others tend not to be; and I suspect that whether someone achieves any substantial degree of wholeheartedness in his life depends rather heavily upon genetic and other modes of luck." ("Wholeheartedness" here stands for the undivided (autonomous) volition of one's own will.) However, he adds: "Perhaps this is not actually so different from what Saint Augustine had in mind when he supposed that it is a matter of divine fiat." In any case, it is not in our power to want to love if we do not love. (*The Reasons of Love* (Princeton, NJ; Oxford: Princeton University Press, 2004), 99).

27. VE 35.

28. On what it means to make sure of the orders of rank, see VE 83f.: The ways of understanding are in an ascending order (*Dasein, Consciousness in General, Spirit,* and *Existence*). They form an order of rank, and it is true that the following one can only be real under the condition of the preceding one, but "the isolating closure of the preceding from the following means a specific break in communication."

29. Thus, at the turning point, a twofold process is to be accomplished: First, from planning and certain knowledge of the possibilities of events to philosophical thinking of the *Encompassing*, and then from there back to thinking in that world of knowledge and planning. The first turn in thinking leads to the transformation of man by this thinking, the second to the effect of this transformation in the *World*, with the consequence of a new direction in the course of events.

30. VWZ 41, 43.

31. Ph 2, LII.

32. GP 62.

33. W 39.

34. Ex 14.
35. Ex 15.
36. W 158ff.
37. W 453 and others.
38. Ph I, 53.
39. W 111f.
40. W 930, 933ff., 953f.
41. GP 461.
42. These general terms characterize *Ideal Types* in the sense of Max Weber, which, from a scientific point of view, provide points of comparison that can be used to describe political institutions in a value-free manner.
43. PW 379f.
44. Søren Kierkegaard, *Krankheit zum Tode*, ed. Emanuel Hirsch, (Düsseldorf: Diederich, 1957): "Self means precisely the contradiction that the *General* is posited as the *Individual*."
45. PW 411. Jaspers thus adheres very closely to Kierkegaard's definition of the *self*.
46. PW 381.
47. PW 382.
48. PW 382.
49. Ph 1, 285.
50. Ph 2, 10.
51. IU (1946), New Annotated Edition by Oliver Immel, in *Schriften zur Universitätsidee*, Karl Jaspers Gesamtausgabe I/21 (Basel: Schwabe, 2016), 103–202, 115.
52. Jaspers illustrates this *Idea* with the example of the *Idea* of life:

> To objectify this *Idea* would be an illusion that makes life disappear. In the whole of an organism, however, life is fully present as an infinity of purposeful relations which we can never recognize, but which we can make fruitful for knowledge if, in progressing into the infinite, we do not lose the infinite. The categories to which we resort, categories such as growth, assimilation, correlation, regeneration, reproduction, irritability, adaptation, etc., are only particular versions of the *Idea* of life. (GP 474)

53. W 52, 57. With this in mind, what was said in the Introduction about the peculiarity of this study becomes understandable: that we keep coming back to previous topics, spiraling and reconsidering them in a new light.
54. See, on the whole Jaspers's presentation of this train of thought in: GP 474–479.
55. The theoretical use of *reflecting* power of judgment also includes its application in the field of knowledge of nature when it comes to living organisms. The marvelous purposefulness manifested in them is inexplicable and incomprehensible to the mind in a nature governed by necessary causal laws. It is as if they had been created by a superhuman artist whose intention we do not know. But guided by the thought that there must be such an inner intention of nature in every organism, we also make progress in the knowledge of organisms" (GP 476, 480, see also note X).
56. GP 501.
57. For these three aspects, see PW 478–484.

58. PW 480.

59. UZG 321.

60. Karl Jaspers, «Wo stehen wir heute? (1960)», in *Das Wagnis der Freiheit. Gesammelte Aufsätze zur Philosophie*, herausgegeben und mit einer Vorbemerkung versehen von Hans Saner (München; Zürich: Piper, 1996), 185–198, 196f.

61. Ibid., 197.

62. Ibid.

63. IU (1946), New Annotated Edition by Oliver Immel, in *Schriften zur Universitätsidee*, Karl Jaspers Gesamtausgabe I/21 (Basel: Schwabe, 2016), 120–122.

64. Aut 77.

65. Aut 79.

66. Jaspers recalls, for example, Jakob Böhme's distinction between God and the Other, the *Ungrund* in God (ChT 76).

67. On this topic see ChT 26–28.

68. On Jaspers's interpretation of Job, see PGO 332–351.

69. VuD 163.

70. Ibid.

71. ChT 35f.

72. This list is partly based on Jaspers' alternatives in VuD 161.

73. See MW 67ff.

74. See KlSch 102.

75. See KlSch 103.

76. KlSch 102.

77. According to Jaspers, there is a chance that even in a struggle in which there seems to be no more common ground, one can "unite with the opponent in the overarching *Humanity*" (KLSch 103). See also Ph 1, 184: Out of the (transcendent) unity there can be kinship even in the fiercest struggle between opponents. Or: W 221: "The last conflicts are not the last, behind all of them there is the *One*."

78. See Jaspers's distinctions: Solidarity of being human in general, solidarity of the rational, covenant for specific purposes, covenant by contract (promise) and forgiveness (VuD 158).

# Chapter 7

# The Decision between Direct and Indirect Communication

The merit of Jaspers can be seen in the fact that—in the post-metaphysical age—he held on to the fundamental existential questions of philosophy and pointed out and explored the still possible ways to *Transcendence*—in the orientation toward the *World*, in the *Illumination* of *Existence*, in the reading of *Chiffers*. But the truly philosophical aspect of his achievement is probably that he not only tried to make himself aware of what he was actually doing when he set out on these paths to *Transcendence* but also radically posed the question of how what we experience on these paths can be communicated at all. In this way, he achieved for philosophy what had already characterized him as a psychopathologist: the development of a *methodological consciousness*.

The philosopher he followed in this matter was not Kant but Kierkegaard. Through him, he gained the insight that all philosophical communication must be indirect.[1] For Jaspers, the distinction and decision between *Direct* and *Indirect Communication* is the fundamental philosophical decision par excellence.[2] It is at the root of his distinction between scientific knowledge and philosophical *Illumination*. The distinction is already present in his *Die Psychologie der Weltanschauungen*. There he characterizes it as follows: While the philosophers of *Direct Communication* appear either as teachers of principles, who demand "loyalty and obedience to the truth as seen and formulated," or then as teachers of totality, such as Aristotle, Thomas Aquinas, and Hegel, who prescribe the way for all as a matter of course, the "prophets of *Indirect Communication*"—Socrates, for example, Kant, Kierkegaard—"turn inward as individuals to the individual, appeal to the life that is in the other (. . .) They push back when one wants to follow them worshipfully, they love the freedom in the other."[3]

But what exactly is the difference between *Direct* and *Indirect Communication*? A key passage can be found in Jaspers's essay on the 100th anniversary of Kierkegaard's death:

> What I communicate directly as a constant content, as a matter that I think, everyone can understand in agreement and take possession of as the same thing. The thinker himself is indifferent. The matter is valid. But if the matter is of such a nature that it does not exist as a generally known object, but only in unity with the being of the thinker, it can only be communicated in such a way that the thinker is present as himself, transforming himself with the truth of thought. Since this is the action of his free *Existence*, he cannot know truth as a content detached from himself. He cannot be told what to do. In other words, what is really important can only be made tangible, illuminated, and achieved indirectly through the forms of the direct.[4]

Directly communicable, as much is immediately clear, are thoughts that have no connection to ourselves and that anyone can think in the same way that anyone else could think them. Indirectly communicable, on the other hand, is when the thought concerns me personally, that is, when it is of such a nature that it makes a significant difference in my life how I relate to the thought, both as the communicator and as the recipient of the communication. In the way I think the matter, I change myself and at the same time change the matter I am thinking about. To illustrate: the content of the equation "2+2 = 4" is true regardless of whether I think of it or not, and can therefore be communicated directly. The statement that radical moral *Conversion* is possible for humans at any time seems to be formally of the same kind as the statement that humans have two legs, but it is objectively meaningless. As we have already seen, its objective meaninglessness is shown by the fact that it belongs to the kind of transcendental statements that lead to contradictions, paradoxes, and tautologies. For how is it possible to make a beginning out of oneself—in a world of causalities? The principle of contradiction to be avoided, which applies to our cognition and our actions in the world, is suspended in transcendental thought: both the yes and the no are true, and both must be held in resistance to the thinking of the *Understanding*, which sees only an either/or everywhere. Such concepts have, as Jaspers says, a thoroughly antinomic character.[5]

As propositional statements, they have the form of ordinary propositions, but I have not understood them unless I understand them as a message addressed to myself. This indirectness hidden in general propositions underlies every sentence that promises to give an answer to existential and metaphysical questions. The indirectness consists in the fact that it is not the proposition itself that is the answer, but the question to me, whether I want to be guided in my life by such a proposition or not. The decision demanded of me—that it is up to me and me alone—is the only possible answer to the already discussed basic situation of man, that he "exists as a single, finite being," which "is at the same time conscious of a *General*"[6] and which therefore has to solve in his life the task of becoming that "figure of the self," which "as an *Individual* is at the same time the *General*."[7]

## THE NATURE OF CONCEPTS RELATED TO EXISTENCE AND TRANSCENDENCE

The antinomic character of transcendental thought indicates that the concepts used here—if they have any function at all—cannot be used to make descriptive statements: there are no identifiable objects to which they could refer. And it is our choice whether to reject them as meaningless or to cling to them—admitting to ourselves that we can only illuminate ourselves with such concepts.[8]

Jaspers vehemently maintained this distinction between concepts of *Reason* and concepts of *Understanding*, creating separate categories for them. As we have seen, he distinguishes three kinds of concepts: concepts that refer to *Phenomena of Reality*, *Signa of Existence*, and *Chiffers of Transcendence*. *Signa of Existence* are categories whose meaning can only be understood by those who try to make their lives transparent on the basis of them. What *Unconditionality* is, for example, can only be understood by those who know themselves under an unconditional claim and who try to create continuity in their lives by repeating their unconditional decision. The message that there is something *Unconditional* only becomes true when I make it true. And I understand it only to the extent that I want to make it true. In short, the *Signa of Existence*, if they are to be understood, require an *Inner Action*, as Jaspers says in the language of Kierkegaard, by which I decide what will become of myself and which leads to a permanent education of myself.

Where *Possible Existence* refers to *Transcendence*, as if *Transcendence* were an object that appears in the *Subject-Object-Split*, all the images and ideas we form and all the statements and constructions we create are either meaningless speculations that reach into the void, or what Jaspers calls a Chiffer.

For thousands of years, everything that has been understood as an image, idea, or a concept of *Transcendence* has been passed off as knowledge. With the modern concept of science and the methodologically grounded existence of real knowledge and cognition, these cognitive claims of metaphysical statements became obsolete. Kant's demarcation deprived them of their ultimate legitimacy and revealed the impossibility of considering *Transcendence* as a *Phenomenon of Reality* or as graspable in concepts and images of the phenomenal world. But now comes the new aspect added by Jaspers: only when these pictorial and imaginary worlds lose their *Corporeality* for us do they acquire their true meaning. They become *Chiffers*.

Of course, *Chiffers* have a corporeal existence, belong to the *Phenomena of Reality*, and are subject to the causalities of the world of appearances. But if I see in them only realities or thoughts that are to be regarded as necessarily true, I have already missed them as *Chiffers*. What makes them *Chiffers* lies on a different level. It is the fact that such phenomena *exist* at all in their uniqueness: a rose of such beauty, a landslide of such force, a thought of such depth.[9] It is as if a light passes through them. It shines into them from somewhere else—from where the *Origin* of all *Being* lies. That light can illuminate everything I think and do. The glowing realities or believed realities become signs as if *Transcendence* were speaking through them. But we do not know what these signs mean. And yet, it is as if they contain a message that is addressed to me and only to me, and that gives me, as this individual, as a *Possible Existence*, something to understand. A message that therefore does not exist for others and has no objectivity. And yet it contains the possibility of becoming a message for others as well. For Jaspers, "the greatest example" of reality becoming a message is Kierkegaard's search for signs of God that would allow him to understand what God wants with him.[10] External events can be interpreted in this way as fate imposed upon me and as a call to will what fate has decreed for me. The *Chiffer* as an encouragement, so to speak, to be on the right path.

Jaspers' theory of *Chiffers* is based on four premises: (1) No image, no *Idea*, no concept can capture what *Transcendence* is. (2) It is therefore wrong to try to form an image of *Transcendence*. The biblical commandment, "Thou shalt not make unto thee any graven image or any likeness" is therefore for Jaspers, as it was for Kant, one of the most *sublime* passages in the Jewish code.[11] (3) However, the *Idea* of *Transcendence* is irrefutable, and when we try to think *Transcendence*, we cannot do it any other way than with the help of images, ideas, and concepts taken from the world of appearances. They are indispensable to us. (4) But they have no cognitive value; they have only an existential meaning: through them, *Transcendence* becomes *present* to us for certain moments, and they become *Chiffers*. It is in these moments that time and eternity touch, as it were, and the finite and the infinite coincide. But these formulae are themselves only *Chiffers* with which we try to make the incomprehensible comprehensible.

But to what extent does it actually make a difference to us whether we think of *Transcendence* as corporeal, tangible, or veiled in *Chiffers*? Jaspers illustrates the difference with the example of the eternal punishments of hell.[12] The fear of hellish punishments in the flesh has conquered people for centuries and encouraged them to restrain their behavior. But when the punishments of hell are *Chiffers*, "something completely changes." Action and punishment are no longer separated in time—the action now and the punishment later. In the *Chiffer*, hell itself becomes present with the action, but is now robbed of its corporeality. The fear of hell's punishments is now replaced by the fear of ourselves, the fear that we might lose ourselves and become guilty. Hell punishments in the flesh appeal to our will to be happy; they force us to obey, just as a despot can force us to obey. Hell punishments as *Chiffers*, on the other hand, appeal to us as free people, as moral beings who have the freedom to do good for its own sake, not out of fear of punishment. A God in the flesh is a God who makes us slaves, but a God as a *Chiffer* is a God who sets us free.

Jaspers often quotes the words of Kant: By denying us his knowledge, God has given us freedom. But freedom, and this is the fifth, central premise of Jaspers's *Chiffer* theory, is more powerful than all corporeality: where the *Non-Sensual* is "really present, it is rather the other way around. For where the senses no longer see anything before them, and yet the indelible *Idea* of morality remains, the power is insurmountable."[13]

A philosophy such as the Kantian-Jaspersian one, which protects us from the deception that *Transcendence* exists as an appearance in the world or can be thought of in analogy to appearances in the world, can rightly claim to be a philosophy of freedom.

However, the most central point in the nature of a *Chiffer* remains unclear: What does it mean to say that *Transcendence* is *present* in a *Chiffer*? How can *Transcendence* be present in the here and now? For Jaspers, there is only one criterion for this: its presence does not show itself in the fact that what has become a *Chiffer* for me is transformed, but that I myself am transformed in perceiving the *Chiffer*. Only this effect can make the proximity and reality of *Transcendence* tangible.[14]

We have already encountered the same idea in connection with the search for the *Unconditional*. There it was about the question of what I should will, about the decision that is a gift to oneself. Now it is about the question of what I can hope for if I do what I ought to do. Since failure is part of this world, this cannot mean hoping for happiness and success. Rather, it is about being able to do what I have chosen to do unconditionally, and not to fail because of myself—by "failing myself."

The only hope that counts is therefore the hope of "help from the ground of things that can never be taken into account." We can trust in it "to the extent that we do what we can in truth and love—to the extent that we become worthy of our freedom." But without ever being allowed to rely on it.[15] Being unsettled and coming to rest are therefore the main effects that Jaspers associates with being addressed by a *Chiffer*. This calmness is not the deceptive reassurance that allows us to hope optimistically for better times in our *Dasein*, but the calm that we long for in the experience of a *Borderline Situation* and in the deepest despair.

## Reading Chiffers and Dialectical Thinking

*Chiffers* can only speak to us not only if we are willing to listen to the *Chiffers* but if we are also able to read *Chiffers*. We have already seen examples of what this means: for example, in the *Illumination* of the relationship between freedom and grace using Augustinian and Pelagian *Chiffers*, or in Job's struggle with his theologian friends to find an answer to the question of God's justice in the face of evil and wickedness in the world. For each of the *Chiffers* brought into play, there is an opposing *Chiffer*; and each has its truth, and yet none may suffice on closer examination. Jaspers says that the effect of the movement of thought set in motion by the *Chiffers* is to "suspend the *Chiffers*." The aim of reading *Chiffers* is to enter and remain in this movement.

But how exactly does it work? There is no other way to become aware of *Chiffers* than to think about them. Triggered by questions that seek to explain the inexplicable, we end up in theological and philosophical speculation. The categories we use here are the same ones with which we move cognitively in the world of appearances; we speak of being, nothingness, something, causality, and so on, but we must always be aware that they have no application here, and that we do not know what the categories mean with which we try to think beyond all these categories, using concepts such as *Reason*, *Origin*, or *Transcendence*. These concepts are themselves only new *Chiffers*, and we never get out of the *Chiffers*.[16]

We remain captives of our categories. The greatest bondage is that we can only ever think in terms of distinctions, distinctions between what something is and what it is not. This is why we inevitably end up in dualisms, in opposites such as God and Devil, good and evil, right and wrong.

But where is the *One* of *Reason* if we always end up with opposites? The will to the *One* cannot be satisfied with these dualisms. Following this will, Jaspers, in his practice of reading *Chiffers*, tries to show both the truth and the falsity of the opposing *Chiffers* and thus to suspend them. This, too, is an act of liberation that prevents us from falling prey to a *Chiffer*. We may never get away from *Chiffers*, but the urge is always there to think beyond all *Chiffers*, to where there are no more *Chiffers*. Neither Job nor his friends are right; they fail because of the inscrutability of God; neither Augustine nor Pelagius is right; the paradox of freedom given to us remains.

But how does this go together, this urge to go beyond all *Chiffers*, to want to think the unthinkable, and on the other hand, to be reminded again and again by Jaspers that we find ourselves in a battle of powers between which we have to decide and between which we have always already decided? This contradiction can only be resolved if we remember the two movements of *Existence* that are bound up with inner *Conversion*: the opening to the most

*General*, to *Transcendence*, and the anchoring in *Existence*, in the here and now.

This tension must be endured. And it remains only as long as the individual succeeds in holding the two extreme poles together within himself.[17] This cannot be achieved by a single act of strength, but only by constant movement, ascending to *Transcendence* and descending again to the place in the world from which this movement emanates and where decisions must be made. Jaspers's favorite metaphor for this double movement is the image of the two wings. If we don't want to crash on our flight, we have to flap two wings: the wing of *Reason*, with which we stretch out into the greatest possible expanse of the *Absolute*, and the wing of *Existence*, which connects the *Absolute* to the *Individual*, to the here and now.[18]

*Chiffers* are, so to speak, vehicles of ascent; they are *Pointers* to *Transcendence*. When we follow the pull of *Reason*, transcending ourselves, we cannot help but leave behind all divisions, connect the seemingly contradictory and mutually exclusive, and try to grasp the most distant in the whole of our thinking. Thinking opposites together is the maxim. As a result, the concepts that come into play turn out to be inextricably linked. They form *Polarities*. Polar means that what is designated by one term presupposes what is designated by the other term and vice versa, as in the paradigmatic case of the magnetic field: no north pole without a south pole, no south pole without a north pole.[19]

The polar concepts are opposites that seem to be mutually exclusive. And yet they belong together and must be held together. This holding together and thinking together is the form of dialectical thinking that goes back to Heraclitus.[20] Let's take the example of the dual concepts of *Loneliness* and *Communication*. The two terms suggest that it is an either/or proposition. If I am alone, I am without *Communication*; if I am communicating, I am not alone. But a deeper understanding reveals that only those who can be themselves in *Loneliness* are able to communicate at all (communicate in a deeper, existential sense). The incompatibles belong together. And it is our seemingly paradoxical task to open ourselves to both sides and to seek both: *Loneliness* and *Communication*.

Jaspers's work is full of polar terms. Some of them are included in the double titles of his collections of articles and lectures: that is, *Hope and Worry*, *Fate and Will*, *Appropriation and Polemic*. Polar concepts belong together, even if it is not always possible for us to think of them as belonging together. The world conceived as infinite harmony and the world conceived as diabolical work are two such polar codes between which there seems to be no mediation. And yet even this contrast must be rejected as inadequate if we are to embark on the flight to *Transcendence*.

But with the descent that begins when the wing of *Existence* beats, there is also a narrowing, an intensification that requires a choice. In the realm of

*Reason*, everything is possible and everything must be held together, but when it comes to becoming real in space and time, only one thing is ever possible, and it is up to us to decide which of the many possibilities shall become real for us.[21] On the way back, therefore, we will no longer have to deal with polar concepts, but with antithetical concepts. They open a fork in the road, an either/or that demands a choice, as we have already seen in the great ultimate alternatives.

The question of descent already separates the two sides: either to remain in *Transcendence* or to return to the here and now. The first path is again divided. On the one hand, there is the path of the intimate seeker of God and the *Mystic*, for whom there is only one goal: to be completely absorbed in *Transcendence*, to reach a place where there are no more *Chiffers*. On the other hand, there is the path of the *Metaphysician*, who believes he can recognize *Being* in the realm of *Reason*, and who forgets himself in the contemplation of this supposedly universally valid content. The third and alternative path is that of the human being who wants to be an *Existence* filled with *Transcendence*.

Jaspers has already discussed this fork in the road at length in his *Psychology of Worldviews*. There he defines the first path as the path of *Mysticism*, the third as the path of the *Idea* or *Ideal Existence*,[22] for which he was probably modeled on Max Weber: "the consciousness of the *Absolute* and an action and behavior that are carried in their *Unconditionality* by the living seriousness of the *Absolute*."[23] The second path does not seem to him to be a real alternative; he speaks rather contemptuously of "fabricated metaphysics," which serve "metaphysical edification," form student associations, theosophical and spiritualist cooperatives, and represent a great danger because of their artificiality and inauthenticity.[24]

He describes the third way, that of *Ideal Existence*, as follows: The eternal *Idea* must enter into the finite; only in this way does the finite gain "meaning and eternal significance" and become "connected with a whole and eternal." For man living in time and space, trapped in the *Subject-Object-Split*, this is the only way. For him, "the finite and the individual, the temporal moment, the decision in the *World* must be as important as if the Eternal were decided only here, as if it depended on this temporal decision."[25] This is unmistakably the path that Jaspers himself took, and of which he says that it is the path that the Occident has taken, while the great Asian thinkers chose the path of *Mysticism*.

It doesn't take much imagination to see the implications of this decision for all other decisions in the realm of *Reason*, and ultimately for our lives. Here is just one example: If we regard it as futile to ever reach the infinitely distant *Transcendence*, and as futile to mystically sink into it, and instead consciously choose the path of *Ideal Existence*, the question still remains as to how *Transcendence* can become present in the here and now. Does it happen, as believers in revelation assume, through a one-time revelation for chosen people at a specific point in time, or does it happen through the fact that things in the world can become *Chiffers* of Transcendence at any time and for everyone? So which side do we take, faith in revelation and in the corporeality of *Transcendence*, or *Philosophical Faith* in *Chiffers*?

For Jaspers, as we have come to know, such dichotomies are not abstract opposites between which a rational choice can be made. They, too, are embodiments of opposing spiritual powers that draw us into their struggle and thus make it impossible for us to attain a neutral standpoint from which to overlook them. We have always been a party—long before we chose to be a party, because of the traditions we have stood for from the beginning. When Jaspers says of the *Ideal Existence* that it is the path of the Western man and the mystical path that of the Asian man, this is more than a mere statement; it is also a commitment, an affirmation of the spiritual world in which he grew up and is "rooted." It is loyalty to what was once direct authority. This is why Jaspers is not merely being ironic when he adds to Kierkegaard's statement that he believes in Jesus Christ because his father told him to: that he, Jaspers, does not believe in Jesus Christ because his father did not tell him to. This may sound strange only if one does not also consider the second point: that one owes allegiance to *Authority* only so far as it stands the scrutiny of *Reason*.

In the end, however, the decisive criterion in this examination of an ultimate position remains the question of whether I am prepared to stand up for the truth of what I believe, even to risk my life for it. Scientific truth stands on its own; it does not require my commitment. Philosophical truth, on the other hand, is bound to the person who stands for it with his life. That is why Galileo, following Jaspers' oft-cited example, rightly renounced his scientific truth in order to save his life; Giordano Bruno, on the other hand, could only prove his philosophical will to truth by dying for his truth.

## PHILOSOPHICAL COMMUNICATION AS INDIRECT COMMUNICATION

After this somewhat lengthy excursus on *Chiffers* and *Chiffer* reading, let us briefly consider their significance in the course of our investigation, in order to return to the question of communication. The starting point was the methodological question of what we are actually doing when we, trusting in *Reason*, try to think beyond the realm of *Understanding*, to transcend it. According to the first hint, we can only approach that which encompasses us, whether it is immanently encompassing or transcendent, by illuminating it. With the help of the reflective power of judgment, we conceive of a *General*, which does not correspond to any objectivity and therefore does not convey any knowledge or insight, but can become the guiding principle of our thoughts and actions—always assuming that we also want to be guided by it. The tacit appeal to our will associated with any *Illumination* requires a special form of communication: *Indirect Communication*. To shed light on this, we have clarified the nature of the concepts used in *Indirect Communication*. Where it is a matter of illuminating *Existence*, they are called *Signa of Existence*; where it is a matter of illuminating *Transcendence*, they are called *Chiffers*. What they have in common is that they are meaningless without the *Possible Existence* of the reader, who, addressed by them, transforms himself inwardly. This is their inherent indirectness. What is said can only be heard in the *Loneliness* of the individual. But it always presupposes communication with the other. This communication, in turn, remains meaningful only if it also becomes an opportunity to try out in *Inner Action* what has been said and to experience it as one understands it: "transforming with the thought truth."[26]

Without this way of personal self-understanding, of "doing one's free *Existence*," no philosophical communication is possible. However, one cannot move the other person by simply telling him that he should go this way, and even less can one suggest it by compelling arguments. The most I can do is hope that if he follows my train of thought, something will be awakened in him and set in motion. The appeal of philosophical communication, of which Jaspers repeatedly speaks, lies in the inherent possibility of hearing what is demanded of me.

If we understand the indirectness of philosophical communication in this way, it also becomes clear why Jaspers sees *Indirect Communication* not only in philosophical works but also in the possibilities for action that people show us in their physical *Dasein* or through the traditional image of their *Dasein*: Through the indirectness at work in them, they become models, examples, or counter-images for us.[27] Ultimately, however, the *Chiffers of Transcendence* are the epitome of *Indirect Communication*. Here we only have what is directly given: the phenomena of the world of appearances. Their depth is revealed only to those who know how to perceive the indirect in them.

Suppose we were to accept Jaspers's dichotomy between *Direct* and *Indirect Communication*, and we were to opt for *Indirect Communication*: What would change in the presentation of our philosophizing? Kierkegaard answered this question with his deliberately chosen form of *Indirect Communication*: he lets pseudonyms speak and refuses to take any responsibility for the content of their works, except for the so-called edifying writings published under his name. The pseudonymous works are to be understood as the writings of a third party, which he, Kierkegaard, claims to understand no better than any other reader.[28]

It is this *Indirect Communication* by Kierkegaard, which has become "intention and plan," that Jaspers rejects for himself. He does not hide, he does not withdraw ironically, but allows us to participate in his own reflections, which—in their lack of results—place themselves in *Limbo*. But when he does this, he always does so with a clear awareness of what he is doing. Although his methodological awareness is supported by the *Basic Knowledge*, the insight into the phenomenality of the world, the presentation of his philosophical thoughts is based on a fundamental decision that transforms the philosopher himself. It is the decision for a philosophy that wants freedom, that wants to recognize "what is absolutely valid for it in historical concreteness," and that does not "negate itself by obedient submission to demanding authorities or an allegedly objective authority, that is, 'renounce freedom for freedom's sake.'"[29] Jaspers's decision is reflected in a clear intention: the will not to create the indirect in a planned way, but to express it through the style of his philosophizing.

But how is this possible? Jaspers's paradoxical answer: through *Maximum Directness*. His explanation is as follows:

> It belongs to the nature of philosophizing and is insurmountable: we must always speak objectively, we can only think clearly along objective lines, and in order to make the philosophical present in it, we must melt the objective again and make it disappear (. . .) We build by destroying what we have built. But this is philosophically bright and eloquent if it does not happen by chance and is not disturbed by other moments, but succeeds in a purely methodical process.[30]

Philosophy's commitment to the objective clarity of *Understanding* is at the same time a rejection of a philosophy that appeals to the emotions and seeks to achieve its goal with "ecstatic speeches, vivid views, surprising claims to power."[31] No false concreteness is the motto:

> Rationally communicated philosophy as such must have an open flank, which it is up to the thinker to complete. It must not already offer the concrete, which is either conquered in the sciences or communicable in the visions of the poets (. . .) The greatest efforts of philosophical thinking (. . .) are directed towards the attainment of the genuine, not empty, but effective *Unconcreteness*.[32]

As a reader of Jaspers, one can't really complain about a lack of *Unconcreteness*!

But how does this go together: leaving everything to the freedom of the reader or listener and still wanting to have an effect? Is it enough to use the unavoidable directness in such a way that, if it reaches the reader, it makes indirectness possible? Beyond the indirect appeal, is it not sometimes necessary to give further guidance—not only by the direct message that one hopes for an indirect effect, but also by the author's direct appeal to the reader to pay attention to the indirect in the message and not to take what is said directly for what is actually said? This direct appeal is undoubtedly always present in Jaspers,[33] even more so in his lectures and talks than in his writings, and more direct in his political writings than in his philosophical works.[34] But this variation makes little difference. Whether direct appeal or only indirect appeal, whether hortative or indicative language: in any case, the reader has understood what has been said only if he takes it not as a cognitive communication in the medium of the *Understanding*—as something that can be repeated in the same or different words and called a teaching—but as an appeal to himself—to the *Reason* within himself to make the leap to his own action: through corresponding *Inner Action*.

To dare this leap into one's own *Existence* is the high demand that Jaspers places on his readers and that he repeatedly tries to demonstrate, most vividly with his now-familiar image of the two wings that must beat together in order for what is said in the text to achieve "fulfilled meaning and upswing." The flapping of one wing is the willingness to think, to "objectively grasp" what has been developed and can be referred to; the flapping of the other wing is the "resonance of the *possible Existence*" of the reader, who allows himself to be included in what he is reading, who is receptive "to the indirect in the movement of thought"[35] and who faces the "hard challenge" of "finding himself with good will and bright *Reason*, in the willingness to be given the gift of *Transcendence* in his own freedom."[36]

But what can we hope for from a philosophy of *Indirect Communication* that does not depend on results, on "true" propositions, on a so-called worldview, or on recipes? Ultimately, according to Jaspers, only one thing: "the recognition, practice, and consolidation of an inner philosophical attitude from which our power of judgment in concrete situations arises, not as a calculable consequence, but as a proof of *Possible Existence* that has made itself certain."[37] Since this attitude can only be attained if I myself take the philosophical path, if I educate myself—out of my own *Origin*—as Jaspers would say.

It could appear that the goal of Jaspers' philosophical writing is ultimately to make itself superfluous, as superfluous as the shell that the hatched chick leaves behind. But this appearance only exists as long as—in addition to the necessary *Loneliness* of standing within oneself—the second moment is not taken into account: that self-education is only possible jointly, in uninterrupted communication with the other—with all the others who, "in saying the *General* as a form of existentially illuminating thinking," turn to themselves and to me as a *Possible Existence*, in order to allow both to come to themselves.[38] Whatever I think must therefore remain in constant communication with everything that has ever been thought.

## NOTES

1. "The elaboration of philosophizing in writings (. . .) contains the insurmountable indirect in contrast to all the directness of the sciences. (. . .) Kierkegaard's indirect communication, which we reject as an intention, has brought this inevitability of philosophical communication to clarity as a methodological consciousness" (Aut 117; see also AB 297).—For more on *Indirect Communication*, see Anton Hügli, "Jaspers' Darstellung von Philosophie—eine Form der indirekten Mitteilung?," *Jahrbuch der österreichischen Karl Jaspers Gesellschaft*, 28 (2015), 9–36.

2. W 648: The modes of communication are not "indifferently juxtaposed." "The most radical difference is that between *Direct* and *Indirect Communication.*"

3. PW 376f.

4. Karl Jaspers, «Kierkegaard. Zu seinem 100. Todestag» in *Aneignung und Polemik. Gesammelte Reden und Aufsätze zur Geschichte der Philosophie,* ed. Hans Saner (München: Piper, 1968), 312–329, 314.

5. They reveal the "antinomic structure of the world" already emphasized by Jaspers in *Die Psychologie der Weltanschauungen*, which becomes existentially experienceable in the *Borderline Situation* and which Kant uncovered in the form of the paralogisms of pure *Reason* and the antinomies for every thinking that goes toward the infinite (PW 229–247). Since antinomic contradictions do not cancel each other out, but collapse into themselves, the contradictory moments can be regarded as one and the same and therefore also appear in the form of tautologies or circles (cf. Ph 2, 13f.).

6. PW 379.

7. PW 411.

8. Therefore: "Statements of being in existentially illuminating philosophizing meet freedom." I examine in freedom what I want to be and produce through myself that which becomes comprehensible only through this production (for me and any other, *Possible Existence*) (Ph 2, 10).

9. In this way, anything can become a *Chiffer*—just by the fact that it is. See NPL 165: "It is as if everything that is, by the very fact that it is, is a language of *Transcendence*. We hear language as real language, experience reality in it in a concrete historical situation in a historically unique form that cannot be generalized."

The historical references that Jaspers cites as the source of his concept of *Chiffer* are revealing (NPL 166):

> Kant—in his moral interpretation of the beautiful forms of nature—called sense and form a *Chiffer* of nature. W. v. Humboldt adopted the term for natural philosophical thought. Schopenhauer spoke of "hieroglyphics" in the same sense—Klages dealt with the "reality of images" as forcefully as he did magnificently.

10. Prov. 49.—Jaspers gives indications of how he also looked for such (*Chiffer*-like) signs in his own life. See, for example: When the call came from Basel, "we felt strange. The sign of destiny, the finger of God—to speak in *Chiffer*—was ambiguous (. . .) The unity of destiny and will should arise, but it was not yet there" (SchW 166, see also 181, 182).

11. *Karl Jaspers,* «Immanuel Kant. Zu seinem 150. Todestag», in *Aneignung und Polemik. Gesammelte Reden und Aufsätze zur Geschichte der Philosophie,* ed. Hans Saner (München: Piper, 1968), 242–250, 246; GPh 528. Immanuel Kant, „Kritik der Urteilskraft," in *Akademie Ausgabe*, ed. Königlich Preussische Akademie der Wissenschaften, vol. 5 (Berlin, 1908, reprint 1968), 165–486, 274.

12. ChT 30.

13. ChT 31, here too Jaspers follows Kant (see GPh 528).

14. Cf. W 458f.

15. KlSch 139.

16. That is why, according to Jaspers, Hegel's attempt to break out of all categories is illusory: cf. ChT 74:

> There is Hegel's great attempt to break out, who demonstrated in his logic the relativity of each of our categories. That was the great liberation. But then came the new fetter: the whole of the categories he developed were to be the thoughts of God before the creation of the earth.

17. The significance of this "holding together" is also expressed in Kierkegaard's formula that man is a "synthesis" of "infinity and finitude, of the temporal and the eternal, of freedom and necessity, in short, a synthesis" (*Krankheit zum Tode,* ed. Emanuel Hirsch (Düsseldorf: Diederichs, 1957)), Jaspers may also have been guided by Kierkegaard's formula in his *Illumination* of the relationship between *Existence* and *Transcendence*.

18. Ph 2, 11. Only through the double movement do we attain independence from the world:

> Independent *Existence* can be lonely with its *Transcendence*; it knows the Archimedean point outside the *World* as possible, but it returns to *Dasein* and its communication as the only place of assurance and proof of what it has experienced alone and beyond. It lives in the *World* and out of the *World*; it knows the limits and essentially moves along them. Actual independence therefore sees its *Dasein* in polarity: life in a common generic substance, in the course of the *World* and the law—and the personal emergence of *Existence* as an individual; being protected in a whole—and pushing towards the boundaries; *Dasein* that is round in itself—and *Dasein* in time; seeing a given world in its order and hierarchy—and going on adventures in a questionable *Dasein*. No beginning and no end are known in this independence, no goal is the last. (Ph 2, 168)

19. More on the polarities in Jaspers's work, cf. Anton Hügli, «Das Nahe und das Ferne, das Einzelne und das Allgemeine, das Zeitliche und das Ewige. Über die Grundpolarität in Jaspers' Denken," in *Karl Jaspers: Filozofia Wieczysta—Filozofia Czasu*, ed. Czeslawa Piecuch (Krakow: Wydawnictwo Naukowe UP, 2021), 15–36.

20. What Heraclitus calls *logos is* the oneness of opposites, "the counter-striving union as with bow and lyre," the agreement of the incongruous (cf. Hermann Diels, Die *Fragmente der Vorsokratiker*, ed. Wilhelm Kranz, Bd. 1, 5. Aufl., B (Berlin: Weidmann, 1934), 162, 22 B 51, 152, 22 B 8. On Jaspers on Heraclitus: GP, 651–659, esp. 652.

21. Cf. UZG 198:

But the overcoming of opposites is stranded in the concrete alternatives of the real situation. This happens wherever thought cannot remain within itself, but is required to realize itself in space and time. Here only those are free who can decide. He who decides takes upon himself a lack of freedom. By giving up possibilities, he realizes himself freely, but in a limited way. Through realization, freedom becomes substantial, but on the way to a lack of freedom.

22. Cf. PW 440–462.

23. Max Weber, «Eine Gedenkrede (1920)», in *Aneignung und Polemik. Gesammelte Reden und Aufsätze zur Geschichte der Philosophie,* ed. Hans Saner (München: Piper, 1968), 409–423, 421f.

24. PW 70f.- In *Philosophie* he then speaks, probably meaning the same thing, of a "prophetic metaphysics" as a method to be rejected, which believes it has taken the step "to the knowledge of what actually is" and wants to "impose the absolute certainty of Transcendence" on the individual in objective language "as if it were a universally valid truth" (Ph 3, 31).

25. PW 460.

26. Karl Jaspers, «Kierkegaard. Zu seinem 100. Todestag« (1955), in *Aneignung und Polemik. Gesammelte Reden und Aufsätze zur Geschichte der Philosophie,* ed. Hans Saner (München: Piper, 1968), 312–329, 314.

27. Jaspers, W 648.—An example of this form of *Indirect Communication* for Jaspers may have been the philosophical claim that Max Weber—through his unconditional will to truth—awakened in him. He became his great role model and the *epitome* of a philosophical existence. His essence is "the consciousness of the *Absolute* and an action and behavior that is carried in its *Unconditionality* by the living seriousness of the *Absolute*. What was unique about Max Weber was that this essence radiated from him without him recognizing and demonstrating the *Absolute* in a concrete way" ("Max Weber: Eine Gedenkrede" 1920), in *Aneignung und Polemik. Gesammelte Reden und Aufsätze zur Geschichte der Philosophie,* ed. Hans Saner (München: Piper, 1968), 409–423, 421f.

28. Søren Kierkegaard, *Abschliessende unwissenschaftliche Nachschrift zu den Philosophischen Brocken*, Zweiter Teil (Düsseldorf; Köln: Diederichs, 1958), 339–344.

29. Ph 1, XLVIII.

30. Ph 1, LII.

31. Ph 1, L.

32. "Letter to Jean Wahl," January 30, 1938 (in *Schriften zur Existenzphilosophie,* Karl Jaspers Gesamtausgabe I/8 (Basel: Schwabe, 2018), 164–167, 165f.). However, the general information Jaspers gives on his method of presentation is again rather "vague."

33. This is what Jaspers says about himself in all directness: I want reason to be in the *World* (Prov 54).

34. This also earned him the accusation of being a moralizing writer and a "political moralist" in his political writings, which often fell into a "preachy tone," for example according to Hermann Lübbe, "Die Masse, der Nationalsozialismus und die Atombombe, Karl Jaspers als politischer Moralist," in "*Wahrheit ist, was uns*

*verbindet." Karl Jaspers' Kunst zu Philosophieren*, ed. Reinhard Schulz, Giandomenico Bonanni, and Matthias Bormuth (Göttingen: Wallstein, 2009), 391–410, esp. 399.

35. Ph 1, XXIX The image of the two wings is unmistakably inspired by the basic idea from the *"Psychologie der Weltanschauungen"* that it is part of the "basic situation of man" that he "exists as a single, finite being," which "is at the same time conscious of a *General*" and which therefore has to solve the task in his life of becoming that form of the self which as the *Individual* is at the same time the *General* (PW 379–381).

36. Ph 1, XLIX.

37. Ph 1, LII.

38. cf. Ph 2, 61: "I cannot become myself without entering into communication and cannot enter into communication without being lonely."

# Chapter 8

# Jaspers's Philosophy as Unconditional Will to Communicate

## WORLD PHILOSOPHY AND THE CONCEPT OF AXIAL AGE

Jaspers could not open the wing of the *General* far enough. When he realized that the ground on which he had felt at home until 1933 was breaking up beneath his feet, and that the Nazi state was initiating a previously unthinkable break in communication, the entire European tradition was put to the test for him. To what extent were Western intellectuals themselves pioneers of the horrors that were now unfolding, to what extent were they "creators and guardians" of that which was capable of resisting them?[1] Where could one still find orientation?

What had previously been Jaspers's inclination now became a clear goal for him: if one was looking for orientation, one had to look to the truly Great ones and seek dialogue with them. Worldwide, beyond Europe. With one goal in mind: to search philosophically for the conditions of the possibility of *Universal Communication*,[2] in the knowledge that there is no one right philosophy. And that honesty requires us to know what we do not want to know and to see the greatness of even the strangest thinkers. In short, philosophy must be critically interrogated and constantly re-appropriated in all its manifestations.

Jaspers now began to study Chinese philosophy more intensively, with Confucius and Lao Tzu, and sensed there an "origin of humanity" which he admired and which he perceived as a contrast "to the barbarism of his surroundings." In 1938, in an exchange with his friend Heinrich Zimmer, an Indologist from Heidelberg, he also turned to Indian thought, with an ever-growing respect for "what was thought there."[3] It was the same questions and the same effort to find answers through independent thinking, and the same awareness that what constitutes the human being must have an eternal *Origin*. For Jaspers, therefore, it became increasingly clear that an equally original philosophical awakening must have occurred in the West, in India, and in China at about the same time and without having been influenced by one another. It is the discovery of the epoch that he would then call the *Axial Age* and for which he set the period between 800 and 200 B.C.[4]

The *axis* consists of the "totality of spiritual events that have liberated man by making him aware of his finitude and incompleteness and of his possibilities for redemption."[5] It represents the decisive turning point in human history. The following statement applies: "No one can lay any foundation other than the one laid from the beginning."[6] The concepts and categories developed during the *Axial Age* still dominate our thinking today. The religions that people still profess today were created during this period. With the *Axial Age* in mind, we Westerners can become aware that not only our chronology but also the biblically based claim to exclusivity of our religion is untenable, that God can also be heard beyond the West, "wherever he speaks to us through people who have experienced *Transcendence* in all seriousness."[7]

Since the *Axial Age*, there has been a global unity of philosophy that can only be represented by a universal history of philosophy. However, Jaspers was aware that writing such a *World History of Philosophy* would be an impossible task for a single person, and that it would require dozens of collaborators just to process the immense amount of material already available. Nevertheless, he decided to attempt the impossible himself. Not, however, with an encyclopedia intended to be complete, which no philosopher would ever be able to review, let alone appropriate. Rather, he wanted to do what only an individual can do:[8] philosophize with the great thinkers. A "concise presentation of the basic schemes of historical conception, constantly illustrated by significant examples" should suffice for this purpose.[9]

Jaspers's idea of a *World History of Philosophy* represents a radical break with the conventional, chronological way of writing the history of philosophy. In his eyes, each of the great thinkers stood on their own, was unique, and could not be explained by what had gone before. Nor could they be understood as a mere prelude to something later, not, as with Hegel, as a mere stage in the movement of the *Absolute Spirit* toward a final goal. For Jaspers, therefore, it was not succession but juxtaposition that was decisive—juxtaposition in the unlimited space of *Reason*.

Jaspers's idea was that there is a timeless republic of philosophers, and the boundaries between them run through time. The only thing that distinguishes them is their rank and greatness. The *reflecting* power of judgment can at best identify affinities between them and classify them according to ultimately subjective points of view. Thus, according to Jaspers, Socrates, Buddha, Confucius, and Jesus belong together as the key figures of humanity;

Plato, Augustine, and Kant as the "procreating founders of philosophizing"; Anaximander, Heraclitus, Parmenides, Plotinus, Anselm, Spinoza, Lao Tzu, and Nagarjuna as the "metaphysicians who think from the origin," and so on.

But how does one measure the greatness of a philosopher? Jaspers gives three main criteria. The greatness of a philosopher—this is the *first condition*—can only become visible if there is a work that is characterized by universality and that helps us "to come to an awareness of our *Existence*, of the *World*, of *Being*, of the *Godhead*" and "to illuminate our path through life as a whole, beyond all particular purposes."[10] Where there are no works, as in the case of Socrates or Buddha, or where they are lost, as in the case of Confucius, there must be accounts of his thoughts and actions that confirm his greatness. The *second condition* is the demonstrable influence on the thinking of later great philosophers and wider circles, and the inexhaustibility of his work, which continues to this day.[11] Finally, the *third condition* is the inner content of his work: that it is bound to time but always stands above time, that it is *original* in the sense that something impossibly new comes to light in it, and that the philosopher is inwardly independent, founded in himself as "*Existence* before *Transcendence*," which, however, understands itself in an incomplete way.[12]

For Jaspers, this third condition is the most important beyond the criteria that can be at least approximately objectified: A philosopher is great to the extent that he is able to awaken the *Possible Existence* of the individual to a *Real Existence*, that is, he not only helps to achieve rational insight but also has the power to bring about the rise to *Existence*. Again, however, it is up to the individual to ensure that this effect occurs: "The purer the will, the truer the thought, the more clearly the will and truth of the great speak." "He who I see as great reveals to me what I am."[13]

Jaspers thus exposes himself to the accusation that can and has been rightly made against him: Does this not ultimately mean a complete *Subjectivization* of the history of philosophy? If, in the end, there is only the struggle of powers, and everyone must see where he stands, is not every judgment of a philosopher arbitrary and capricious? In any case, beyond all scientificity? This question, however, calls for a counterquestion: Would scholarly research on philosophical texts be possible at all if it were not ultimately supported by that which appeals to the researcher as meaningful? And would anything essential be visible in them at all if they were not related to ultimate constructions of meaning?

Jaspers was aware of this problem. He confronted it with the attitude that characterizes his method of *Indirect Communication*: to communicate the indirect (addressing each individual in his freedom) with maximum directness. Directness requires distance and objectification. The philosopher in question is to be presented as himself, as far as possible. This requires the objectivity that academic research thrives on: emphasizing the historical conditions and the context in which the work stands, finding out everything that is historically known about the author, omitting no facts, declaring nothing to be a private matter, or exaggerating it mythically. The aim is to raise awareness of "what a philosopher has thought," perhaps even "without having said it explicitly himself."[14]

The context in which all this takes place is the history of philosophy in its entirety. But how does Jaspers bring this together: to grasp the individual great philosopher in his uniqueness and yet not lose sight of the history of philosophy as a whole? To seek the supra-historical nature of his thought and yet not forget that he remains ultimately historical? Again, it seems to be a question of either/or, of exclusivity. But on closer inspection, it is again a polarity. Expressed schematically, it is the polarity of the vertical and the horizontal, of the expansion in time and the transversal to time.

Philosophy has its beginning in time and expands in time. But the fact that what appears in time is philosophy can only be determined with regard to the supra-temporal *Idea* of philosophy. Every great philosopher contributes to the realization of this *Idea*, without being able to claim that what he realizes is also the whole of philosophy. If we follow the horizontal, spread of philosophy over the centuries, we move in the explorable realm of facts, but if we ourselves strive to participate in the life of the *Idea*, we move in the supra-historical space of *Reason*, in the timeless republic of philosophers. Jaspers's world history of philosophy follows both the horizontal and the vertical. These two directions are juxtaposed here.

## PHILOSOPHY IN ITS TEMPORAL APPEARANCE

It will never be possible to survey the history of philosophy in its temporal manifestation. One can only ever penetrate it to a certain extent under certain aspects. In his last draft[15] of a *World History of Philosophy*, Jaspers distinguishes between five aspects: First, the historical aspect (guided by chronology and geography); second, the factual aspect (based on the problems and systems of thought); third, the genetic aspect (the origin of philosophy from myth, religion, poetry, language); fourth, the practical aspect (related to the realization of philosophy in the practice of life); fifth, the dynamic aspect in the space of "powers," "in which a struggle of powers takes place through philosophizing."[16]

Each of these aspects would have to be treated separately and independently of the others, and would require its own chronological presentation. But even if all this were possible, the whole of philosophy would not be exhausted. Above all, the essential would be missing: the people behind these objectivities, who, like us, are searching for the Ground of *Being* and the direction of their lives, and with whom we would therefore like to connect. "They bring more than what is revealed by these five points of view. They reveal the essence of philosophy."[17] Jaspers therefore concentrated entirely on the personal aspect of the history of philosophy and made the presentation of the great philosophers his main task.[18] The first volume of his monumental work, *The Great Philosophers*, published in 1957, bears witness to this, as do the monographs and articles that appeared before and after it. But even this task was too big, and in the end, the work remained a torso.[19] The posthumously published volumes of his legacy show the dimensions in which it was conceived.[20]

## PHILOSOPHY IN ITS SUPRA-HISTORICITY

The path to philosophy leads to those who have already walked it. Therefore, there is no philosophy without the history of philosophy. This is Jaspers's credo. For philosophy does not consist of thoughts, theories, and systems; it is not a doctrine. Unlike science, the "matter" here is inseparable from the person who thinks it.[21] And because every individual is historical, this thinking itself is subject to time. Philosophy wants the whole, but this whole can only be grasped to the extent that an individual person is able to express it in his or her lifetime; it is not objectified in a cumulative body of doctrines but must be brought to life anew in each individual.[22] Creating the conditions for this personal appropriation of what the great philosophers have realized is what Jaspers is concerned with in *The Great Philosophers*.

Jaspers's aim in portraying a philosopher is to search for the unity of his thought and for that "single unity" in which all great philosophers meet.[23] The first step is to reproduce his thoughts and actions as faithfully as possible. Just as art history needs reproductions, the historian of philosophy must use the representations he constructs. They should be as comprehensible as possible, to create "images" of the patterns of thought that a philosopher has produced.[24] But with the constant reminder that these images can never replace the reading of the original texts themselves.

Only when all this has been accomplished can the conversation with the philosopher begin, guided by the critical question of the interpreter and the readers who follow him: What thought can I embrace, and what must I reject inwardly? This is the process of interpretation and evaluation, of one's own philosophizing, which must be clearly separated from the presentation of facts. It must be a conversation at eye level because even the great philosopher is a human being like me; he too can make mistakes and go wrong. Therefore, no philosopher can be an authority to be obediently followed, and no work is a sacred text in which absolute truth can be found. Philosophers are models of the highest order in their way of searching, who can encourage us to follow this path ourselves.

However, the individual only acquires the right to enter into dialogue with the great dead if he is willing to educate himself to understand them and thus allow himself to be educated by them. They show themselves to us willingly—but only to the extent that we know how to question them properly.[25]

To question is to examine, according to the Kantian maxim of self-thinking.[26] But in order to examine, we need the right tools, or to be more precise, the very tool that has been called the *Organon* since certain writings of Aristotle were summarized under this title, and that has been called *Logic* since the Stoics. The development of such an *Organon* was Jaspers's second major project, parallel to his *World History of Philosophy*. This work served the sole purpose of providing the tools with which philosophical thought could be developed. He called it *Philosophical Logic*.

## Philosophical Logic

Jaspers's Philosophical Logic is more than the formal logic handed down by Aristotle. It is at the same time what was called *Metaphysics* after Aristotle, later *Prima Philosophia*, what Kant finally began with his *Transcendental Logic*, and what Hegel carried out in his metaphysical logic as a theory of categories. In short, it is a discipline that attempts to encompass all actual forms of thought, all known categories, and methods, but, unlike Hegelian logic, without claiming to be a conclusive system of all possible forms of thought. In his later works, Jaspers refers to this logic only as *Basic Philosophical Knowledge* (*philosophisches Grundwissen*).[27]

Jaspers's starting point is the fundamental idea that truth only exists for us if we also know in what sense and to what extent what we believe to be true can be true. So there is no truth without knowing when something can be considered true. Since every claim that something is true is synonymous with the claim that things are as we say they are, every consciousness of truth is linked to a consciousness of *Being*. To know what is true is to know what is the case. This makes it understandable why Jaspers's *Philosophical Logic* sees itself as metaphysical, as a doctrine of what exists. But since, after Kant's fundamental insight into the phenomenal nature of the world, the claim to be able to recognize *Being* as such falls away, all that remains instead of the knowledge of *Being* is the *Illumination* of the being which appears to us, the being which encompasses us and in which we find ourselves. This is precisely where our investigation began: with the ways of grasping and the corresponding ways of knowing and being true.

In retrospect, we can now see that from the very beginning we were in the midst of what Jaspers calls *Philosophical Logic*. This is not surprising, however, since the question of the possibility of communication, the possibility of understanding and being understood, requires us to gain clarity about the forms we use to communicate with ourselves and with others. *Philosophical Logic*, then, as Jaspers can formulate it, is work "on the preconditions of the possibility of universal communication."[28] Its goal is "to become the *Organon* of thinking communication."[29] For it is concerned with the question of communicability per se, with the question of how communication is possible and where the limits of communicability lie.

But what benefit can we expect from such *Philosophical Logic*? Do we have to wait for this logic before we can talk to each other in a meaningful way? Certainly not. People have always talked meaningfully to each other without ever having heard of logic. But whenever they have tried to determine what is really true, right, or valid, they have necessarily considered the way to arrive at the truth, the methods to be used, the arguments to be presented, and the conclusions to be drawn.

Logical reflection is therefore indispensable, especially in situations or times when, as in Greek sophistry, everything is doubted, general confusion prevails, and nothing is taken for granted. But also in times when new knowledge and new ways of knowing need to be methodologically validated and methodological clarity needs to be created. An example of this is Bacon's *Inductive Logic* at the time of the emerging natural sciences, or *Hermeneutics* as the logic of understanding among theologians, philologists, and historians in the nineteenth century.[30] Logic, then, is not a remote matter, but one that is extremely close to life and, not least, of *existential* importance. This should be made clearer.

If a dispute arises in a game as to whether a move is still part of the game or not, there is only one way to come to an agreement: remember the rules of the game, or redefine them. It is the same with thinking about logic: when there is doubt about whether something is true or not, the only option is to think together about the conditions for believing something to be true. It is also the best weapon in the fight against concealment, deception, and pretense, and against all forms of untruth. The crucial step here is to look away from all content and focus solely on the way in which that content has been arrived at and the form in which it is expressed. The hope is that on the level of form a consensus can be established that has not been possible on the level of content, and perhaps never will be. It could be the common ground on which all can find each other.

Jaspers hoped that his *Philosophical Logic* would provide such a common ground for universal communication. For him, logic is that part of philosophy in which there is no "compelling truth" in the sense of scientific knowledge, but at least a scientifically analogous way of thinking in which "perhaps rational discussion and agreement are possible."[31] In contrast to genuine philosophical thinking, which begins anew with every great thinker and deals with the same fundamental questions over and over again, there is something like a progress of knowledge over the centuries in philosophical logic. For example, Kant's *Transcendental Logic* (based on his fundamental idea of the phenomenality of the world) is such an irreversible step in *Basic Philosophical Knowledge*.[32] This is the reason for Jaspers' insistence on Kant's insight in this study as well. But the analogy with scientific progress also implies that *Philosophical Logic* is never complete and must remain open to the future. Hence Jaspers' decisive rejection of any conclusive system in the sense of Hegel.

What is new in Jaspers's draft of a *Philosophical Logic* is his attempt to explore the logical foundations of truth-consciousness in all its forms and ramifications, and to relate them to one another in order to make their possibilities and limitations visible.[33] His project is based on the conviction that there are an infinite number of forms of truth and truthfulness, so that none of them can be the only truth, and yet what we seek is the one truth or the truth of the *One*. In this will to the *One*, as we have seen, lies the power of *Reason*. Jaspers's *Philosophical Logic* is therefore best understood as an attempt to become aware of what being reasonable requires of us.

It is the *Reason* in us that is expressed in the logical foundations of our thinking, and *Philosophical Logic*, if you like, is the *Organon* of a *Reason* that becomes aware of itself and explains itself. Since it is part of the task of philosophy to undertake this explication, Jaspers's statement that he saw it as his mission to help bring *Reason* into the world becomes understandable. He assumes that Kant also understood the task of philosophy in this way, when Kant says that philosophy is called upon to administer the "depository" of the records of humanity, in which everything is thoroughly recalculated and examined.

Does philosophy then have a lease on *Reason*? This assumption is contradicted by the fact that what constitutes *Reason* is also a whole that encompasses us, which we can never survey and therefore can at best illuminate. If we try to determine what *Reason* actually consists of, we ourselves already need *Reason*. It is like the hare and the hedgehog. Wherever we go in search of truth, *Reason* is always already there. Therefore, in order to get at the workings of *Reason*, *Philosophical Logic* must go where *Reason* has already been thought, spoken, and acted upon. And this must be as far-reaching as possible. Every form of certainty and truth, every way of knowing, must be illuminated. First and foremost, those forms of knowledge that have made a breakthrough in the sciences themselves, but also in the thinking of everyday life, in all fields of experience and practice.

In *Philosophical Logic*, too, nothing may be omitted, forgotten, or set aside. No way of knowing and believing may be declared to be the only possible way of thinking according to reason.[34] Every method and every category must be seen in its limitations and placed in relation to all other methods and categories. What are their presuppositions, how far do they go, and what are their limits? These are the guiding questions for all ways and forms of thinking.

Just as the use of *Reason* already precedes every use of *Reason*, so for us later generations, every reflection on the logical foundations of the use of *Reason* is already preceded by such a reflection. That is why any subsequent reflection is not possible without recourse to the reflection that has already taken place. And that is why, here too, none of these historical reflections can be ignored. But in order not to drown in the endlessness of this endeavor, we must try to gain an overview by ascending, as it were, to those thinkers who have carried the reflection of *Basic Knowledge* to the highest heights. The need to cling to the great philosophers who have achieved this shows once again, from a different perspective, why Jaspers attaches so much importance to the study of the great philosophers. And why, for him Kant, after Plato, towers above all others. Only those who have climbed this summit, he says of Kant, will understand all the other philosophers.[35]

The great philosophers have demonstrated their own thinking and made us aware of how we can think. We can learn to think from them. They become our teachers to the extent that we try to understand the forms and ways of their thinking. This also allows us to turn their thinking against them where it does not seem consistent enough to us, instead of allowing ourselves to be uncritically drawn into their spell. It also allows us to understand them perhaps better than they understood themselves.[36] What matters is not what they believed and what truths they proclaimed, but the forms of thought they used and the spaces of thought they opened up.

The metaphor of the spaces of *Reason*, which Jaspers liked to use, illustrates impressively the importance of the formal in *Philosophical Logic*: whatever claims to be true must be able to find its place in the space of thought opened up by logic. But this space itself is empty; the content by which we can live must come from somewhere else. The forms of thought are, so to speak, the algebraic equations into which the numerical values still have to be inserted. But the forms of thought are as indispensable as the air we breathe, on which we do not live, but without which we cannot live.

Nothing can replace reading the original works when it comes to participating in the thought experiences of the great philosophers and practicing *Philosophical Logic*, educating oneself, as Jaspers says. But this path can be all too difficult, blocked by rocks and debris. Very few people have the time or the strength to even set out on this path. That is why we need those whose job it is to facilitate and smooth access to the great philosophers: the professors of philosophy.[37] Their task is the least important in philosophy, but it is indispensable.

Jaspers considered himself a professor of philosophy. He modestly refrained from presenting himself as a great philosopher and repeatedly warned against such confusion. He saw his task solely in "making contact with the great philosophers as accessible as possible." For him, however, this meant not using apparent simplicity to conceal their depth, but rather to make philosophy itself tangible, to make the seriousness of philosophizing palpable.[38] The great help for this is the *Basic Philosophical Knowledge* that he acquired in his own dealings with the great philosophers and that he set out in his *Philosophical Logic* and still wanted to set out: by reproducing the "concepts that have become scholastic, textbook-like," by "training in categories and operations of thought, in questions, answers, refutations, and justifications."[39]

Training in *Philosophical Logic* involves the greatest effort because it requires a reversal of our natural, object-oriented attitude. This is for the well-known reason that we are not concerned with acquiring knowledge of objects but with gaining clarity about how we can come to know these objects. However, if this shift succeeds, it can now become philosophically "natural" itself. A "new, deeper nature" then becomes "the basic attitude of my being."[40]

How important this logical and methodological work was to Jaspers is also shown by the fact that he repeatedly modified the *Basic Knowledge* he had acquired and tried to convey it with the greatest possible simplicity and depth, right up to his last works. He believed, not least inspired by Kant's similar hope that the path he had "paved" could be turned into a "military road" by later generations, that it might one day become common knowledge.[41]

It remains to be seen how wide this "army road" can become. But one thing is certain: without a *Philosophical Logic* at hand, as Jaspers tried to develop in the wake of Kant, one will remain without criticism in philosophy, without instruments and criteria for examination and scrutiny.

This *Philosophical Logic* cannot be summarized, but it can be understood in terms of its *Origin* and its *Goal*. Its *Origin* is the will to see everything we think in context and to search for the overarching unity; its Goal is to arrive at the *One* who is the ground of all unity—the transcendent *One* as the *Encompassing of the Encompassing*, as the One in which everything is. From this *One* emanates a "pulling force" that overcomes all divisions and draws us toward it. Selfhood, as the will in us to be one with ourselves, is itself already captured by the pulling force that emanates from the *One*. According to Jaspers, only those who feel this force in the desire for unity within themselves are willing and able to embark on a search for the distant *One*. Only those who allow themselves to be guided by *Reason* in their search for the *One* can also create unity within themselves. *Reason,* as the urge toward the *One*, is therefore already "*Existence* itself, which is connected with the One."[42]

Jaspers' concept of *Reason* here takes on features that he undoubtedly borrowed from Neoplatonic philosophy, culminating in Plotinus. But is this not a contradiction, this turn to Plotinus, the great metaphysician and mystic, and Jaspers's commitment to Kant's critique of traditional metaphysics? Only at first glance does it seem that there is a contradiction. At a second glance, however, the unifying factor becomes apparent. What unites the Neoplatonic metaphysics of unity with Kant is the insight that *Transcendence* eludes all cognitive thought. For this reason alone, Jaspers's appropriation of Plotinus's metaphysics of unity could fit so easily into the framework of Kant's *Basic Knowledge* (remember his image of Kant as the summit from which other thinkers first become comprehensible).

Crucial to Jaspers's turn to Plotinus, however, was that Jaspers was not only a faithful interpreter of Kant but also Kant's sharpest critic, clearly aware of Kant's limitations. One of these limitations in particular made Jaspers the defender of a Plotinian type of metaphysics. It is the limit that Jaspers calls Kant's "unsurpassable sparseness."[43] Kant's sparseness is the flip side of his great strength: that he relies solely on the power of the formal, that he wants to bring the forms to consciousness in their "purity" (without admixtures from other sources) and thereby opens up spaces (the space of *Reason* and the *Transcendental*), but then leaves everything open because he denies himself any fullness of content. He remains with the critical examination of what already exists. He remains with the transcendental question of the "conditions of the possibility of" (of knowledge, of what has validity), but Kant refuses to go where *Reality* shows itself: in the *Existence* of the individual, in the researching sciences, in historical contemplation, in the "looking visualization" in poetry and art, and also in the manifestations of *Transcendence*. Kant's critical philosophy is a transcendental philosophy, but not a philosophy of *Transcendence*. Therefore, Jaspers concludes, Kant's thought must be supplemented:

> Between the imageless God and the breadth of experience and the vision of beauty there is the immeasurable world of *Chiffer* language and in it the struggle for the historical meaning of one's own *Existence*. There is the possibility of an *Illumination of Existence* that goes beyond the *Illumination of Reason*, without undoing it or even limiting it.[44]

## PHILOSOPHICAL EROS AND THE ROLE OF LOVE IN JASPERS'S WORK

In his critique of Kant, Jaspers points to that part of his own thinking which is not to be found in Kant and which, where it is to be found in other philosophies, "does not refute Kant but complements him, namely in the purifying *Reason* of his own thinking."[45] As we have seen, Jaspers has found such a supplement in Kierkegaard and his concept of *Existence*; he is now also concerned with such a supplement in the case of Plotinus and the Platonic tradition—with the *Philosophy of Transcendence* that is missing in Kant, and especially with what he misses most in Kant: a philosophy of love that makes it possible to see in what sense *Reason* itself is already love, and how *Reason* functions in love.[46] The "tractive force" which, according to Jaspers, emanates from the *One*, is a Platonic metaphor and just another name for the love of the soul for the *One* praised by Plotinus, the *Eros* which, for Plotinus as for Plato, is the "ultimate moving force" of all philosophizing.[47]

Against the Christian tradition, however, Jaspers, along with Plato and Plotinus, rejects the idea that God is a lover or even love itself: God as the *One*, if seen in this way, would be "falsely transformed into a human being" and would lose its *Transcendence*. "For in love, God becomes tangible, but God is not love."[48] As for Plato,[49] love is also for Jaspers a *Medium*, an intermediate state between poverty and wealth, a search that in its insufficiency is already fulfillment; directed to the future because it still lacks what it seeks, but already present in every moment of its existence and therefore, although in time, as it were transversal to time.[50] Love is what truly connects, the *Bond* between all that was previously separate and distinct.[51] But to be such a *Bond* is also the essence of *Reason*. This is why Jaspers can rightly say that *Reason* in itself is already love.

Why is love so important for Jaspers? It is probably the insight that thinking alone is not enough, that thinking ultimately remains indifferent to the object and leads to the false belief that to think an object is also to know it. This false belief can then manifest itself in judgments such as: "This is how it is; this is how it has always been; this is nothing more than (. . .)."[52] The "I think" of consciousness does not move anything and is not moved by anything.[53] Therefore, it is not able to open itself to what its object can become in truth.

But where does motion come from? Movement only comes from *Existence* and it is only in *Existence*. And what moves *Existence* is love, which we cannot will, but which is the *Origin* of our will, going through all kinds of grasping. How Jaspers conceives of this can best be seen if we try to follow him in his Phenomenology of Love.

Love itself is also something that encompasses us. It can never be grasped as the one universal, the only love, but can only be illuminated in its various manifestations, from sexual love to metaphysical love, love for the metaphysical ground in the *One*.[54] The all-pervading sexual love, which sustains all love and can also participate in the most sublime, even in the metaphysical, as is beautifully demonstrated in the enthusiasm of Giordano Bruno, is the one pole of love and a sign that there must be a unity of all ways of loving. But love finds its fulfillment only with the other pole, love from the metaphysical ground, the pull of the *One*.

In the field of tension between these two poles, the different forms of love move through all the *Modes of the Encompassing*:[55] As the infinite drive of desire and the desire for more in vital *Dasein*, which seeks its immortality in perpetual generation and giving birth; as the intellectual love of *Consciousness in General*, which finds its immortality in the timelessly true contents and in its drive for proof and the fertilization of knowledge; as the love for the whole of an *Idea of the Spirit*, which holds together the community of those who are in the service of this *Idea* and says yes to all that partakes of the *Idea* and becomes aware of its immortality in the forms and shapes of the *Idea* in its time-typical manifestations; as the *existential* love, which gains eternity in time in its unconditional determination to be faithful to the unjustifiably unique and individual.[56]

None of these ways of loving can be the only way. Only in the combination of all forms does love find its true fulfillment; for man—in the multitude of his *Modes of Encompassing*—is always one. Any isolation and absolutization of a single form is a disastrous narrowing of what makes a person human.

Philosophically disastrous, however, is also the disregard of the hierarchy of the *Modes of Encompassing*, in that in philosophical reflection one way of love is declared to be at the service of another, the one above as being at the service of the one below, but also vice versa, the one below as being at the service of the one above.[57] Jaspers explains this thought using the example of sexual love, which one thinks of first and foremost when one speaks of love, a view that Jaspers does not share, however, because he ultimately understands love only as personal love, love between people: "Being human demands that it takes precedence over being sexual. Men and women are human beings first and sexual beings second."[58]

Purely schematically, Jaspers distinguishes three forms of sexual love, each of which has its own reality: Sexuality as the reality of vital being; eroticism as the reality of spiritual, sexually related play; marriage as the reality of the legal and moral order; metaphysical love, which strikes like a bolt of lightning, which no one sees except the person himself, at the moment when he meets the person to whom he is forever devoted as the only one in an unconditional, noncontractual bond. This love is no longer a reality of the world of appearances but is incomprehensible, as if it came from somewhere else.[59]

What is separated in this scheme, however, are only moments of what is contained in the word "love" and cannot be separated. But it is neither imaginable nor conceivable to unite what belongs together in a single life; the moments enter into battle with each other like the conflicting divine powers in the Greek Olympus: the Greek serves Aphrodite, the goddess who ennobles the sexual into beauty, but at the same time also Artemis as the adversary of all that is sexual, or Hera as the protector of marriage.[60] Even if these powers are never united, it becomes clear how disastrous it is when a single moment isolates and dominates: when erotic play becomes an end in itself and one lurches from one love affair to another; when marriage, with its constraints of rights and duties, becomes a prison; or when metaphysical love elevates the object of its love to the unattainable supernatural.[61]

What is shown here in the example of sexual love applies to all forms of love. In each of them, there is an opposite tendency: the tendency for the individual moments to fall apart and become separated and isolated, or the tendency to hold the moments together and soar into infinity. It is only the ever-new choice that can bring about the turning point from dispersion and disintegration to a new upswing. This is another sense of the *Conversion* of which Jaspers speaks repeatedly.[62]

The never-ending task that love sets for us is to gather ourselves together from dispersion. But this is also a double movement (think of the image of flying with two wings): Love must soar into *Transcendence* in order to draw strength from the *One* from whom all being springs, but this soaring must not become an escape from reality; it must be translated into action in the world, which is no longer a return to distraction, but is guided by the *One*, trusting in the sustaining ground.

The dual movement of love does not take place somewhere in the abstract; it is bound to love for the other person, to a togetherness that exists only between individual people and that connects the selfhood of one with the selfhood of the other. This distinguishes love from all other forms of togetherness: it is more than empathy in compassion and joy, more than experiencing the same situations together, and more than perceiving and understanding what the other person experiences, means, thinks, and wants.[63] All this may be the starting point for *Existential* love, but it is only fully present where those who are connected to each other are concerned with their own selfhood and that of the other: in *Existential Communication.*

This sounds as if Jaspers is preaching the happiness of self-sufficient togetherness. But he clearly rejects this: love would shrink if it consisted only of love for the other person—always only seeing the other person, being absorbed in him, and merging with him is "love that perfects itself in lovelessness."[64] Communication can be fulfilled only through factual content. To the extent that communication absorbs these contents as shared, it unfolds itself. And vice versa, only by loving people does factual content become essential.[65] Love for others is love for Being. And it culminates in love for the being of the *One*.

We experience what *Being* is only in communication. To be able to create and use the means of communication for the advancement and guidance of ourselves without being subjected to them is, according to Jaspers, the impetus for philosophizing and, in the hands of the philosopher, becomes *Philosophical Logic*.

So let us return to it. But not without first noting the decisive insight for the question of universal communication: Since all philosophizing that is born of love aims at the *One*, it is the search for the *One* that connects people as human beings in universal communication. Since the *Axis Age*, humanity as a whole has been on its way under these auspices. However, as Jaspers warns, not in such a way that anyone can claim the *One* for himself or herself with awareness:

> The *One* is to be proclaimed, the *One*, this one God, is the only God, and I know him, I know him, I have heard him, and everyone should follow him. But the other way around: whoever hears the One God or the One of *Transcendence* can only approach the *One* in the *World* by creating unity in the *World*, previously unity with myself, identity with myself, now unity among people, communication. What connects leads to the *One*.[66]

## NOTES

1. Auto 121.
2. Auto 120.
3. KorrPhil, "Karl Jaspers an E. Frank," 294.
4. GPhil 240–245. Jaspers had already become aware of the *Axial Age* in the early 1940s during his work on *Die Grundsätze des Philosophierens*, see GPhil, Einleitung des Herausgebers, LXI f.
5. GPhil 62.
6. This sentence, with which Schelling refers to the appearance of Christ, is transferred by Jaspers to the *Axial Age* and is repeatedly quoted by him when he speaks of the "floating" spiritual guidance that has come to humanity from the *Axial Age*. This has a completely different authority, which can only be heard by individuals, than the authority of churches and institutions (cf., for example, PG 104, and note 182).
7. GPhil 62.
8. Auto 121.
9. Auto 121.
10. GP 40, 39.
11. GP 39.
12. See also the editor's introduction, KJG I/15.1, XII f.
13. GP 31.
14. GP 96.
15. His legacy contained an *Einleitung in die Weltgeschichte derPhilosophie* conceived by Jaspers even before *Die großen Philosophen*, with a somewhat different structure (cf. WGP, in particular the preface by Hans Saner, 5–9).

16. GP 8.

17. GP 9.

18. He considered it so important that he decided to remove this work from the overall complex of the *Weltgeschichte der Philosophie* (see Jaspers in his letters to K. Piper dated February 19, 1954, June 24, 1955, December 6, 1955, and May 11, 1956, VÜK, III/8.2, 196, 229, 245, 247, 254–256).

19. The accounts of Empedocles, Anaxagoras, and Democritus for the second volume of *The Great Philosophers* had already been completed. In addition, the book on Schelling had already appeared as a separate publication in 1955. A number of other philosophers planned for Volume 2 are the subject of articles in collections and journals: Solon (1948), Xenophanes (1967), Epicurus (1960), Schopenhauer (1960); there are also three essays on Kierkegaard (1951, 1955, 1964). The artists, poets, and scientists included in Volume 3 are: a study of Leonardo as a philosopher (1953), two essays on Goethe (1947, 1949), and another essay on Max Weber's political thought (1962), in addition to the Max Weber memorial speech (1920) and the Weber monograph of 1932.

20. GPN 1/2. Here, in brief, is what these two volumes should be about, for which Jaspers had already collected and prepared a wealth of materials, drafts, and texts in addition to the works mentioned:

Volume II

The Designing Metaphysicians:

Worldly Piety *(Weltfromme Anschauungen):* Xenophanes. Empedocles. Democritus. Poseidonius. Bruno.

Gnostic Dreamers of Truth: Origen. Boehme. Schelling.

Constructive minds: Hobbes. Leibniz. Fichte.

The Looseners:

Drilling Negatives: Abälard. Descartes. Hume.

The Great Revivalists: Pascal. Lessing. Kierkegaard. Nietzsche.

The Buildings of the Creative Folders: Aristotle. Thomas. Hegel.

Volume Ill

*Philosophers in poetry* (from the Greek tragedians to Shakespeare, Goethe and Dostoevsky), in research (natural scientists from Kepler to Einstein, historians such as Ranke and Burkhardt),

*in political thought* (from Machiavelli to Tocqueville, plus "utopians" such as Rousseau and Marx),

*in the will to educate and in literary criticism* (from Cicero to Erasmus and Voltaire to Schiller and Humboldt),

*in the wisdom of life* (such as Epictetus, Seneca, Epicurus),

*in the practice of life* (statesmen, monks, doctors),

*in theology and in the teaching of philosophy* (such as Proclos, Wolff, Erdmann).

21. GP 62, cf. the concise formulation in Einf 123: Philosophical thoughts cannot be applied like a "doctrine in the sense of rules," "rather they are the reality of which one can say: in the realization of these thoughts man himself lives or: life is permeated with thought."

22. GP 62–64.

23. GP 93.
24. GP 94.
25. GP 13.
26. Einf 144f.
27. The term *Basic Knowledge* (*Grundwissen*) is already used in W 28, 44, but then becomes central in PGO 111–151.
28. Aut 121.
29. W 7.
30. W 12.
31. Cf. Ent 98; PGO 149; Sch 317.
32. GP 619: After Kant, metaphysics can no longer have the same character as before. "Whoever today skips Kant's critical clarity and the realm of compelling scientific insight must be confused."
33. W 3f.
34. W 4.
35. GP 615.
36. Jaspers also turns this word of Kant against Kant himself.
37. Jaspers's characterization of the role of the philosophy professor is particularly revealing in: GPN 2, 1015–1018.
38. GP 14.
39. GPN 2, 1016.
40. W 10.
41. GP 616.
42. W 131.
43. GP 603.
44. GP 604.
45. GP 604.
46. GP 606.
47. W 991, 992, 1004.
48. W 1012.
49. W 1012: "Love does not belong to God, the perfect *One*, nor does it belong to *Dasein* as the absolutely unknowable, which knows nothing of itself. It is the way of man. Plato has illuminated it forever."
50. W 990.
51. W 1014.
52. W 998.
53. Cf. W 988.—Not to have seen this is another of Kant's limitations mentioned by Jaspers (GP 605).
54. Cf. W 1001.
55. W 1001.
56. W 993–997.
57. W 1014–1017.
58. KlSch 153.
59. So, Jaspers's formulations in W 999, KlSch 148f.
60. KlSch 155.

61. W 1000.
62. Cf. W 1008.
63. W 1010.
64. W 1007.
65. W 1011.
66. ChT 55.—Jaspers indiscriminately uses sometimes *the One* (in German *das Eine* or *der Eine*), sometimes *the One God* or *the Godhead* (W 690, 692), because he is not interested in the name, but only in expressing the idea that what is at stake cannot be grasped by any name or concept. The changing names are merely instructions for thinking of the *Absolute* as liberated from all conceivable determinations and as *Chiffers* through which *the One* can reveal Himself to us.

## *Chapter 9*

# The Idea of the One and Negative Theology

### THE IDEA OF THE *ABOVE BEING*

The urge of *Reason* (filled with love) toward the *One* and *Only Being* is preceded by a *foreknowledge* of the *Infinite*. But where does this *foreknowledge* come from? It has its origin in the fact that when man becomes aware of his finiteness and his dissatisfaction with finiteness, he also becomes aware of the fact that the *Infinite* must exist as something completely different, as *True Being*.[1] Without this *foreknowledge*, there would be no search for the *One*[2] and no reflection on the question of the nature of that *One*. And without this reflection, there would be no experience that any attempt to think the *One* will inevitably fail. No matter under which category I try to grasp it, whether I seek it under the concept of the possible, the real, the necessary, or whatever, what I manage to grasp is never *Being* itself, but only a kind of Being, an object within the *Subject-Object-Split*, but not beyond it. There is hardly a better name for the fact that the *One* transcends all categories than the one used by Plotinus: the *Above Being* in the sense of Plato's *Beyond Being (epekeina tes usias)*.[3]

However, one could also call the *One Non-Being* to express "that there is no being in any category that signifies *Being*."[4] The paradox remains: once we have grasped the *Idea* of the *Absolute*, we cannot get rid of it; even if we want to deny it, we must have already thought it. But we cannot think the *Absolute* either, because we cannot say what it is or what it is not.[5] This is the deeper meaning of Jaspers's statement that we have already encountered: "It is conceivable that there is what is not conceivable."[6]

But how can we think what we cannot think? Isn't that a hopeless task? There is at least one way: thinking in *Negations*. A way of thinking in which every statement is taken back. This means that the *Absolute* "cannot be determined by any predicate, cannot be conceived as an object in any conception, in any conclusion, but all categories can be used to say that the Transcendent is neither quantity nor quality, neither relation nor ground, not one, not many, not being, not nothing, etc."[7]

The knowledge of the unthinkability of the Absolute is knowledge of not knowing, the *docta ignorantia*, the *Knowing not Knowing* of *Nicholas of Cusa*. However, this is not a *Not-Knowing* that ends in *Nothingness*, but a "fulfilled *Not-Knowing*"[8] that "indirectly brings the *One* as *Transcendence* into the present."[9]

The path that Jaspers is taking here is the path of so-called *Negative Theology*, which—and this brings us back to Plato and Plotinus—was the theology of Platonism and extends to our time via Cusanus, Meister Eckehart, and Schelling. In the form of the doctrine of the radical negativity of the *Absolute*, however, it can also be found in Asian thinkers, such as Lao Tzu and Nagarjuna, which Jaspers included in his presentation of the *Great Philosophers*.

When a thinker attempts to approach the *Absolute* by rejecting any positive labeling of the *Absolute*, he is carrying out the movement that Jaspers calls *Formal Transcending*. But what is the purpose of this movement if it never reaches its goal?

It might seem a way out to say of the *Absolute* that it is the complete Other of everything categorically determined, in short, the negation of everything negated. But seeking refuge in the category of the *totally Other* leads, as Jaspers rightly points out, "to the false idea that God is a different being from the being of the *World*, as if there were two kinds of being, God and the *World*."[10]

A consistently *Negative Theology* must therefore also negate the idea that God is "the *completely Other*." God is also the *completely Other* in relation to the *completely Other*, nothing of this and nothing of that, but as such not simply nothing, but rather, as Plato put it in incomparable terms, *Beyond Being*, removed from all being, transcendent. But it is precisely in this absolute negativity that the positivity of the *One* lies. For only the distant God, who is removed from all contemplation and all conceivability, who has nothing beyond himself, can become the reference point of all and everything and be the ultimate, absolute *Reality* for *Existence*.[11]

The reversal occurs as soon as one draws this distant God close, into the realm of the conceivable, and wants to make him one's own God, a person who turns to me—as the zealous God, the wrathful God, the fatherly loving God. Thus the true *One* becomes the false, whose will and command are directed against the other whom it excludes, "*Unconditionality* turns into fanaticism, worldly freedom into blind obedience to absurdities."[12]

Once again, it may seem that if all this has been properly considered, then everything has already been considered. This insight is easy to have, and philosophy is already at an end, as Hegel reproaches.[13] Jaspers, on the contrary, sees this as the most difficult job: it requires a constant "extraordinary effort to prevent the settlement of *Transcendence* in any form in the *World*" and to fight against the *Understanding*'s inescapable tendency to objectify what cannot be objectified.[14] Jaspers's *Philosophical Logic* can be understood as an attempt to undertake this endeavor.

Jaspers calls this way of thinking *Transcending Thinking*, *Transcending* in the sense of thinking beyond the objective. Again, his model is the speculative metaphysics of Plotinus.[15] For him, its purpose is to translate the statement of the *Negative Theology*—that God eludes all determination—into a movement of thought, through which its truth is continually proven—through a "self-destroying dialectic," a "thinking that cancels itself out," a "non-thinking that illuminates itself by not thinking something and not thinking nothing."[16] In the collapse of *Understanding,* it achieves the thinking of the unthinkable.[17] Among Plotinus scholars, the term *Negative Dialectic* has become established for this kind of thinking.[18]

But how exactly does this dialectic work? We have already encountered it in isolated examples. But Jaspers tried to illustrate it in detail, especially in the second volume of his *Philosophical Logic*, which he no longer published.[19] It has become a lesson in self-illuminating *Reason*.[20]

## THE NEGATIVE DIALECTIC

The starting point for thinking the unthinkable is the thinkable, or more precisely, the categories with which we try to penetrate everything thinkable, categories such as unity and duality, form and matter, possibility and reality, reason and consequence, and so on. As categories of thought, knowledge, and being, they have a clearly definable meaning. But they lose all meaning when they are used *Transcending* in order to think *Transcendence* with their help. Jaspers distinguishes three methods for such a *Transcending* use of categories: the analogical method, the method that reveals their logical illusory nature, and the method of self-referential, circular use of categories.

The use of categories is *Analogous* when they are applied directly to the *Absolute*, thus emptying themselves of meaning. To say of the *Absolute*, for example, that it is necessity may appeal to us existentially and soothe a restless heart, but we are left empty-handed as soon as we try to understand what necessity actually means here. It cannot be a logical necessity, nor a causal one. But what other kind could it be? It is beyond any determinability.

The second method is the use of categories in *statements that are beyond comprehension* simply because they are tautological or contradictory. Tautological like the biblical phrase "I am what I am"[21] or the enigmatic words of Max Weber on his deathbed, "The true is the truth."[22] Or paradoxical, like

Heraclitus's sayings about the unity of all opposites: "Whole and not-whole, concordant discordant, harmony discord, and out of everything one and out of one everything." Straight is crooked, up is down, the beginning is the end, the immortal is mortal, the mortal is immortal, etc.[23]

The third method is *the self-referential use of categories*, for example in the formula of the Absolute as the ground of itself (*causa sui*),[24] the absurdity of which has already been mentioned.

But what can be gained from studying these methods of *Transcending*? On the one hand, the "proof" of the "truth" of *Negative Theology*: why every attempt to categorically determine the *Absolute* must fail, and why the biblical prohibition of images of God has its truth. On the other hand, however, the ground is prepared for what, according to Jaspers, is the only thing that counts: that it is precisely in this failure that the *Absolute* can be "touched" in all its incomprehensibility. Even if we never know what the *Absolute* is, it is precisely through the failure of the *Transcending* movement of thought that we can become certain of the existence of the *Absolute*. This certainty, which is possible for us, is the highest and final certainty; it must be enough for us. Jaspers expresses it again and again in different formulations: that the *One* is, is enough, that *Being* is, is enough, or—most often, based on the existential experience of Jeremias—that *God* is, is enough.

But there is always the caveat that this certainty may not materialize. Transcending thinking leads to inner certainty only indirectly—only insofar as it finds an "echo" in *Existence*.[25] What *Transcending* thinking can do on its own is to "prepare and remember, illuminate and examine, assure and protect" the actual, the ascent to *Transcendence*.[26] Transcendental thought, in a word, is nothing but the *Chiffer* language that has become communication, and what is communicated can itself become a *Chiffer* for those who understand the message.[27]

## USING CATEGORIES TO THINK BEYOND ALL CATEGORIES

Since our thinking never comes to rest, and since no *Chiffer* can be the only *Chiffer*, the openness of *Reason*, and therefore the *Philosophical Logic* that illuminates it, demands that we seek out all conceivable categories in order to carry out the *Transcending* movement with ever-changing categories. But where to begin? Jaspers proceeds by first sketching out a possible systematic order of groups of categories and attempting to characterize the specific type of *Transcending* use of the categories assigned to them, in order then to carry out the transcendental movement on the basis of the individual categories within these groupings.

It would seem obvious to organize the categories according to the *Modes of Encompassing*, from the categories of *Dasein* to the categories of *Transcendence*. But Jaspers rejects this idea for two main reasons: First, because the categories pass through all *Modes of Encompassing*, and second, because there can be no categories of *Transcendence*, since *Transcendence* eludes all categories. Instead, he proposes a division into three spheres of categories: the sphere of the *Objective in General*, the sphere of *Reality*, and the sphere of *Freedom*. They differ in the kind of being that determines them: being is object for me, being is reality, being is freedom.

For us—through our intentional directionality—*Object* is everything that we touch, recognize, illuminate, and understand in our thinking. So *Object* is categorically always *Something*, something that is one, something that is related, something that is different, something that is opposite, etc. These are universal categories that run through all thinking, but do not themselves determine anything—a *Something*, for example, can be anything that ever becomes an *Object* for me.

Thought is filled with content only when it meets *Reality*. And the characteristic of *Reality* is that it resists me, and I have to resist it. *Reality* therefore exists in every way of being grasped, from empirical *Reality* to the *Reality* of *Existence* and *Transcendence* (whose *Reality* is experienced in being given to myself). However, since only empirical being is categorically determined, the categories of *Reality* are not universal, but only particular. They are the basic forms in which we encounter the tangible, the experienceable—in short, the *Real Being* (e.g., time, space, body, matter, motion, life).

The title *Categories of Freedom* is actually misleading. For it is not about being as a *state* of being, but about a state of being that can only become out of and through *Freedom*, and is always only *in the process of becoming*. Clear examples of this are nomological categories such as purpose, norm, and law, which only become *real* when I *realize* them through my actions. Not only action in the *World* but also the cognition of *Reality* is a doing, and a doing is also the (objective) thinking that takes place in the affirmative and negative judgments that result from *Freedom*.

From this point of view, all categories could be described as *Categories of Freedom*. But this would obscure an essential, philosophically significant difference. Insofar as *Freedom* finds its realization through action in *Reality*, through recognition of *Reality*, or through grasping the rightness of formal thought, it is always bound to another that is not itself *Freedom*. There is no *Freedom* without a counterpart and without *Reality* as its opponent. Conversely, *Freedom* can only be "experienced" indirectly, only through the fact that its effect is manifested in this other. However, it does not manifest itself as an *Objective Reality* that can be recognized by the *Understanding*; it only becomes visible to those who know themselves to be free and therefore recognizes the possible *Freedom* in the actions of others—as they do in themselves. The principle that like is recognized only by like applies here.[28]

Yet the function of *Freedom* is different when it comes to illuminating the *Non-Objective*, the *Encompassing*. The categories formed by *Reason* and the *reflecting* power of judgment have being only to the extent that *Possible Existence* makes them its own. Nothing is recognized here, but the *Encompassing*, which I am as *Existence*, secures its *Freedom* by deciding to live in precisely these categories. "Therefore, freedom is the *Goal* and *Origin* of such thinking."[29] In order to establish this difference between *Categories of Objectivity* or *Reality* and *Categories of Freedom*, Jaspers, as we have already seen, also refers to them as *Signa of Existence*.[30] Examples of this are categories such as decision, choice, and the *Unconditioned*.

But what about the categories and their use in the ascent to *Transcendence*? Any category out of these three groups can be used transcendently. Each has its own kind of failing dialectic. Three examples may illustrate this.

Let us take the *Modal* categories of the *Possible*, the *Actual*, the *Necessary*, and the *Accidental* as examples from the *Categories of the Objective*, the category of *Time* from the *Categories of Reality*, and the category of *Freedom* itself from the *Categories of Freedom*. The crucial first step is always *Absolutization*: the assumption that the *Absolute* can be thought by means of the category in question.

## Categories of the Objective

Is *Absolute Being* possible at all? This seems to be a reasonable question. Its nonsense becomes apparent as soon as we realize what it means to be possible. The word *Possible* has two meanings: First, to say that something is possible can mean that it is logically possible. Logically possible is anything that does not contain a contradiction. Second, it can mean that it is really possible because it can be conceived in the categories of being real, or really possible in the sense that it is compatible with the conditions and forces of real being. When these conditions and forces are present, the possible becomes real. What is real is possible, but not all that is possible is real.

In what sense is *Absolute Being* possible? Since there is nothing outside the *Absolute*, there is no difference here between the initially possible and the subsequently actual. Either we say that the *Absolute* is the identity of possibility and actuality—in contrast to actual existence, therefore, not only possible as actual but already actual as possible—but then we do not know what this is supposed to mean. Or we insist that the *Absolute* also recognizes the separation between the *possible Absolute* and the *real Absolute*. But then we are not with the *Absolute*, but with something that exists in the *World*. The inconceivable identity of *Possibility* and *Reality* can, however, become for me existentially a *Chiffer* in which the *Absolute* shines in its incomprehensible absoluteness.

We are no better off when we resort to the category of *Necessity*. In categorical thinking, what is necessary is what must follow from something else according to logical or empirical laws. What does not obey such *Necessity* we call *Coincidence*. In the *Absolute*, however, there is not the *One* and then the *Other* that could arise from it, but the *One*. If this *One* is necessary, then it is absolute *Coincidence*. A *Necessary Coincidence* or an *Accidentally Necessary* or whatever—that is, a further unthinkability. But this failing thought is at the same time another possible *Chiffer* for the reassurance of the One.

## Categories of Reality

We run into other difficulties when we insist that the *Absolute* is *Reality*. If it were a reality of the kind of empirical being to which the *Categories of Reality* are tailored, then it would be empirical *Reality* a second time. As the absolute *One*, however, it cannot have another *Reality* beside itself. It would have to be, if you like, the full and whole, the *one Reality*, which, however, if it really is the whole, must not exclude the empirically real in all its severity. But how is this to be conceived?

*Reality* as empirical *Reality* appears to us in three stages: as dead matter, as living organisms, and as conscious individuals. The corresponding categories are *Matter*, *Life,* and *Soul.*

*Matter* is the substance underlying all empirical being, the modifications of which are the individual phenomena. While these modifications arise and pass away, *Matter* is that which does not arise and does not pass away, but remains permanent.

*Life* is the self-contained individual existence of an organism as a process with a beginning and an end. This organism is related to the environment and undergoes certain metamorphoses determined by rules; it is purposefully moved and in constant change.

The *Soul* is the consciousness of such an organism that feels its well-being and its lack, is guided by instincts, has self-contained inwardness, and wants to maintain itself in its world.

What happens when these categories are made absolute? *Transcendence* is then conceived in three typical forms: (1) *Being* is *Substance*, all that exists is indifferent and disappearing appearance, movement, and opposites are mere illusions. (2) Everything is *Life*, what is not alive is merely the residue of *Life*; *Being* is an immense organism in constant motion. (3) *Being* is *Soul*, everything is consciousness, and individual consciousness is only a partial form of this comprehensive consciousness.

But the *One* cannot be *Substance* without its modifications, *Life* without death, or consciousness without the unconscious. It is always both at the same time and something more, namely the unity of everything: *Substance* and its modifications, *Life* and death, the *Conscious* and the unconscious. But if we try to think of these mutually exclusive categories as identical, we fail in all our thinking. This failure, in turn, can become a *Chiffer* for the unthinkable *One* of *Transcendence* that it announces.

### Categories of Freedom

In opposition to the naturalization of *Transcendence,* there is a way of thinking that tries to think of the *One* in *Categories of Freedom*: Deity not as *Nature* but as *Consciousness*, not as *Substance* but as *Personality*, not as *Being* but as *Will. Freedom*, however, always exists only in interaction with *Nature*. It is the realization or the struggle to overcome *Nature*. *Human Freedom* is therefore always finite and limited. If it is to become real, it requires communication and thus always *Another*. If *Freedom* is transcendently absolutized, one would have to imagine a perfect *Freedom* that has no *Nature* toward itself, but is itself *Freedom* and *Nature* in one. *Transcendence* would have to be conceived as a being without communication, as "a being that is itself without relatedness."[31] But it is incomprehensible to the *Understanding* how such a paradoxical identity of *Freedom* and *Nature* and such a self-referential being can be conceived. For us, *Transcendence* can be brought together with *Freedom* in only one way: not by thinking of *Transcendence* as *Freedom*, but by becoming aware of it as the ground of our existential *Freedom*—in being given to ourselves.

## CONCLUSION

These three examples of *Formal Transcending* impressively demonstrate what will be proven anew with every category we take up: its inadequacy when we try to think of it *transcategorically* as a category of the *Absolute*. But each time anew, the thinker is confronted with the question of what this failure means for him existentially, whether it becomes a *Chiffer* or not. This *Formal Transcending* must be practiced,[32] and the field of practice is the entire space of traditional metaphysical speculation, which must now be critically penetrated with a methodologically trained consciousness. Not every category will appeal to us to the same extent; there may be preferred and less preferred categories. But one category seems to be more important than the countless others: the category of the *One*. For what we are trying to grasp in each of these trains of thought is the *Absolute* as the *One*. The *One*, as Jaspers summarizes,[33] is the great theme of philosophy since Plato. It is present in man's innermost self, in the "pull" toward the *One*, as that which gives coherence to my life. Only the *One* has nothing outside itself; only the *One* unites the many that oppose it. But we do not think of the *One* as the category of the *Absolute* either; it is a *One* that also embraces the *Other* that is opposed to it. For this reason alone it cannot be the *Numerical One* from the list of formal categories, which by definition has a second beside it. Jaspers speaks with Kant of a *Qualitative One*, but this too is not conceivable, but only *Chiffer*, "who lets the power of the *One* of *Transcendence* shine in the *Numerical One*."[34] The category of the *One* is, if you like, the *Chiffer of all Chiffers*, running through all *Chiffers*.

But only as *Chiffer*, as the infinitely distant *One*, can it break through all absolutizations and fanaticisms; it refuses to be appropriated and stands beyond all partisanship and ideologization, beyond all worldly institutions and authorities. It allows us to resist the evil that, in the name of the *Numerical One*, claims to be the only truth and the only chosen one, and turns against all others with ruthless violence.[35]

Only the *Distant One*, in its incomprehensibility, can make people forget all differences and unite them in the thought of that *One*. But because this *Distant One* remains hidden from us, it is up to each individual to decide whether he or she will believe in this *One*. The struggle for this belief is the goal of communication, which connects people universally. The purpose of Jaspers's philosophizing is to draw attention to this and to lead people to this communication. However, the prerequisite and goal of this philosophizing is *Faith*.

*Faith* is basically required for everything we do seriously[36]—both in the subjective sense, which concerns us, and in the objective sense, which concerns the world. I need to have *Faith* that it is my task to do what I want to do—to put myself at the service of science, for example, to fulfill my political responsibility, to remain faithful to my love for this one person. Faith is what moves me and what fulfills me at the same time, because it allows me to transcend myself and to be connected to the *Origin* of all *Being*.[37] The connection with the *Origin* therefore allows me—and this is the objective side of faith—to believe that it is meaningful and necessary for the world in which I live that I do here and now what I have decided to do.[38]

Because it depends on *Faith* and *Faith* alone, philosophy, with the *Illumination* of *Faith* as its goal,[39] serves man in everything he wants and everything he does. But philosophical thinking alone is not *Faith* itself. It prepares it, it creates space for it, it accomplishes what Kant expressed in his famous words: "I had therefore to suspend knowledge in order to make room for *Faith*"[40]—namely, the supposed knowledge that believes to know where one can no longer know.

In the course of this book, we have repeatedly encountered what *Faith* means here: the belief that there is something *Unconditional*, that there is *Freedom* and selfhood, that there is *Transcendence*, or the *One* we have just been talking about, and, above all, the belief in the possibility of "understanding one another without limitation,"[41] the belief that it depends on each individual what becomes of him and of the *World*, and the belief in an ultimate meaning that, despite the deepest shock of living through *Borderline Situations*, enables people to recover and gives them the confidence to go on living.

It is now time to deal specifically with this *Faith*. Jaspers calls it *Philosophical Faith*. It is the central theme of his philosophizing after 1945, and two of his most important late works—*Philosophical Faith* (1947) and *Philosophical Faith in the Face of Revelation* (1962)—bear this term in their titles. For Jaspers, the question of Faith is closely related to everything that was important to him in his work and in his life, and to what he considered the most important thing in the life of every human being.[42]

## NOTES

1. This *Foreknowledge* is related to the experience that we still measure everything finite against the (*supra-natural*) *Idea* of the *absolutely Great*, which, according to Kant, constitutes the *Sublime*.

2. AP 638.

3. Plato, Politeia, in *Werke*, ed. Gunther Eigler, Bd. 4 (Darmstadt: WBG, 1971), 509 b. Cf. PGO 410.

4. Ph 3, 37; GP 683.

5. Ph 3, 37. Jaspers already points out this paradox in *Die Psychologie der Weltanschauungen*:

> The human mental structure is such that the *Absolute* is, as it were, a place for man where he must inevitably place something, whether he does it practically, without knowing it for himself, in his life, or whether he thinks it for his consciousness. He must (psychologically he cannot do otherwise) put something there, be it *Nothing*, be it the thesis that there is no *Absolute*. It has been said of fanatical atheists that they worship their Non-God. (PW 184f.)

6. Ph 3, 38.

7. Ph 3, 38f.

8. IU 121, 302.

9. IU 122, 302.

10. W 690.

11. W 691.

12. W 693.

13. See Jens Halfwassen, *Auf den Spuren des Einen. Studien zur Metaphysik und ihrer Geschichte* (Tübingen: Mohr Siebeck, 2015), 331–349.

14. Ph 3, 39, see also W 111.

15. Cf. Jaspers's account of *speculative Transcending* in Plotinus, GP 678–694.

16. Ph 3, 39.

17. GP 685.

18. Cf. Tolga Ratzsch, *Karl Jaspers und Plotin. Eine Untersuchung zu den Quellen von Jaspers' Metaphysik der Transzendenz* (Baden-Baden: Alber, 2023), 220.

19. Published posthumously by Hans Saner, in PLN.

20. As the following is an overview, I will largely dispense with individual references. The editor's preface PLN XVII-XXXI provides a good overview of the whole volume.

21. Ex. 3,14, quoted in Ph 3, 67.

22. Ph I, 145.

23. GP 632.

24. Ph 3, 38.

25. W 42.

26. W 878.

27. Cf. Ph 3, 153f.: "Speculative thought is the *Chiffer* writing that has become communicability. It interprets, but its interpretation is not an understanding of *Being*, but in understanding a touching of the actually incomprehensible of the substance of *Being*."

28. Cf. NPL 204f.

29. NPL 203.

30. According to Jaspers, however, the common designation *Category* is justified insofar as all three groups of categories are "formal determinations that require a content in order to show their meaning" (NPL 203).

31. Ph 3, 65.

32. According to Jaspers' advice, *Transcending Reflection* is part of the daily routine of philosophical living.

> By following philosophical trains of thought, I assure myself of the *Actual Being*, the *Godhead*. (. . .) I seek to assure myself of the time-independent or the eternal in time, seek to touch the *Origin* of my *Freedom* and through it *Being* itself, seek to penetrate to the bottom, as it were, of a co-knowledge with creation. (Einf 119)

33. PGO 214–219.

34. PGO 216; ChT 56.

35. Cf. ChT 55.

36. Cf. Prov 72: "Every person needs a basis of *Faith* for everything they take seriously."

37. UZG 267.

38. A particularly telling passage is found in Jaspers's *Philosophical Autobiography*:

> That is why so much depends on what the individual wants to live and work for. He must know where he stands. His own being and the course of things depend on his finding it relevant what he does, even in his most minute decisions. It is of eternal significance before the *Transcendence*, through which, by surrendering to it, he first becomes himself,

> there unthreatened by success or failure. It is of temporal significance through his work in the *World*.

What will become of the *World* "depends on each man in a way that is incalculable for him as a whole" (Aut 135).

39. Cf. PGO, 99: Philosophy

> is not science in the sense of the modern sciences. Rather, what belongs to these is excluded from philosophy. What remains for philosophy, and what has always been its substance, is not cognition in the sense of universality for every mind, but is a movement of thought for the *Illumination* of *Philosophical Faith.*

40. Kant, Immanuel, *Kritik der reinen Vernunft,* ed. Raymund Schmidt, 2nd ed. 1930 (reprint Hamburg: Meiner, 1956), B XXX.

41. PGO 150.

42. However, *Faith* only became the subject of his philosophizing later. "Since my *Philosophie* (1931)," writes Jaspers, "*Philosophical Faith* has been publicly advocated by me as the meaning of philosophical doctrine. I formulated it explicitly in the essay *Philosophischer Glaube* (1947)" (Aut 119).

# Chapter 10

# Philosophical Faith

Why use the term *Philosophical Faith*? Once again, we are dealing with a *Mode of the Encompassing*: *Philosophical Faith*, in the sense meant here, is the epitome of what ultimately sustains a person in the conduct of his life, from which he lives and in which he finds his footing in the face of *Borderline Situations*.[1] It is "the substance of his personal life," the historical ground "from which he is given."[2] This last formulation may be irritating: Is not *Transcendence*, as has always been said up to now, that other through which I am given to myself? Why should it now be *Faith*?

The emphasis on *Faith* is entirely logical if one considers that the transcendent *One* is not a counterpart separate from me that—according to a concept of causality that is in any case mistaken—could have an effect on me,[3] but rather that which encompasses everything and, in particular the *Subject-Object-Split*. Therefore, there is neither an *Objectivity* that determines the content of *Faith* nor *Faith* a *Subjective* truth that, instead of being determined by the object, determines it. Rather, *Philosophical Faith* is both in one: both the *Content* itself in which we believe and the *Faith* from which we believe this *Content*.[4] It is not God, but the God we conceive that makes us what we are, the God we see in the *Chiffers*.[5] And therefore everything depends on what we believe and how we believe.

Like everything else that is encompassing, *Philosophical Faith* cannot be determined objectively, but can only be *illuminated* through the *reflecting* power of judgment, which allows individual moments of *Philosophical Faith* to become bright in generalizing statements—through the contrast to what it is not.

## PHILOSOPHICAL FAITH IS NOT RELIGIOUS FAITH AND NOT A BELIEF IN REVELATION

First, *Philosophical Faith* is not *Religious Faith. Religious Faith,* as Jaspers understands it, is bound to a particular tradition, to a community, to a creed, to a sacred event in the world, and to cultic actors; *Philosophical Faith*, on the other hand, knows no dogmas and creeds, no organized community and no cult; it is the *Faith* of individuals who are denied the opportunity to live unquestioningly in the peace of an authority.[6] It is a *Faith* that can only be *given* to those who, in communication with their philosophical companions in the invisible realm of *Reason*, have set out on the path of philosophical *Illumination* of *Being* and of the self—with the instruments of *Basic Knowledge*, through *Formal Transcending*, in the experience of *Borderline Situations*, in the reflection of *Existential Relations* to *Transcendence*, in the reading of *Chiffers*, guided by the unreserved will not to accept anything incomprehensible, but to "convince oneself by presentness."[7]

Since the process of self-assurance is never complete, *Philosophical Faith* can at best be consolidated in provisional schemata, but the questioning always begins anew.[8] Nothing stands in the way of an understanding between *Religious Faith* and *Philosophical Faith*, provided that the religious believer distances himself from himself and allows himself to be open to this process of self-questioning.

Second, *Philosophical Faith* is not *Belief in Revelation. Belief in Revelation* appears historically in the following form:[9] Prophets proclaimed what God told them, churches and priests declared texts to be sacred and inspired by God and claimed to interpret them correctly, apostles testified that God had become man in Christ. For each of these three forms of revelation, an authority must decide who was a true prophet, which writings are inspired, and who was an apostle with valid testimony. *Belief in Revelation* is without support if it does not follow this authority. Such final authorities are the churches. Jaspers likes to quote Augustine in this context: "I would not believe the Gospel if the authority of the Catholic Church did not persuade me to do so."[10]

These authorities must be believed. If this belief is lacking, the writings and testimonies considered sacred are writings like all others, of special rank only for those who believe in revelation. Who belongs to the believers in revelation and how long this belief lasted and continues to last can be researched historically, but no research will ever be able to prove that the claim to canonization by the ecclesiastical authorities is justified. This is where Lessing's apostrophized "nasty" gap between historical facts and eternal truths opens up.

In contrast to the *Belief in Revelation, Philosophical Faith* knows no instances before which one's own thinking and examination may stop.

Whatever claims to be revelation, and whoever proclaims truth as a prophet or apostle and claims absolute authority, must be subject to the same critical scrutiny as any other human authority. Referring to revelation and elevating it to the only valid truth for all people is tantamount to breaking off communication, as Jaspers painfully experienced time and again in discussions with theologians.

Does this mean that there can be no revelation for *Philosophical Faith*? Does Jaspers not also claim a kind of revelation when he uses modes of speech in such a way that *Transcendence*—on the path of *Formal Transcending*, when reading *Chiffers*, or in the certainty of the *Unconditional* for me—is "experienced," "felt," or "present"? Such "experiences" can indeed be understood as analogous to a revelation,[11] but from the point of view of *Philosophical Faith,* there are two crucial differences: (1) What is "revealed" in this way is not *Transcendence* itself, but *Transcendence* that has become a *Chiffer*. (2) A Chiffer is a *Chiffer* only for the individual in his historical situation: it is addressed to him and only to him, and it is exclusive only in the sense that it applies to him alone. Every person, however, can be addressed by *Chiffers of Transcendence* at any time. "Revelation" in the broader sense is therefore never historically unique, never bound to a single place and time.

## WHAT REVELATION MEANS FOR THE PHILOSOPHICAL BELIEVER, AND WHETHER THE GAP BETWEEN PHILOSOPHICAL FAITH AND BELIEF IN REVELATION CAN BE BRIDGED

For *Philosophical Faith*, the truths of *Belief in Revelation* are a source of possible *Chiffers*, and the Bible, as a reflection of the deepest existential and religious experiences of people throughout the centuries, is one of the most precious sources of all. What *Possible Existence* "hears" from these *Chiffers*, however, is not the "voice" of the God who reveals Himself, but that of the God who is forever hidden in His unknowability. God revealed versus God hidden: this is probably the ultimate difference between *Belief in Revelation* and *Philosophical Faith*.[12] But in the face of all these differences, how can there still be an understanding between philosophical believers and believers in revelation?[13]

It seems impossible that philosophical believers and believers in revelation could ever meet. For how can a believer in revelation, for whom God has truly spoken, consider any other truth to be possible? And how can a philosophical believer, having come to the insight that there can be no incarnate revelation of God, suddenly believe in such a revelation? It would be natural for both sides to dismiss the truth of the other as an illusion. Or, at best, to adopt the kind of tolerance that acknowledges with contempt or indifference that there are people who, in their stubbornness, do not want to admit what alone can be true.

For the philosophical believer, this attitude would be falsehood par excellence. For if he truly believes in all-encompassing *Reason*, he cannot exclude the possibility that what he does not understand is possible for other people. Therefore, the thought of this possibility causes consternation and uneasiness. And the hope that it might also be possible for the believer in revelation—even if full of pain at the lack of grace for the other—to meet the unbeliever in his sense with unreserved respect, to listen to him seriously and, in covenant with him, to tackle the tasks that confront us human beings in this world.

## UNBELIEF AND NIHILISM

The second opponent of *Philosophical Faith* is *Unbelief* and *Faithlessness*. Both deny *Transcendence*. For them, there is only *Immanence*, whatever that may be for them: sometimes it is *Dasein*, sometimes it is *Reality*, sometimes it is the *World*. The only difference between these two attitudes: *Unbelief* is still belief insofar as it elevates particular realities to the *Absolute*, whereas *Faithlessness* denies any absoluteness—it is the standpoint of *Nihilism*. For Jaspers, philosophy is so closely linked to *Philosophical Faith* that he can judge both *Unbelief* and *Faithlessness* as *Un-philosophy*. However, *Un-philosophy* has been a companion of philosophy from the very beginning, and *Unbelief* is a widespread spiritual force today. Let's take a closer look at them.

First, *Unbelief*: what exactly is meant by the absolutizing of particular realities? Examples of this are *Demonology* and the *Deification of Man*.[14] The word *Demonology* sounds strange to modern ears. It is reminiscent of a worldview that we think we have left behind: the belief in evil or friendly mythical forces in the world that perished with Christianity or were domesticated as angels, mediators, or messengers of God and the Devil.

According to today's belief, there are no more demons. But the *Demonic* is still there, as Jaspers reminds us with reference to the following facts:[15] It is there in a diffuse form, like the word itself, for example, wherever an uncontrollable, inscrutable force suddenly threatens to overwhelm us. Thus we speak of the demonic nature of technology when the technical world we have created develops a power of its own and begins to turn against us, or when we say that nature, which we have exploited, is now striking back at us. Animals can also be seen as demonic, or people who are like animals. Conversely, the trust in nature that can come over us when we feel safe in a peaceful landscape and, to generalize, want to entrust ourselves to the "guidance" of nature for our salvation, is also demonic. But this feeling of safety lasts only until unpredictable and unforeseeable natural disasters thwart our will and the seemingly benevolent power of nature turns out to be a hostile and now even more demonic counterforce.

Another form of demonization is human *Idolatry*: individual people are enthusiastically worshiped, elevated to superhuman status, to the ideal that one would like to be but can never be. However, to participate in this *Higher* and blindly submit to it is itself seen as salvation. Throughout the centuries, there seems to be a greed among the masses for the cult of man. This is most evident in the glorification and deification of military leaders and rulers: Alexander became a son of God, the Roman god-emperors were part of the state cult. Caesar, Napoleon, and other potentates went down in history as *Idols*. In the course of their mythification, what they actually were as people was reinterpreted, veiled, and glorified. This tendency continues today in the personality cult of autocrats such as Putin, Xi Jinping, or Erdogan; the fanatical masses surrounding football players, band leaders, actors, self-styled gurus, etc. are another recent manifestation of this disastrous tendency to glorify *Idols*.

A more subtle form of *Disbelief* is scientific superstition, which considers what is scientifically recognizable to be the *Ultimate Reality*, and for which everything that goes beyond this—*Transcendence* as well as *Existence*—is considered non-existent. Science, which now wants to be philosophy itself, ignores the factual fragmentation of the world, which is expressed in the ever-increasing fragmentation of disciplines. It wants to re-establish the supposedly scientific worldviews, declare the partial aspects of the *World* to be the *Ultimate Reality* and reduce all being to these aspects, with the popular formula that the world is *nothing other than—nothing other than* matter, or life, or information or whatever. But such worldviews have long since become obsolete.[16] Scientific superstition, which does not know how to distinguish between belief and knowledge, loses both at the same time—belief and knowledge.

What all forms of *Unbelief* have in common is that they are no less believing than *Religious* or *Philosophical Faith*, but in their belief, they elevate to the *Absolute* things that, as immanent in the *World*, have only relative, finite, and conditional significance and therefore can be shown to be relative, finite, and conditional at any time once the illusion fades. When this happens, *Unbelief* shows its true face: it becomes *Nihilism*, which has lost all illusions. For which there is no more truth or *Absolute*, for which nothing is valid and everything is permissible. Since *Nihilism* knows no other being than that of *Immanence*, it is right in everything it asserts: that there is no God (for how could one prove the existence of God as the existence of an object in the world with the means of knowledge of *Immanence*), that there is no connection between God and man (for how could there be a reference to God without God), and that the only obligations that exist are obligations to persons and authorities in the world, which are only respected because they have the sanctioning power to enforce their laws and orders. What keeps the nihilist alive is not a goal that breaks through *Immanence*, but the drives of vitality, the lust for life, the will to power. When these drives do not blindly determine him, but are affirmed in the sense of Nietzsche's *Pessimism of Strength*, *Nihilism* in turn becomes a belief in the unconditional value of the *Vital*.

In addition to this *Nihilism of the Philistines*, as Jaspers calls it,[17] there is a very different kind of *Nihilism*, one that arises out of indignation at the terrible things that happen in the world and that people do to each other. It is the indignation of Ivan in Dostoevsky's *The Brothers Karamazov*: Ivan recalls the unjust suffering, the children tortured to death, and the immense, unpunished shamefulness through which the world exists. And then he pronounces his verdict: "'I give thanks from the very beginning for every higher harmony. It's not worth a single tear of that tortured child (. . .)' 'I don't want harmony, out of love for humanity I don't want any (. . .)' I am not rejecting God, I am just sending Him back the ticket of surrender.'[18] The very *Idea* of God—God as omnipotent, omniscient, and all-good—becomes the standard for rejecting God and the *World*. If God were really truth, goodness, and love, He would have created man and the world differently. So God is not omnipotent or not all-good.[19]

## NIHILISM AS A GATEWAY TO PHILOSOPHY

The *Nihilism* of people who have experienced terrible things, or who have become nihilists simply by imagining the terrible things that have happened to others, can horrify us again. It is as if they have fallen into a madness more terrible than the madness of nature. Struck by horror, they may be ready—out of revenge, out of anger—to do even more horrible things than what they are horrified by. This will never be condoned: evil remains evil, even if it is a reaction to evil that has already happened. But what can we say to the nihilist? Everything else that is said seems misguided. One might rather ask how it is possible that we do not all become nihilists. Are the experiences that turn nihilists into nihilists not telling enough? After all that has happened in human history, how can we still believe in a harmony of *Being*?[20] Anyone who is honest must admit that the despair that speaks from the nihilist must affect all those who have reached the limits of our being in the world.

Jaspers took *Nihilism* more seriously than almost any other thinker after Nietzsche and Kierkegaard.[21] His philosophy can be seen as the attempt to overcome *Nihilism* in itself, to gain *Faith* from *Unbelief*. "He who does not know the experience of *Unbelief*," was his key sentence, "also does not carry out a self-conscious *Faith*."[22] For him, this is also the crossroads for philosophy: whether it has passed through *Nihilism*. *Un-philosophy* should therefore not simply be dismissed. It is not superfluous or accidental. It is the philosophy on the borderline, where the turning point can take place, the *Conversion* that can only give us inner peace.

But how can this *Conversion* take place? Certainly not by proclaiming and professing a different *Faith*, not by direct attack or, worse, by moral condemnation. Jaspers sees only one path: the path of illuminating the ways of thinking that keep us trapped in *Nihilism*.[23] Only by resorting to the instruments of *Philosophical Logic* can the untruth be revealed (dialectically) in the intrinsically true of all forms of *Unbelief*. Jaspers demonstrates this with the examples of *Demonology*, the *Deification of Man*, and *radical Nihilism*.[24]

The truth of *Demonology* lies in the fact that all things and events of the empirical world have a physiognomy through which something *Supra-Empirical* can be seen, and which is the origin of the abundance of those figures of which mythology tells. Only an impoverished soul cannot be addressed by this. In philosophical *Illumination*, these sensual, non-sensual phenomena are the starting point for what Jaspers calls the *Chiffers of Transcendence*: the transparency of physical, mental, and spiritual realities toward *Transcendence*. *Demonology* is untrue because it claims to see the transcendent in physical form, but it remains true in that *Transcendence* can exist for us in no other way than by speaking to us through things and events in the world.

The *Deification of Man* has its truth in the fact that the other human being is the only being to whom man can turn and who can be his model and counter-image, object of love and companion on the path to truth. The untruth lies in the fact that no human being can be more than a human being, finite and fallible. Any absolutizing of a human being or a human instance confuses something particular with the *Encompassing* from which it itself comes. *Nihilism* proper, on the other hand, for which the ultimate is nothingness, is as irrefutable as the opposing belief in a God who guarantees harmony.

What helps beyond this contradiction, however, is the insight, which can only be gained through philosophical *Illumination*, that our lives and our thinking are bound up in dialectical cycles. Jaspers refers to the perpetual circular process that is already evident in the physiological and psychological.[25] Opposites are always bound together: such a passive self-surrender in active action, as can be observed in digestion, breathing, and sexuality; such an active action on the basis of a passive surrender to an event independent of us, as in arbitrary action supported by a process removed from arbitrariness; such in thinking, which depends on ideas that occur to us; such in will, which cannot be willed. In the existential, it is the dialectic of seizing oneself in being given to oneself, a will that is a transcendent must.

Finally, as we have seen, every transcending thought reveals the continuous polarities in which the one can exist only through the other: *Loneliness* only through *Communication*, *Existence* only through *Transcendence*, *Reason* only through *Being*. Even the seemingly ultimate opposition of *Nothingness* and *Being* is itself such a polarity, which, as a *Chiffer*, can point beyond itself to the *One* that stands above all *Chiffers*.

This now sounds as if we simply have to realize that we are constantly moving in dialectical circles in order to see that *Nihilism* and *Belief in Revelation* therefore also cancel each other out in a higher position, in which this opposition proves to be not an either/or, but a both/and. But this is not how Jaspers thinks, and not what constitutes *Philosophical Faith*. This higher standpoint is a fictitious standpoint that could only be taken by an observer who looks down on human beings from above with God's gaze, as it were. But we are not observers. We are parties to this dispute.

A movement in this eternal dispute can only come from one side: from people who have looked into the abyss of the *World* and for whom *Nihilism* has become present as a self-experienced possibility. Jaspers is thinking of personal but also historical experiences. He is thinking of the *Nihilism* that Nietzsche and Kierkegaard announced and that every thoughtful person must have experienced in 1933, and at the latest after 1945, in view of the disintegration of previously valid norms, the general bottomless condition, and the loss of any supporting *Faith*.

To experience *Nihilism* is to stand at the absolute zero of *Existence*, at the point where all bridges are broken. There is only salvation for those who, in their desperation, manage to cast their anchor so high on the eternal ground that they come to rest far above all the rationalisms and schematisms to which they have been clinging. This is the *Conversion* of which Jaspers speaks repeatedly. It gives rise to what he calls *Originality (Ursprünglichkeit)*, and which he believes is possible for every human being. It is the possibility to set out on the path to the eternal *Origin*, with the unending question of what is left when nothing seems to be left. Filled with the will to know the truth and nothing but the truth.

The story of Job's desperate struggle with God can be read as a *Chiffer* for this movement beyond *Nihilism*. All the elements are contained in this story: The zero point of *Existence* in Job's despair over the terrible evils that have befallen him, the righteous man; the rejection of the self-righteous answers of his theologian friends who believe in revelation and think they have the true doctrine; his will not to refer to traditional doctrines but to understand God from within himself; and then, at the end, the divine judgment that condemns the theologian friends and puts Job in his place with the words "Where were you when I founded the earth," but which—and this is the decisive moment—at the same time approves of Job's tireless search for truth and justice.

According to Jaspers's interpretation, the struggle between Job and the theologians is the struggle of "two incarnated powers whose *Origin* lies at the bottom of human possibilities" and which provides the archetype of what is still recognizable today in the struggle between philosophy and theology, "albeit weakened and less serious." There is "indignation and contempt" on both sides, but not of the same kind: on the one hand, the indignation of fanaticism that clings to dogma; on the other, "the indignation of free *Faith* that is turned toward *Transcendence* and wants truth."[26] No authority recognized by either side can judge who is right. "Man must choose at his peril."[27]

In the abstract, it is a choice between *Dogmatism* and *Freedom*. This choice seems to be identical to the general choice already discussed between *Autonomy* and *Heteronomy*, between wanting to judge for oneself or having one's judgments predetermined. However, the dimensions of this choice need to be clarified once again. Only then will it become clear what this choice means, and what those who choose *Freedom* are choosing.

## THE DECISION BETWEEN DOGMATISM AND FREEDOM AND THE DECISION ON WHICH IT IS BASED

### The Contrast between Abstract and Concrete Thinking

A dogmatist can be recognized by the fact that he relies on the dogmas and doctrines laid down by his tradition and his authorities and sticks to them at all costs, regardless of the situation. The only thing he can perceive about a situation is whether it provides a case for the doctrinal assertion. If there is anything for him to choose, it is the abstract choice between different doctrines. He is then either a follower of one doctrine or another. An example from moral philosophy may illustrate this.

There are two opposing doctrines in moral philosophy, which can be summarized as follows: According to the first doctrine, morality consists of a set of rules like the Decalogue, and the only good is the good disposition, which consists of following the rules for their own sake, regardless of the consequences of doing so. The second doctrine contradicts this: it is only in the good consequences that the goodness of our actions becomes apparent, and therefore the rules can only be considered valid as long as they produce good consequences. The first doctrine is that of the *Ethics of Conviction (Gesinnungsethik)*, the second that of the *Ethics of Success (Erfolgsethik)*. The contrast seems irreconcilable. The classic example of this dispute is Kant's objection to Benjamin Constant's arguments in defense of the *Ethics of*

*Success* in his pamphlet *On a Supposed Right to Lie out of Philanthropy*. In it, Kant argues that lying is not permissible under any circumstances. According to Jaspers, however, the real opposition lies not in the either/or of the *Ethics of Success* and the *Ethics of Conviction*, but elsewhere.

Jaspers, as a worldview psychologist, has already described exactly where this "elsewhere" lies in his comparison between the *Rationalist* and the *Living, Existing Human Being*. They differ in the way they make their choice in relation to the either/or of the *Ethics of Success* and the *Ethics of Conviction*. For the *Rationalist*, there is only the abstract choice; one chooses once and for all which side one wants to be on, one is either an *Ethicist of Conviction* or an *Ethicist of Success*. The *Living Person*, on the other hand, does not know such an abstract choice; for him there is only "a concrete choice in the moment (. . .) which is followed by rational interpretations and justifications without exhausting it." For both, choice means "a commitment, a definitive and obligatory one." This commitment arises in the first case "from the *General* and the insight," in the second case "from the living act in a very concrete situation."[28]

To make this contrast between the *Rationalist* and the *Living Person* a little clearer, let us return here to the distinction between *determining* and *reflecting* power of judgment that is central to both Kant and Jaspers (though Jaspers does not use it here): The *Rationalist* is the type of person who knows only the *determining* power of judgment (the "insight from the *General*"); the *Living Person*, on the other hand, is the type for whom the *reflecting* power of judgment comes first, because he knows "that he must continually choose, and that he exists all the more vividly the more decisive and certain his acts of choice are."[29]

To "choose constantly" means (and this is the only way to understand this statement by Jaspers) never to see the situation merely as a case of an immovable moral rule, along the lines of: thou shalt not lie, to tell the untruth now would be a lie, therefore I should not do it. Rather, taking into account the particularity of the situation and the interests of those affected by it, I should find that maxim of action which I can make the law for everyone else in any relevant similar situation. In the first case, the *determining* power of judgment is sufficient (to subsume the individual case under the general rule); in the second case, the *reflecting* power of judgment is required, which enables us to find the general rule, the maxim of my action, for the individual case.[30]

What Jaspers describes here as the type of the living person is, although he does not use the term here, the type that Max Weber describes as the *Ethicist of Responsibility (Verantwortungsethiker)*,[31] and which—with his anchoring in the concrete situation—breaks through the sterile opposition between the *Ethics of Conviction* and the *Ethics of Success*.

Although the *Ethicist of Responsibility* knows, again in Jaspers's words, that objectified "norms and tables of values" belong "to the space of *Existence*" as "necessary means of self-illumination," he considers it a "distraction" to be content with the scheme of a value order":

> Instead of an infinite immersion in that which is historically opposed to me, in order to discover from it its values in one's own ascent with it, (. . .) everything individual is merely classified into existing compartments of a *General* and thus regulated (. . .).

But every hierarchy has its historical *Origin* and does not tolerate a "shift into valid objectivity."[32]

What the *Ethicist of Responsibility* rejects is the tendency to leave it to the generalization once found, as a cushion for all future cases. He rightly emphasizes that the judgment of the *reflecting* power of judgment, which arises from the situation, is inevitably exposed to the risk of failure, to the "possibility of fall and ascent," "which overlaps all objectification and allows no peace of mind."[33] There is no shift to an a priori valid objectivity, it must be added, but objectivity is also necessary here, because the examination of the decision to be made necessarily requires objectification in the form of universalized maxims of action. Otherwise, Jaspers's demand that every action, if it is to be considered good, even an action out of love, must be placed under the condition of the moral law, could not be fulfilled.[34] For him, every determination is therefore always only provisional, leaving room for constant (unrestricted) correction[35]—with a constantly renewed view of the respective situation.

The *Success Ethicist* also seems to see only the situation. But what he sees of the situation is the opportunity for the possible success of his actions, measured against what he then considers to be good, in the best case—in the sense of *Utilitarianism*—the greatest possible happiness of all those affected by the situation,[36] in the worst and most common case what is considered good in his society: be it the good of the family, the interests of the state, the power of the party, and the like. But all this is done without reference to the moral law and its demand for universalization. The *Ethicist of Success* thus easily mutates into an unscrupulous so-called *Pragmatist* who knows how to adapt to any situation. For the *Ethicist of Responsibility*, on the other hand, it is essential to test his maxims of action against the moral law. This is the only way to achieve unconditionality in his actions—by following the moral law for its own sake. And this is where he differs from the *Success Ethicist*, who has become an agile *Pragmatist*. Because of his unwavering commitment to the moral law, however, he can also be described as the *True Ethicist of Conviction*,[37] for whom it is not the moral rule once established that is important, but only the commitment to the universalizing demand of the moral law.

## *The Living, Existing Individual* versus Dogmatism and Rationalism

The big question in our context, however, is this: What makes individuals take the positions outlined here, the abstract either/or of the *Ethics of Success* and the *Ethics of Conviction* on the one hand and the *Ethics of Responsibility* on the other, not just as textbook knowledge, but as a challenge to themselves: that it is about them and that they have to decide where they want to stand? The answer to this question is also the answer to the original question of this chapter: What could lead the individual to reject the abstract either/or of *Nihilism* and *Belief in Revelation* and to choose *Philosophical Faith*, in short, to choose not *Dogmatism* but *Freedom*?

The key figure here is the *Living, Existing Individual* of the young Jaspers, whose model is probably the *Existing Thinker* of Kierkegaard.[38] For what constitutes his *Liveliness*? The best way to see what it consists of is to ask what its counterpart, the *Abstractly Choosing Individual*, lacks. As its basic characteristic, we found that it lacks the *reflecting* power of judgment. But a closer look reveals that it is not that it lacks this capacity, but that it does not need it at all. And why doesn't it need it? Because there is nothing that connects it to the situation in which it lives and that would make it delve deeper into it. That's why it doesn't ask itself where it is and what the place it is in requires of it. It is, as it were, bottomless, without *Substance*, as Jaspers would say.

Because the *Abstractly Choosing Individual* does not want to know where it is and what it is actually doing, it does not need to judge and therefore does not need the *reflecting* power of judgment. The *determining* power of judgment, with its recourse to immovable general concepts under which one can subsume oneself and one's situation, does the job perfectly well.

But how does the bottomless, unreflective person get into this position? Because he is in love with his commonplaces, his rationalisms? No, because he cannot love them at all. What he lacks is that which binds people to a place and makes them present in the first place: Love for the individual person, for something historical that exists only once, in this place and at this time. Those who love want the beloved to be there and to be able to be there, to have, in a word, *Reality*.[39]

And where the *Real* is concerned, or more precisely, where something is real or becomes real, there is also the call: what will become of what you love and of the world to which it belongs depends on you. You are responsible. Now show who you are, what you really want, and what you really can do. Not just for show, not just halfway, but absolutely, truly. And this is the only way to know yourself, the only way to become who you are. All this is lost to the unloving: the situation, the bondage, the *Reality*. Worse, he doesn't know who he is. Nor does he exist in the true sense of the word. He is never himself, but someone else, another.

But if his lack of judgment is only due to another fundamental lack, his lack of love, which in turn leads to his unreality and lack of *Existence*, then the question arises: Is this his fault? Where is the intention, the will, without which there is no decision? Can someone want to love if he does not love?

Is it possible to appeal to him to love at last? The question itself is absurd. Love is not in our power; it is like a power that seizes us from outside, that is given to us, as Jaspers repeatedly emphasizes. And yet—is this the full truth? Can I be a lover, a hater, a loveless monster, or whatever, in the full sense, without *being aware of* how I love and what I love (or hate)? And isn't that, in turn, a prerequisite for being able to judge and, in the end—after the moral examination that is only now possible—to say yes or no to what moves me?

This process of *Becoming Aware* can be misunderstood as if it were simply a matter of determining who or what I am, that is, which case I am, according to the usual repertoire of psychological clichés. In reality, however, it is about coming to terms with what I really want. But I can only do this by first sketching out the possibilities that I can accept or reject; technically speaking, by first finding the *General* under which I want to place myself. But for that, I need—*reflecting* power of judgment.

## The Independence of the Sincere Person. Exemplified by Hannah Arendt and Her Eichmann Book

It is clear from the previous considerations that nothing happens by itself. I can only become aware of my impulses if I *want* to become aware of them, I can only judge them if I *want* to judge myself, and I can only act according to this judgment if I *want* to act accordingly. Nothing works without *Will*. But here a special *Will* is required: the *Will* to tear away the veil of self-deception in which I am wrapped, the veil of idioms, rationalisms, and gossip. This *Will* has a name: it is the *Will to Sincerity*. The *Sincerity* that Kant, Nietzsche, and Kierkegaard put at the top of the list, and that Jaspers also puts at the top. And without it, everything these thinkers condemned would go hand in hand: forgetfulness of *Existence*, bottomlessness, loss of *Freedom* and *Self*. So, is not wanting to be sincere the downfall?

This is how Kierkegaard saw it and placed it under the moral category of good and evil: The Origin of evil is the radical will not to become transparent to oneself. I have the choice to become transparent to myself (and thus achieve *Freedom* in the long run) or to close myself off. If I choose to close myself off, I have already lost my *Freedom* by that very choice. But where does this *Will* to remain closed come from? According to Jaspers, Kierkegaard "grasped the *Origin* of this loss of *Freedom* to a depth that no one before him had reached."[40] He locates it in the resistance of a desperate person who desperately wants to be neither himself nor not himself but cannot be either. He wants to hide himself, from himself and from others, does everything to avoid revealing himself, until he bursts out and desperately reveals himself, only to use this revelation itself as a pretext for the desired closure.

In her reflections on Eichmann and the *Origin* of evil, Hannah Arendt demonstrated the dimensions to which this kind of evil can lead and the topicality it can acquire. If we pay attention to the external, publicly accessible behavior of a deeply dishonest person, all that becomes visible is the insubstantiality of his actions. It is the *Bottomless Evil* of which Hannah Arendt speaks and in which she sees the entire *Banality of Evil*: monstrous deeds committed by puppets and *Hanswursts* of the caliber of Eichmann, who cling to a web of commonplaces, unable or unwilling to confront their situation and judge for themselves. The monstrosity of their deeds was so outrageous that no reflection was needed[41] to recognize them—according to any moral code—as outrageous: as something that should never have happened.

This evil is bottomless because this type of person is never anchored in a situation. He lacks the *clairaudience (Hellhörigkeit)* that, according to Jaspers,[42] characterizes Hannah Arendt, the *Love* for the *Individual.*[43] Therefore, he cannot be moved by the fate of his victims or be outraged by what is done to them. To do his so-called duty, to be so-called decent, like a real Nazi has to be decent, that is his ultimate goal, in which he is absorbed. The commonplaces he invokes are the bridges and railings he clings to in order to rise above all that is *Present* and not to have to deal with any situation, not to have to remember anything he has done. Those who do not want to remember cannot put down roots in the past, and because this evil has no roots, Arendt diagnoses, "it has no limits, it can develop to unimaginable extremes and spread over the whole world"—and thus become the *Greatest Evil.*[44]

Pulling on his strings, a *jumping jack* like Eichmann is the antithesis of the self-contained, independent person embodied by Hannah Arendt herself in Jaspers's eyes. In his characterization of her *Independence*, the *reflecting* power of judgment once again takes center stage: Her *Independence*, he says, is shown in the fact that she refuses any flight into generalities, always aims at the example, and also sees the particular case even in Eichmann's case, which must be seen in its particularity, instead of resorting to the usual clichés and declaring him a monster.[45] The secret of her *Independence* lies, in a word, in the fact that she always starts from the particular, from what is given in the situation, in short: from the *present*.

To visualize the importance of *Becoming Present (gegenwärtig werden)* for Jaspers's philosophizing, a few keywords will suffice. The present moment is the only *Reality* that exists for us, and only when we realize this fact do we become aware of the *Encompassing* in which we find ourselves, and of which we can only assure ourselves in the constantly failing movements of our thinking. But since everything that is present immediately becomes past, it must be constantly represented in order to endure for us. Only by remembering can the past continue to affect us and move us to carry it into the future through our thoughts and actions. We are reminded of this by the now familiar maxim of *Reason* that nothing should be forgotten, nothing left out. But this maxim speaks of a voice that transcends the present and yet must be present in every moment. It speaks of an *Unconditionality* that transcends all temporal conditions: as an eternal reminder not to cease to remember. Hearing this voice and following it is what enables us to make a new beginning of ourselves again and again. This is the *Originality (Ursprünglichkeit)* given to man, as Jaspers calls it, and which Hannah Arendt, in her famous interpretation of Augustine's words, traces back to the fact of our birth: "In order that there might be a beginning in the world, man was created, before whom there was no man."[46]

*Originality* and *Becoming Present* go hand in hand. And every *Becoming Present* calls me into the scene, demands an answer from me, and thus awakens my *Possible Existence*. But this answer is not available anywhere; no tradition, no authority, no God can give it to me. I have to find it myself and see if I can live with it. To gain *Originality* is, according to Jaspers, the *Innate Nobility of Man* that characterizes the *True Man* in human history. But precisely because he stands in the *Loneliness of Freedom* within himself, he is all the more in need of all the others who, for their part, strive for "the ever new *Originality* of *Reason* and *Existence*," in the knowledge that I can only become truthful if I have a counterpart who wants truthfulness himself: "only through truthfulness, and not without it, can the good become."[47] Conversely, this means that evil begins with untruthfulness.[48]

Being truthful or *Sincere*, which is the same thing, includes everything that makes up the *Independent* human being who lives out of his own *Origin*. He knows that all that is essential is *Historical*, and that we ourselves must be *Historical*: responsible for what we think and do in the here and now. He is also aware of his insurmountable limitations: that he, trapped in the situation, will never be able to gain an overview of the situation and what it encompasses. The realization of this has consequences for all *Basic Philosophical Knowledge* (which Jaspers tried to capture in his doctrine of the *Encompassing*), but no less so for our existential relationship to *Transcendens,* as can be shown exemplarily in the question of *Theodicy*. Let us therefore return to it a second time.

## The Sincere Man and the Theodicy Question for the Second Time

Anyone who loves the *Individual* and *lives in the Present* shares the indignation at the terrible and evil things that people do to each other, which

Dostoevsky's Ivan Karamazov expresses in a unique way.[49] On the other hand, he does not close his eyes to the beauty and goodness that exist in the *World* despite all the horrors. But he forbids himself any judgment of the *World* as a whole, both a judgment like Schopenhauer's, that the *World* is so bad that it can only just exist, and the judgment of modernity, from Leibniz to Hegel, that the *World* is a glorious harmony in which everything has its place and its meaning. He is opposed to all the arguments that have been used in the history of Western thought to explain or justify the evil and wickedness in the world: be it *Gnosticism* with its doctrine of the evil creator God and the good redeemer God, be it *Christianity* with Augustine's concept of freedom and sin, or be it modernity with Leibniz's *Theodicy*. For Jaspers, as for Kant, the only valid answer is the one given to Job.

Jaspers's position on the question of *Theodicy* becomes clearest when we contrast it with Leibniz's *Theodicy*.[50]

The basic concept with which Leibniz tries to come to terms with *Malum* (as the epitome of all evil and badness) is the concept of *Compossibility*. Not everything is possible at the same time. Therefore, God is subject to boundary conditions that He cannot change. Even though in His goodness He aims at the good per se, He cannot have a perfect *World*, but only the best possible *World*. In other words, in addition to the good that is sought, one must also accept—out of consideration for the *Compossibilities*—the evils that are necessarily associated with that good.[51]

The word "accept" indicates the secret principle that Leibniz follows: Everything has its price. God's wisdom is shown in the fact that He knows how to calculate correctly and to select precisely the *World* that offers the best possible value for the lowest possible price. The term that best describes this calculability is the word *Compensation*.[52] What makes Leibniz's God seem excusable and just is the fact that He always knows how to provide the necessary *Compensation*. The concept of *Compensation* in *Theodicy* differs from the concept already in use in the Middle Ages: *Compensation* is not simply revenge, penance or punishment for an offense, but rather—and this is where its modernity lies—an equalization of positive and negative accounts, balancing the *Mala* suffered by appropriate *Boni*.

This *Idea* of *Compensation* is fully realized in the philosophy of history, which Voltaire created as a new discipline and which, as Hegel explicitly states, now assumes the function of *Theodicy*. The mala are certainly there, in the form of the fall of human freedom and the physical evils that result from it; but in the course of the historical process, divine providence, or, what amounts to the same thing, the antagonism of the forces of nature—oh, the cunning of *Reason*—ensures that it's precisely through this *Mala*, and with the help of this *Mala*, that the real and true *Bonum* comes into being, such as, for example, Hegel's self-realizing *Absolute Spirit* or Karl Marx's *Classless Society*.

Jaspers's objection to this way of thinking can perhaps be summed up in a single sentence: For those who live in the *Present*, there are things that cannot be compensated for by anything; they have absolutely positive or absolutely negative value. The absolute negative is evil. It has no function, serves no purpose, and has no meaning. This is how Kant already saw it with his doctrine of *Radical Evil*, with which he radically breaks through the functional context of the *Bonification* of *Malum*, on which Leibniz based his *Theodicy*.

For Leibniz, the equation was as follows: *Metaphysical Malum*—the inevitable finitude of creation—entails *Moral Malum*, because *Moral Malum* is nothing other than the necessary consequence of our imperfect knowledge, which makes us mistake good for evil and evil for good; the moral or natural consequence of *Moral Malum*, in turn, is *Physical Malum*: one suffers evil because one has done evil, and where we seem to suffer innocently, it is for our education: as a means of improvement. With the doctrine of *Radical Evil*, Kant draws a thick line through all compensatory balances. *Radical Evil* knows no *Compensation*, because even the best consequences of an evil act do not make it a good one. There is no causal connection between the *Moral* and the *Natural Order* of things. Freedom belongs to another realm than natural causality. Therefore, there is no connection between moral good and evil, on the one hand, and physical good and evil, on the other. The most righteous may suffer the worst physical evil, while the most unrighteous may enjoy an all-round happy life.[53]

How does Kant deal with this? His *Sincerity* forbids him from trying to understand what lies beyond all *Reason*: how the experience of an unbearable world could be compatible with the moral wisdom of the *World's* Creator. The existence of a just and benevolent God, Kant concludes, can never be doctrinally proven. The existence of a benevolent God is at most something that a just person can postulate against all evidence and can postulate authentically, as a consequence and not as the reason of his *Morality*.

Kant finds the last word on this allegorically expressed in the story of Job: the claim to the power of *Practical Reason*, which commands us to do good unconditionally, the incomprehensibility of God's ways and faith in God based solely on *Morality*, God's approval of Job's *Sincerity* and his rejection of the *Untruhfulness* of his theological friends, who think they can justify God on the basis of their supposed knowledge in the face of Job's complaints.[54]

What is Jaspers's position on this? He adopts Kant's position, both in the question of *Theodicy* and in his interpretation of Job. Only someone who is *Insincere* can want to give an absolute answer to the question of the *Origin* of evil and wickedness in the *World*, be it that of indignation or the reassuring *Idea* of *World Harmony*. For,

> Is indignation not connected with *Insincerity* when it sets itself up as an *Absolute*? And is the rejection of indignation not insincere if it ignores the truth inherent in the language of indignation? Is the *Idea* of harmony not insincere if it obscures? And is the rejection of harmony not insincere if it treats harmony in the *World* as null and void?[55]

The biblical God's words to Job: "Where were you when I created the heavens and the earth?" become for him the supporting *Chiffer* for the distance of *Transcendence*, before which even the dispute between belief in harmony and nihilistic despair becomes obsolete. For him, Kant's insight into the phenomenal nature of our being, and thus also his interpretation of time as a form of perception of our understanding of the *World* and our empirical self-consciousness, is irrefutable. It is to this insight that he owes the fundamental idea of his philosophizing: that what constitutes us as *Existence*, our *Freedom*, transcends time and the causality of nature, and that the (*Historical*) moment is therefore of crucial importance: as the point at which time and eternity, *Existence* and *Transcendence* meet—in that we decide temporally what is eternal.[56]

On the basis of this notion of *Transversality* in time *(Quer zur Zeit)*, Jaspers finally turns critically against Kant himself by rejecting his *Postulate Theory* (God and immortality as postulates of *Practical Reason*) as "ambiguous."[57] Kant postulates our immortality as a complement to our temporally unfinishable being and as a necessity in order to harmonize virtue and happiness, but understands immortality in the temporal sense as a future existence. For Jaspers, however, the only thing that makes us immortal is *Love* (which Kant never or only inadequately mentions).[58]

But why *Love*? Because *Love* alone keeps us in the moment and thus allows us to experience the *Presence* of the eternal. This becomes more understandable when we consider that when Jaspers speaks of *Love* in this context, he does not mean *Love* pure and simple, but *Love* that is tested with the help of the *reflecting* power of judgment and on the basis of the universalizing demand of the *Categorical Imperative*. For him, then, *Love* is more than an inclination; it is *Reason* in itself.

But what about hatred and the nihilistic will to destroy everything, which oppose *Love* on the third level of evil? As soon as the will to *Sincerity* and the indispensable examination on the basis of the moral law are added, the evil will collapses and becomes nothing.[59] This is why Jaspers insists so strongly that there can only be *Unconditionality* in good, but no *Unconditionality* in evil. The necessary condition of *Unconditionality* is and remains the validity of the general law of morally right action.[60]

There are those who speak of *Greatness*, of being above good and evil. But those who only want to be *Great* and believe themselves to be above good and evil, according to Jaspers's judgment, only become "smaller": they surrender to the vitality of their natural *Dasein*; they take refuge in the "noncommitment of an aesthetic view that regards everything as valid in its own way," or they abandon themselves to evil because they "count on grace in a belief in God that is now itself evil."[61]

But does this mean, conversely, that the good thing about placing the opposition of good and evil in the highest place is that only in this way can one be really *Great*—well understood, in the Jaspersian sense of *Nobility in Man*? Is the *Actual*, the *Self*, the *Original*—or whatever the formula may be—even higher than the moral good and its actual goal? Or would we have to say, in the sense of Kant's *Doctrine of Postulates*: not the highest good—for that remains morality—but that good which, together with morality, forms the *Complete* good, because being good goes together with selfhood, just as virtue goes together with a future happiness appropriate to the subject's worthiness in Kant's *Postulate* of *Practical Reason*? Would selfhood then be something like *eternal* happiness (experienced at the moment of decision and *Ascent*) in the place of *temporal* happiness?[62] The happiness of being one with oneself? And the eternal unhappiness—the "hell," so to speak—of not being able to be that?

Jaspers must have been convinced of this,[63] and Hannah Arendt's reflections on the moral significance of man's dialogue with himself read like a confirmation of this idea. In her search for a justification of the Socratic statement that it is better to suffer injustice than to do injustice, she draws attention to a sentence by Socrates in Plato's dialogue *Gorgias:* worse for him than having to contradict the whole world is "that I alone do not agree with myself, but have to contradict myself."[64] The core of this sentence is that, even if I am one, I am always two in one, I have a self opposite me with which I can be in harmony or disharmony. "If I do wrong, I am condemned to live in unbearable intimacy with a 'wrong-doer,' whom I can never get rid of."[65] No one could wish to have to live and communicate every day with his own enemy.[66] Indeed, for Hannah Arendt, this seems to be the secular equivalent of hell, with no possibility of forgiveness.[67]

Because the conversation with myself never ends, in order not to get caught up in myself, I am necessarily dependent on the dialogue with the other, or the others, who continue this dialogue with me—in solidarity with me and with the same will to truthfulness, which is a prerequisite for being able to agree with myself at all. Job's theologian friends are the frightening counterexample. Self-assured in their teachings and fully convinced that they are on the right side, they are, as Jaspers emphasizes in his interpretation of Job, "mercilessly without inner participation in the individual human being's experience of doom."[68]

The young Jaspers would probably have said: *Abstract Rationalists* encounter a *Living, Existing Human Being*, and the great example of such a

*Living, Existing Human Being* would probably have been the old Jaspers's Job,[69] who denies himself the consolation "that comes from a proclamation, a promise by a teaching authority that claims to be instituted by God." What he seeks is the "infinite consolation" that man can only find "by being with other men as companions in a common destiny before *Transcendence*." Job wants not the work of men, not dogmas, but God Himself. And when God Himself then speaks and "leads Job to self-knowledge by pointing to the wonders of His creation, which are incomprehensible to man," no doctrine can be derived from this that the church authorities could now proclaim, for example, as the dogma of the knowledge of ignorance. What the author of the Book of Job has God say is a *Chiffer* that constantly stimulates the movement of wanting to know anew, "always born anew out of questioning and defiance," while *Dogmatic Knowledge* ends "in the dull questionlessness of no longer thinking."[70]

This difference between belief in *Chiffers* and *Dogmatic Knowledge* cannot be emphasized enough. It is precisely at the point where we reach the limit of our knowledge and *Existence* that even the last contradiction, the one between *Nihilism* and *Belief in Revelation*, can break down. It is all too easy to take the step toward the attitude of the *Passive Agnostic*, who stands "indifferent, unaffected" before "that which he cannot investigate and which does not concern him at all" and is content with what can be recognized as universally valid. The *Active Agnostic* is quite different: he is affected by what he does not know; it attracts him, it leaves him no peace. Even when he does not know, he expects that "if he brings it quite clearly and distinctly before his eyes and visualizes it concretely," "something else must come out of it."[71]

*Active Agnosticism*—a catchy formula that sums up what leads to *Philosophical Faith* beyond the opposition of *Nihilism* and *Belief in Revelation*: *Being Present* and *Becoming Present,* being affected by the *Borderline Situation*, by the bursting of all rational "shells," by the experience of *Nihilism* and the never-ending question of the truth of *Transcendence*. But all this only by constantly turning to people who are and have been on this path themselves, and listening to what they have to tell us. Because the questions that people ask themselves in their efforts to understand what is happening to them have been going on throughout human history since the *Axis Time,* every voice from the past is present for us as if it were addressing us at this very moment and as if we were in the same room. At least in the space of *Reason* that Jaspers tried to fathom. Among the many voices from the past, there was one in particular that appealed to him in its simplicity and that he therefore liked to quote again and again:

I come from, I don't know where,
I am, I don't know who,

I'm dying, I don't know when,
I'm going, I don't know where,
I'm amazed that I'm happy.[72]

## The Importance of the Historicity of Man

Even if human beings, as human beings, are companions of destiny in the suffering of *Borderline Situations* and in the search for a foothold, everyone stands in their historical place and in their particular historical situation. It is in this alone that they have their *Presence*, to which they remain bound and to which they must unconditionally commit themselves. Their task in communicating with the other is therefore to allow the historical other to approach them without being unfaithful to their own *Historicity*; to recognize the other in their historical difference and yet to claim *Unconditionality* for their own path; to stand against the other in the struggle of powers and yet not give up solidarity with them, striving to transform the inevitable struggle into a loving struggle that unites both in the search for truth and leads to where the common ground becomes tangible.

The belief that it is possible for us human beings to accomplish this seemingly unsolvable task is the core of *Philosophical Faith* as Jaspers understands it. It does not consist of a specific content and it is not a program,[73] it is the belief in the possibility of communication and the unconditional will to dare to communicate. And this is where the greatest difference to *Nihilism* and *Belief in Revelation* lies: in the decision for or against communication. Hence the apodictic sentence: "Only believers can realize communication."[74] Hence the equally apodictic sentence about those who refuse to communicate: "You can't talk to warriors of faith." *Philosophical Faith* recognizes "devilry" in every will to break off communication.[75]

Once again, the importance of *Being Present* becomes apparent: the belief that communication is possible is not a dream of a distant utopia; it is the belief that it is possible in the here and now—every day—and that I myself can make it possible, as long as I want to. But I can only want this if I am where I am now: in the *Present*, in my historical situation. Illuminating the historical situation in which I find myself and what it demands of me is therefore a permanent task for philosophical believers.

Jaspers set himself this task again and again. That is why Kierkegaard and Nietzsche were indispensable to him in interpreting his time, which is still our time. They saw the coming catastrophe that overtook humanity in the twentieth century and were, so to speak, the storm birds who announced the coming storm. They suffered what has since become the basic experience of all of us: *Nihilism.* The disintegration of all valid norms, the groundlessness, the predominance of *Unbelief* in all its variations, the *Demonology* of today's conspiracy theories, the idolatry of idols and dictators, and the transcendentless *Naturalism* of today's currents of philosophical thought. On the other hand, there is the threat of violence from a fundamentalist, hardened *Belief in Revelation*, whether in Christianity, Judaism, or Islam.

*Nihilism* "taken to the extreme" opened Jaspers's eyes to *Nihilism* as an approach to traditional philosophy and made him see philosophy as a way to overcome *Nihilism*. "Through *Nihilism* to the appropriation of philosophy": this was the real driving force behind his engagement with the history of philosophical thought, and the driving force behind not only taking note of the philosophical tradition in an observational way but also being "inwardly *present*" "as with one's own cause."[76]

"The basic attitude born of *Nihilism*" allows him to see the history of philosophy differently. Three millennia of philosophical history become a single *Present*. We now see the *Origin* of philosophy in its various manifestations, and it becomes necessary for us to keep the memory of the universal tradition alive if we do not want to sink into the nothingness of "a mere moment without past and future."[77] This is Jaspers's *Becoming Present* through the *Presence* of the *Philosophia Perennis*, and the deeper reason for his desire for boundless communication and for his belief in "the possibility in us human beings to really live together, to talk to each other, to find the truth through this togetherness and only in this way to really become ourselves."[78]

However, this attitude should become reality in everyday life, especially in politics. This is Jasper's demand. No evaporation into a distant *Transcendence* that is elevated above all earthly things. But what does all this mean in the face of a world in which the opposing forces seem to be more powerful than everything that unites us, a world in which hate reigns instead of love, violence instead of understanding, lies instead of truth, war instead of peace? In short, a world in which evil is *Real* and proves its *Reality* by its power of destruction?[79] At this point, it is necessary to open a final chapter with the question: how does this philosophy relate to the "evil" world of politics?

## NOTES

1. Even if Jaspers denies that *Faith* was already a topic for him before his *Philosophie*, it is in fact, already there in *Psychologie der Weltanschauungen* as that in which man has his support in the face of the *Borderline Situation*: whether he seeks it in something that prevents him from entering the *Borderline Situations*, or that which helps him out of them. "What support a person has, how he has it, seeks it, finds it, preserves it, that is the characteristic expression of the forces alive in him. If we ask about the type of spirit, we ask *where man has his hold*" (PW 229). Jaspers even explicitly refers to this something that provides support as *Faith* (PW 337).

2. Ex 79.

3. Cf. PGO 485: The *Chiffer*, but not *Transcendence*, is a "counterpart."

4. This is how Jaspers interprets the unity of the separation of two moments of *Faith* made in the old Lutheran tradition: the *Faith* that I carry out by believing, and the content of *Faith* that I grasp, "*fides qua creditur and fides quae creditur*" (PG 14). It is the same figure of thought that we have already encountered in determining the effectiveness of *Ideas*: the *Idea*, because it encompasses, is both (objectively) goal-determining and (subjectively) inspiring to us.

5. Cf. for example the words of Luther quoted by Jaspers: What God I think of, I become myself (ChT 46).

6. cf. Ex 43f.

7. PGO 140.

8. Ibid.

9. Here I follow Jasper's summary of his historical account of the *Belief in Revelation* from the perspective of *Philosophical Faith* (PGO 479ff.).

10. Augustin: *Contra epistolam Manichaei quam vocant Fundamenti,* 5,6 PL 42, 176. Mentioned or quoted by Jaspers: PGO 10, 479f.; GP 375.

11. Jaspers distinguishes between a narrower and a broader sense of the word "revelation." In the narrower sense, it is "the historically determined objectivity of God's action and of God's word"; in the broader sense, revelation "means every kind of objectivity in which man believes himself to become indirectly certain of God's will" (GPhil 61). In this second sense, he then speaks of "being revealed" in relation to the ways in which that which is shows itself to me: in the interpretation of the *World* and the *Illumination* of *Existence*, in individual knowledge and total knowledge, in being thought and in being unthinkable (W 892–903).

12. Cf. PGO 481.

13. Jaspers poses this question himself at the end of his large-scale examination of the *Belief in Revelation*. The following considerations are based on his reflections, cf. PGO 533–536.

14. From a psychological point of view, *Nihilism* is discussed in PW, 285–304, under the spiritual types of *Skepticism* and *Nihilism* as answers to the "first and very last fundamental question of worldview, whether one says yes or no to life as a whole, whether the highest is in *Nothingness* or in *Being*, whether dissolving and ceasing to exist is the ultimate goal or life in action, creation, construction" (PW 285).

15. PG 108–118.

16. Cf. KlSch 26.

17. PG 125.

18. Quoted by Jaspers in W 793f.

19. PG 125: Indignation, defiance, and devotion are therefore the decisive *Existential Relations* to *Transcendence*. (Cf. also Ph 3, 71ff.).

20. PG 128.

21. Jaspers, as a worldview psychologist, was already aware of this fundamental significance of *Nihilism*: "*Nihilism* is psychologically unavoidable as a stage if life is to come to self-consciousness. Everything that is dead and final must first be questioned, must be drawn into the cauldron of *Nihilism* if a new form of life is to emerge. *Nihilism* cannot be escaped by avoiding it, but it must be experienced—which is only

possible through inner despair—if it is to be overcome and become a mere element, which it is in all kinds of *Spirit*" (PW 303).

22. PG 130.

23. PG 130: "A logical visualization of the philosophical ways of thinking, which are a methodically unfolded *Transcending*, and the ways of thinking of objective objectification and fixation, in which philosophy gets onto sandbanks, would have to show what and in what form truth is."

24. PG 126–129.

25. PG 134f.

26. PGO 349.

27. PGO 349.

28. PW 315.

29. PW 315.

30. There is an ambiguity in the word *General* that always causes confusion. People confuse *General* with *Universal*. *Universal* is a proposition that, unlike a particular judgment, contains no individual constants, that is, no proper names, demonstratives, or designators such as "disciple of Plato." *Universality*, then, is a question of either/or. A proposition is either universal or not. The *Generality* of a proposition, on the other hand, is determined by the conceptual scope of the predicates used: the proposition never to lie to a person is more general than the proposition never to lie to a child, and this in turn is more general than the proposition never to lie to small children. There are, of course, differences in the degree of *Generality* or specification, from highly abstract to arbitrarily concrete. It is one of the merits of Richard M. Hare to have emphasized this distinction. See, for example, *Freedom and Reason* (Oxford: Oxford University Press 1961), 30–50; *Sorting Out Ethics*, (Oxford: Clarendon Press 1997), 96f., 142. The demand of the *Categorical Imperative* to act according to that maxim which I can will to become a general law requires a *Universalization*, not a *Generalization*, of the maxim.

The purpose of *Universalization* lies in the effect that can be achieved by excluding individual constants: the creation of impartial judgments. For what is impartiality? Probably the fact that no individual preferences are allowed, no exceptions for me, for example, but that judgments are made that are valid not only for a single case but also for all relevant similar cases—for all situations, for example, in which thoughtlessly telling the truth endangers a human life (no matter which one). Anyone could be in danger in such a situation, especially myself. And that is exactly what is important: that I put myself in the position of all those involved, and especially in the position of the person most affected (as if I were him). The original form of the *Categorical Imperative*, the so-called *Golden Rule*, reminds us of this: Do unto others as you would have them do unto you.

31. Cf. GP 493: The truth is a third, which Max Weber expressed clearly as the *Ethics of Responsibility*.

32. PW 315.- What Jaspers could mean by *Hierarchy* is shown by his discussion of Kant's rejection of the "supposed right to lie out of love for humanity" when he asks rhetorically: Should this strict prohibition of lying still apply "if the other person, who is in possession of all power, criminally wants to destroy me or loved ones?" Not

lying only applies to people, but not to beasts. And this is precisely the other *Hierarchy* that arises from the particular situation—despite all the uncertainty about when people may no longer be regarded as rational beings (GP 491f.).—A comparable case is Jaspers's discussion of whether a physician, following the *Idea* of the physician, should always tell his patient the absolute truth. According to him, the patient cannot have a claim to the truth if he is "not able to bear the truth and to deal with it reasonably" (Karl Jaspers, „Die Idee des Arztes" (1953), in ders.: *Philosophie und Welt*, 169–183. (München: Piper 1958), 173).

33. Ph 3, 86.

34. Ph 3, 86.

35. Cf. VuD 26.

36. This is probably the borderline case in which the judgment of the *Utilitarian* could coincide with the judgment of the *Kantian*, at least with regard to the objective correctness of the judgment. (Cf. Richard Hare's effort to advocate a *Utilitarianism* that incorporates the Kantian point of view, for example in his essay: "Could Kant Have Been a Utilitarian?," Richard Hare: *Sorting out Ethics* (Oxford: Clarendon Press, 1997), 147–166.)

37. Jaspers later also sees him indeed as the *True Ethicist of Conviction* (GP 493).

38. Cf. PW 384.

39. Cf. "Das Unbedingte und das Böse," in *Das Wagnis der Freiheit. Gesammelte Aufsätze zur Philosophie*, ed. and with a preface by Hans Saner (München; Zürich: Piper, 1996), 86–98, 89.

40. PGO 322. Jaspers also seems to share Kierkegaard's view, cf. "Das Unbedingte und das Böse," in *Das Wagnis der Freiheit. Gesammelte Aufsätze zur Philosophie*, ed. and with a preface by Hans Saner (München; Zürich: Piper, 1996), 86–98, 87: Man awakens only when he distinguishes between good and evil. He becomes himself when he clearly decides where he wants to go. "Instead of deciding, we waver and stagger through life. This indecision alone is evil." Becoming transparent means making a clear distinction between good and evil.

41. As Hannah Arendt points out, it was above all ordinary people who could not bring themselves to commit such acts because they still had a counterpart in themselves with whom they could speak (were two in one) (*Über das Böse. Eine Vorlesung zu Fragen der Ethik* (München; Zürich: Piper, 2006), 73, 75))

42. VuD 576.

43. VuD 571.

44. Hannah Arendt, *Über das Böse. Eine Vorlesung zu Fragen der Ethik* (München; Zürich: Piper, 2006), 77.

45. VuD 181, 180; 179: "In its *Independence*, it does not allow itself to be guided by any preconceived clichés." However, we are never immune to them: we always make use of some clichés; it is important to be aware of them, not to allow ourselves to be dominated by them (VuD 577). The fight against clichés is waged with Kant's *Extended Way of Thinking*: through the presence of the other, through the creation of publicity (VuD 769, note 1134).

46. Augustinus, *Der Gottesstaat*, ed. Carl Johann Perl (Salzburg: Otto Müller, 1952), Bd. 2, 269. (De Civitate Dei, XII, 20). On the interpretation and significance

of the fact of being born in Hannah Arendt cf. Hans Saner, «Die politische Bedeutung der Natalität bei Hannah Arendt», in ders.: *Erinnern und Vergessen. Essays zur Geschichte des Denkens* (Basel: Lenos, 2004), 33–58.

47. VuD 563.

48. This must be understood to mean that *Insincerity* paves the way to evil on all levels of evil: through the disregard for what would be duty, through the false belief that one is doing good while following the inclination to "radical evil"; through deception about the extent to which not love but hatred has become the basic drive. So it is not *Ignorance*, as is repeatedly claimed, but *Untruthfulness* (as self-generated "ignorance") that is the source of evil.

49. ChT 35f.

50. For more on the position of Leibniz's *Theodicy* in the history of modern thought, see Anton Hügli, "Die Instrumentalisierung des Malum in der Philosophie der Neuzeit," in *Die Wirklichkeit des Bösen. Systematisch-theologische und philosophische Annäherungen*, ed. Friedrich Hermanni and Peter Koslowski (München: Wilhelm Fink, 1998), 159–183. For a conceptual-historical account see Anton Hügli, «Malum (Böses, Übel, Schlechtes)» Neuzeit, in *Historisches Wörterbuch der Philosophie*, ed. Joachim Ritter und Karlfried Gründer, vol. 5 (Basel: Schwabe, 1980), 611–706.

51. Leibniz, Gottfried Wilhelm, *Essais de Theodicee*, Philosophische Schriften, ed. C. I. Gerhardt (Hildesheim: Olms, 1961), § 119, 169ff.

52. See Odo Marquard, "Kompensation. Überlegungen zu einer Verlaufsfigur geschichtlicher Prozesse," in *Historische Prozesse* (Theorie der Geschichte U), ed. K. G. Faber and Ch. Meier (München: dtv, 1978), 330–362; "Kompensation," in *Historisches Wörterbuch der Philosophie*, ed. J. Ritter and K. Gründer, Vol. 4 (Basel; Stuttgart: Schwabe, 1976), 912–918.

53. Immanuel Kant, «Über das Misslingen aller philosophischen Versuche in der Theodicee,» in *Akademie Ausgabe*, ed. Königlich Preussische Akademie der Wissenschaften, vol. 8 (Berlin, 1912, reprint 1968), 253–272, 261f.

54. See Immanuel Kant, «Über das Misslingen aller philosophischen Versuche in der Theodicee» in *Akademie Ausgabe*, ed. Königlich Preussische Akademie der Wissenschaften, vol. 8 (Berlin, 1912, reprint 1968), 253–272, 264–267.

55. PGO 383.

56. But how do I know if I have made an eternal decision? If I make decisions knowing that the future temporal consequences of my actions are uncertain and that everything will fail in the end. This is why Job is so important to Jaspers. As a *Chiffer* for the fact that only in failure, only then, when I have nothing more to hope for, does the *Eternal* reveal itself to me.

57. GP 607.

58. GP 606.

59. Jaspers shows this impressively in his interpretation of evil in Shakespeare ("Das Unbedingte und das Böse," in *Das Wagnis der Freiheit. Gesammelte Aufsätze zur Philosophie*, ed. and with a preface by Hans Saner (München; Zürich: Piper, 1996), 86–98, 92–97).

60. «Das Unbedingte und das Böse," in *Das Wagnis der Freiheit. Gesammelte Aufsätze zur Philosophie*, ed. Hans Saner, 86–96 (München; Zürich: Piper, 1996), 86.

61. «Das Unbedingte und das Böse," in *Das Wagnis der Freiheit. Gesammelte Aufsätze zur Philosophie*, ed. Hans Saner, 86–96 (München; Zürich: Piper, 1996), 98.

62. See GP 546: "The transformation of all happiness into the supra-sensible, in that it becomes the material of the good will, and thus the permeation of happiness by eternity, brings us to the point where happiness is no longer just happiness. There is no longer the *Ultimate End*, but the *Final End*." "The *Final End* does not lie in the future, for, as supra-sensible, it is independent of temporal conditions—it is in the presence of good will. It is indeed conceived in the image of a future, but without that future having an objective reality." The *Ultimate End*, on the other hand, is happiness in the world. It is infinite and impossible.

63. He recalls, for example, the Stoics' and Spinoza's idea that "evil action carries punishment within itself." He then adds: "In the eternity of erased time, good as well as evil gains reward and punishment not afterwards, but through the action itself" (POG 371).

64. Plato, «Gorgias," in *Werke*, ed. Gunther Eigler, Bd. 2 (Darmstadt: WBG, 1990), 268–503, 482c-d.—Hannah Arendt, *Über das Böse. Eine Vorlesung zu Fragen der Ethik* (München; Zürich: Piper, 2006), 70.

65. Hannah Arendt, *Über das Böse. Eine Vorlesung zu Fragen der Ethik* (München; Zürich: Piper, 2006), 70.

66. Hannah Arendt, *Über das Böse. Eine Vorlesung zu Fragen der Ethik* (München; Zürich: Piper, 2006), 71.

67. Hannah Arendt, *Über das Böse. Eine Vorlesung zu Fragen der Ethik* (München; Zürich: Piper, 2006), 68f.

68. PGO 350.

69. The young Jaspers already mentions Job, but interprets him as one who falls into the "resignation of not comprehending" (PW 251).

70. PGO 370.

71. ChT 10.

72. For ex. PGO 29, 473; ChT 13, 112.

73. At the time of his greatest personal crisis, in the years 1937–1945, Jaspers abandoned this reticence and decided to make clear, at least to himself, which contents of *Faith* guided his personal life. The result is the five principles of *Philosophical Faith*, which he develops in the first part of his unpublished book *Grundsätze des Philosophierens*, and which he says are analogous to a creed. They are formulaic, abbreviated sentences that invite the reader to think for himself and can only ever be seen as moments in a movement of thought, aphoristic formulas, as we often find elsewhere in his work. (On the context of the creation of this work see: Bernd Weidmann in his Introduction to GPhil, Karl Jaspers Gesamtausgabe (Basel: Schwabe 2019), II/1, VII–LXXXV).

These five principles are: "God is," "There is an unconditional demand in Dasein," "Man is finite and unfinishable," "Man can live in the guidance of God," "The reality of the *World* has a vanishing being between God and *Existence*." Never before and never again did he go so far with a personal confession (see: Hans Saner, "Foreword to Karl Jaspers' Principles for Philosophizing," in *Philosophical Faith and the Future of Humanity,* ed. Helmut Wautischer, Alan M. Olson, and Gregory

J. Walters (Dordrecht: Springer, 2012), 9). At that time, his writing was intended only for a close circle of confidants, but in the end he also thought of an anonymous readership. He intended the book as a *Modern Protreptikos*, as an advertisement for philosophy, so to speak, in which a philosopher wants to testify to his credibility by presenting his philosophical attitude to life. For Jaspers, this should be done without any claim to imitation, but as a "hand extended to others, seeking communication" (GPhil 20). Under these conditions, despite his renewed reticence in later years, he included the Five Principles at least partially in his publications even in the first years after 1945, as in *Der Philosophische Glaube* (1947), Zweite Vorlesung, and again in his *Einführung in die Philosophie* (1953), chap. VIII.

74. PG 159.

75. PG 159.

76. PG 102.

77. PG 154f.

78. PG 160.

79. Cf. Jaspers's insistence on the reality of evil against all philosophical arguments that want to see in evil only a lack of goodness without any reality (POG 371–373).

# Chapter 11

# Democracy as Self-Education

## *The Will to Unconditional Communication in Politics*

### JASPERS AND PLATO ON PHILOSOPHY AND POLITICS

The political question par excellence is who or what governs us?[1] And how are we governed? It has been a fundamental question of philosophy at least since Plato and is the question of fate for all of us. Everything depends on whether we are governed with or against our will. A regime of terror can buy the consent of its subjects or try to force it by the use or threat of force. But how do we make possible a state based not on bought or coerced consent, but on free consent?

This question is first answered in Plato's *Politeia*, a work that has shaped the political history of ideas in Europe. For Plato, this question is linked to a crucial philosophical premise, the validity of which is difficult to dispute: A state is more than the rule of men over men. Whoever wants power in the state and over the people in the state must be able to say what that state and its institutions are supposed to be good for, and how what they do serves that good. The power of the ruler derives from the fact that those who are subject to him accept his power because he works for the good to which they all aspire.[2] Where this mutual agreement on the common good is lacking, the state becomes a tyranny, the rule of naked force, the power of bayonets and cannons.[3]

But who can tell us what the common good is that entitles those in power to rule over others? According to Plato's diagnosis, the political disaster that befell Athens and the polis states of his time was due to the fact that this question was neither asked nor answered. The search for an answer led him to his thesis, which provoked his contemporaries and still provokes us today, that there is no salvation for states and the people in them unless the philosophers, that is, those who have insight into the good, are kings or the kings are philosophers.

Jaspers was not provoked by this thesis. He agreed with Plato on the crucial point: philosophy and politics cannot be separated. Their way of thinking "comes from the same source"; they are not separate fields, but both take hold of "the whole human being." "Both take part, if they are serious, in the whole destiny of man."[4]

Just as philosophy "manifests itself in the practical life of the individual," so it "manifests itself in politics." Politics concerns only the basic interests of human beings, that which is common to all people, in which everyone can understand each other in order to give each other the space to develop in freedom through order, law, and contract. Politics wants freedom,[5] but political freedom is only a condition for inner freedom. But because the most elementary aspects of existence are at stake, it is all the more important which way of thinking is expressed in politics.

So what is a politics that is really *serious*? Jaspers already made it clear in his book *Die geistige Situation der Zeit (1931)* that politics as we have understood it up to now—securing the interests of power and "skill for the moment"[6]—cannot be the *Ultimate Goal.* True politics must be oriented toward the ultimate whole, and this ultimate whole cannot be the de facto state. At the decisive *Origin* man encounters "something that transcends state and education."[7] The longing for such an overarching authority grows in the confrontation with the Nazi state. What Jaspers seeks is an authority "above the peoples, a law that can legally help the individual who is raped without rights by his state."[8]

During the war years, he tried to define the philosophical principles that could constitute this authority: it is the *Idea* of a free *World Order* that stands above all the citizens of this world, both citizens and stateless people. The universal *World Order* is no longer characterized by violence but by mutual understanding. It wants eternal peace, as Kant outlined in his principles: peace not at any price, but peace based on freedom and justice.[9]

But how can this peace be achieved? It cannot be realized directly and not overnight, "but it can be promoted by *Spiritual Communication*, by placing all political actions, initially directed to immediate goals, more and more under the standard of this *Ultimate Goal*."[10]

## THE ATOMIC BOMB AND THE NEED TO CHANGE POLITICS

After the World War II, the question of peace became more urgent than ever. With the development and first use of the atomic bomb and the immeasurably increased threat potential of the hydrogen bomb, mankind is on the brink of the abyss. An unprecedented situation has arisen. "Up to now," Jasper concludes,

> man as an individual could take his own life. He could kill and be killed in battle. Peoples could be exterminated. Now, however, mankind as a whole can be destroyed by man. That this will happen is not only within the realm of possibility. From a purely rational point of view, it is probable that it will happen.[11]

> No longer a fictitious end of the world, no end of the world at all, but the killing of all life on the entire surface of the earth is the possible reality to be reckoned with from now on (. . .).[12]

The first thought might be: Fear of these consequences might deter any aggressor from resorting to the nuclear bomb. But this hope is illusory. Wars will continue, and the temptation to use nuclear weapons when one of the belligerents sees fit has not been eliminated. And even less is there any assurance that a new Hitler, in the face of his own downfall, would not be afraid to drag the whole world down with him.

It is therefore difficult to disagree with Jaspers's conclusion: the danger can only be averted in the long term if two demands are met: "First, the atomic bomb must be abolished. Second, a state of world peace must be established, based not on fear alone, but on law."[13]

The first step would only be possible through a binding contract, and the condition for such a contract is mutual control. This is the only way to ensure implementation. But even this step means more than the abolition of the atomic bomb; it required a fundamental transformation of the political world: from the state of mere coexistence between states facing each other like beasts in a state of nature to cooperation, to a community of states based on the law of treaties, the observance of which is ensured by common institutions.

This situation would only be possible if principles such as the following were generally recognized:[14]

1. Contracts are recognized as legally valid as long as they are not amended by new negotiations.
2. The states are guided by the overriding legal concept and renounce their absolute sovereignty.
3. There is worldwide publicity, permission for unrestricted communication, and free intellectual struggle in public.
4. The injustice that happens in one place is condemned all over the world.
5. Unjust political borders and treaties from the past can be revised.

However, the principles that are actually followed and considered inviolable are—to this day—the opposite of a peaceful *World Order*.[15] There is the absolute sovereignty of each state, hence the demand for mutual non-interference and the right of veto in jointly established bodies; there is the arbitrariness of unjust regimes and—despite the Internet—the restriction of communication and free public discussion. There are totalitarian states whose form of rule excludes any control, because it is based on secrecy, concealment, and "state control of all journalism."[16] What we have achieved so far on this path is only a respite. But the disaster remains. We are sitting on an active volcano.

The omnipresence of the nuclear threat has increased many times over since Jaspers wrote his book. This applies to nuclear weapons, which are now not only in the hands of two mutually threatening world powers but also in the arsenals of various states and in the grasp of unpredictable despots such as Kim Jong-un. This is no less true for the so-called peaceful use of nuclear energy, with its incalculable threat potential, about the extent of which the rhetorical talk of reactor and waste disposal safety can always deceive us. Of course, there are different degrees of destruction: the ultimate local destruction like that of Fukushima, the extinction of civilization in general, the destruction of mankind, and of life itself "through the summation of effects up to the life-destroying contamination of the Earth's atmosphere."[17] Nuclear destruction would still be many times greater than the destruction currently in the media spotlight: the catastrophic consequences of human-induced climate change. We have not thought through to the end the magnitude of the impending disaster if we do not see this last and extreme one.

But this is exactly where the disaster begins: not wanting to see the extreme. In our apocalyptic blindness, we do not see that we, as mankind, are "facing a *Borderline Situation* from which everything we are and can be would have to be put into a different basic state, as it were."[18] We are lulled into the belief that by continuing with the old politics, with the help of "intelligently conceived institutions," we can force every state and every individual

> not to make use of the basic human impulses: the urge to use violence—the desire for violence and its daring—the urge to sacrifice oneself in such violence, to die or to win—the urge for ever greater adventure in order to get rid of the staleness of existence.[19]

But this belief is illusory: it only creates "illusory structures" that serve individual states to strengthen their own positions of power and behind which "the preparation for the extreme takes place."[20] The war in Ukraine is a drastic example of this.

According to Jaspers, the first commandment, the commandment of *Sincerity* in politics, is to show the realities and to see the realities without illusions. And what is decisive here is not merely to take note of the facts—as knowledge that does not affect us—but to visualize them in full existential tension. Only when we look into the face of *Gorgo*, without avoiding it, can this gaze "produce both the seriousness and the knowledge necessary for decisions in the course of the world."[21] That is why it is important—through constant repetition, through constant reminding of the facts—to increase fear, the fear that translates into the power to transform oneself.[22] This is not scaremongering, which can only come from ignorance and is pointless. What is needed is not panic, but fear, fear transformed into active concern:[23] to prevent what seems inevitable, but can still be avoided.

Disaster only appears avoidable to us if we realize—and this is part of facing reality—that the impending catastrophe is not a natural event that strikes us like a tsunami or an asteroid hitting the earth, but a disaster that we have brought upon ourselves and that cannot be averted in any other way than by ourselves. To call it inevitable is to give up on ourselves, and it is to want to know more than we can know.[24] For this reason, it is wrong to be hopeless and to sink into passivity,[25] but it is also wrong to trust that everything will work out, that everything will fall into place, that we are on the best path to a secure future with the arrangements we have already made, or that, if all else fails, some god will come to our aid, a prophet or a leader who will save us.[26]

False trust can only perpetuate disaster, and any trust we place in others or in anything else is false: for example, expecting the solution from a particular department, a scientific, economic, or technical authority. The division of labor into departments may make sense when it comes to specific tasks within partial areas, to specialized knowledge and skills, but not when it comes to the whole of mankind. This whole belongs to everyone, and therefore each individual must answer for himself, beyond all departments. And the answer can only be a choice. Beginning with me and extending to the political sphere.[27] Not by abstaining from politics and fleeing the world without doing anything, nor by wanting to be politically involved at all costs, nor by indulging in pure indignation that insists on one's own independence and blamelessness.[28] But by transforming myself[29]—by facing the demands, by changing my life, by asking myself what I am doing to avert disaster and what I am doing to prevent the wrong politicians from coming to power.[30]

But whenever the individual makes a decision and tries to become aware of his decision, he moves into the space of philosophy—philosophy not as another scientific field, but as the space in which we all find ourselves when we are looking for an answer to the question that concerns us all equally: how we should live.[31] We as human beings, not as experts and technicians. Everything else depends on the answer to this question, including politics itself. It can therefore only be, as Jaspers calls it, a *supra-political* answer. It is precisely the answer that has always been taught and repeated, for example, by the prophets of the Old Testament, and that has now become unavoidable—as a necessary condition for the continued existence of mankind: no further life without a change in our attitude and way of thinking, our moral and political will. "I do not think I am exaggerating," writes Jaspers: "Those who continue to live as before have not understood what is threatening."[32]

## PHILOSOPHICAL CONVERSION AND CONVERSION IN POLITICS

The politics we need today—Jaspers calls it *True Politics*—must be guided by the political and moral *Idea* of a universal *World Order*. Only where the *Supra-Political* (*das Überpolitische*) becomes the "driving force" can the "intrinsic lawfulness" of the old, destructive politics be broken through.[33] The *Supra-Political* makes it possible to intervene and change the course of events.

Breaking through the inherent laws of the political (as well as of every other sphere) is only possible because this power, as Jaspers already emphasized in *Philosophie*[34] and in *Die geistige Situation der Zeit*, does not "come from the whole of this World" but has its origin in *Transcendence*. Whoever dares to make the "leap into another, existentially superior reality, which is completely dependent on factual appearance, but which nevertheless determines the course of things as the appearing reality at the decisive *Origins*," is seized by it.[35] This power intervenes in the world in the form of *Unconditional Faith*.[36]

The leap into this other, transcendent reality means a radical reversal. As we have already seen, *Conversion* is the key word not only for understanding the *Supra-Political* but also for Jaspers's entire philosophizing. Its significance should be recalled here.

Philosophizing begins with a reversal. To inquire beyond every horizon into what constitutes that which can never be reached, that which encompasses all horizons, up to the "*Encompassing* in which we are and which we ourselves are": this, and precisely this, is what constitutes philosophical thinking as the epitome of thinking that focuses on the *Whole*. It is based on reversal because the *Idea* of the *Encompassing* is a "thought that releases us from every particular being and forces us to turn back from every solidification."[37]

*Conversion*—as a philosophical movement—is therefore the tearing of oneself out of captivity in rational *Enclosures* (*Gehäuse*) and an upswing toward the *Transcendence* that stands beyond all *Being*; it is the change of perspective from the conditional to the *Unconditional*, from the rationality of the *Understanding* to the all-solid liquefying thinking of *Reason*—from the concealment of reality to the perception of what is. *Conversion*, now not just one of thinking, is the existential response to the *Borderline Situations* of man, which belong "to man as man." It is "the call of the great philosophies and religions,"[38] the call not to cling to the finite purposes of this world, but to gain "a foothold in the infinite."

The transformation of the *Consciousness of Being* goes hand in hand with an inner transformation. *Conversion*, understood as moral-political *Conversion*, is what Jaspers demands of every German in the situation after the collapse of the Nazi regime in view of the immeasurable guilt that Germans had brought upon themselves in the name of Germany,[39] and according to him, Conversion is also the only answer in view of the *Borderline Situation* created by the atomic bomb and the impending nuclear self-destruction of mankind. For it is not enough to find new institutions, "we must transform ourselves, our attitudes, our moral and political will." "What has long been present in the individual, effective in small circles, has now become the condition for the continued existence of mankind (. . .) Without *Conversion*, human life is lost."[40] However, the goal of *Conversion* is not to flee to another reality, but to make a new start from a different *Origin*, which allows us to "break through the political lawfulness inherent,"[41] to intervene in the course of events and give them a new direction.

The source of inspiration for Jaspers's description of philosophical and existential *Conversion* is unmistakably Plato,[42] or more precisely Plato's parables of the stepped way of knowledge and the corresponding stages of being.[43] From the wealth of ideas contained in these parables, Jaspers highlights three interpretations in particular as decisive for his account of Plato. They show how closely he himself follows Plato.[44]

First:

Man's cognition is tied to a *Conversion* (*metastrophe, periagoge*). It does not happen through an external gift, nor through the insertion of eyes (. . .). Rather, just as in the cave the turning of the eyes takes place only with the whole body, so knowledge must turn with the whole soul from the *Realm of Becoming* to the *Realm of Being*. *Education* (*paideia*) is therefore the art of bringing about such a reversal.[45]

Second:

Cognition follows a stepped path. From the empirically perceived, it goes to pure thought (in mathematics)—from pure thought to the *Idea* (from mathematical cognition to dialectical science)—from the *Idea* to the *Beyond of Being* (from *Ideas* to the one *Idea* of the *Good*).

Depending on the aspect, the stages are stages of cognition, stages of human self-behavior in its entire state, stages of being. (. . .) Dwelling on the earlier stages, we have a tendency to speak here as if the higher ones were not there. But talking about them can only be true through the guidance of the higher ones. If there is no guidance (. . .) we remain in perplexity and defiance because we lack the inner relationship to the content of what everything must lead to if there is to be truth.[46]

Third:

Two directions open up for the behavior of the thinking soul: out of the world of appearances into the eternal World (. . .), and then out of the eternal World again to see, understand, and form the world of appearances (. . ..)." The "ascent of thought" is followed by "re-entry into this world: the turning away from the world leads to the turning back," "the turning away from the life of the polis to the eternal realms obliges the return to the life of the state."

Plato's philosophizing, then, unlike that of Plotinus, "does not lead to leaving the world," but rather "takes up the task in the world." But he can fulfill this task only because he is at home in that *Supra-Heavenly Place* from which standards and guidance come.[47]

The *Supra-Heavenly Place* from which standards and guidance come: a poetic paraphrase for what Jaspers calls the *Supra-Political*. But what are the standards for the "guidance" of political action that Jaspers hopes to gain from the *Supra-Political*? His answer is the one we already know: that there are no new insights, no doctrines, no state designs, and no instructions for action. What the turn to philosophical thinking alone can achieve is the *Transformation of Man*, "the recognition, practice, and consolidation of an inner philosophical attitude from which our power of judgment in concrete situations arises, not as a calculable consequence, but as the proof of a *Possible Existence* that has become certain."[48] This is, in a word, nothing less than the *Supra-Political Ethos* to be attained through *Conversion*.

The *Supra-Political Ethos* includes taking responsibility for even the smallest things, doing what is possible here and now—in the unshakable belief that it is up to me and me alone how the world goes on. It is expressed in a willingness to make *Sacrifices*: a willingness to renounce, to abstain, to take risks—in order to bring us back from the forlornness of a life absorbed in consumerism without content.[49]

The *Supra-Political Ethos* is more than a morality "exhausted in do's and don'ts." Morality is also unconditional, cannot be skipped, insofar as it is that which is expressed as a form in Kant's *Categorical Imperative*. But how it is concretely fulfilled by the material of the temporal situation cannot be calculated. The form of the *Unconditional* does not have the content as a deducible consequence.[50]

This is why the *Supra-Political Ethos* needs the *reflecting* power of judgment, and the thinking of *Reason* that goes beyond the rationality of

*Understanding*—to give us clarity about what is to be done here and now—not only because it is right but also because it is important.

The *Correct* is the rational, the plannable, the scientifically recognizable, but the *Important* has to do with the "hierarchy of things," with greatness and nothingness, with depth and shallowness, with value and worthlessness, with the essential and the non-essential. We gain this "power of hearing for the essential and for the order of things" only through *Reason*, not through the calculating *Understanding*. *Reason* teaches us to be modest and to seize what is possible, and keeps us in the tension of not missing what is given to us as an opportunity. This succeeds when the *Reason* of everyday life is first the preparation and then the realization of the great decisions that decide between salvation and disaster.[51]

As a temporal phenomenon of eternal *Origin*, the *Supra-Political* is in polar tension: it is the *Supra-Historical,* but it can only show itself in the historical; it is the *Ethics of Conviction,* which can still have meaning even in failure, and at the same time the *Ethics of Responsibility* through the will to work in the world.[52]

The *Supra-Political* is always present where "foundation and continuation, continuity of effect" are concerned, and where "political institutions, legislation, planning [. . .] are permanently effective," but it is neither plannable nor feasible, and it knows no organization and no objective authority in the world. It arises solely from the freedom that lies within the individual. These "self-seeking" individuals form the *Community of the Reasonables*, which grows out of small circles and, like the *Invisible Church*, runs through all social groups.[53] The individual proves that he belongs to this community simply by wanting to work for it.[54] But what is needed is a clear idea of what *Being Reasonable* actually means. Let us recall the main features of *Reason* as outlined in chapter 6.

## REASON, CONVERSION, AND THE SUPER-POLITICAL

*Reason*, as we have learned, is the thinking that begins where all scientific knowledge and all "planning" and "doing" oriented toward the interests of *Dasein* and predetermined purposes ends, in short, where there is nothing more to know in the sense of *Understanding*. *Reason's* thinking is driven by the question of the meaning and purpose of my life itself, what I can believe in, what I can hope for, and where I stand within the *Whole* that encompasses the *World* and myself. Because *Reason* is concerned with the *Whole*, it seeks unity in everything.

It does not want to grasp any unity, but to seek the true and only unity. In every premature and partial grasping of unity, if it is to be the final and absolute one, it knows itself to be lost. For it wants the *One* that is all. Therefore, it must omit nothing that is, drop nothing, exclude nothing. Like itself, it is boundless openness.[55]

The search for unity has one condition: The seeker must become *One* himself. Jaspers recalls the "unforgettable sentences" of Plato and Kant: that man is only himself when he is at one with himself, when he does not contradict himself, and that the greatest disaster for him is "that he falls apart into himself, meaning this and that at the same time, and being, without reference to each other, in the whirl of chance."[56] To attain selfhood through *Reason* and *Reason* through selfhood: this double requirement may best explain why, for Jaspers philosophical *Conversion* is always also a moral *Conversion*, and moral *Conversion* a philosophical one.[57]

*Reason* must go beyond *Understanding* without losing *Understanding*, according to Jaspers' short formula for the relationship between *Understanding* and *Reason*. He describes what this means in concrete terms as follows: *Reason* is able to refrain from everything; it can—with the help of *Understanding*—penetrate to the most abstract, to the question of why there is something and not nothing at all—a mental game, it seems, which, however, by leading to the groundlessness "makes us aware of the presence of *Being* as that which is incomprehensible to us, impenetrable, which already exists before all our thinking and approaches us."[58]

With this thought as a guide, we can swing out "from all finite bondage to where we come from, to that which is still before all the *World*." But this most abstract of all thoughts has a transforming power: leaving everything behind and relating to this *One*, we become aware for the first time of what is historically unique in the appearance of this world, and it allows "everything that is to be there again in a new, wondrously transparent way, speaking as never before."[59]

It does not have to be the most abstract thought. The work of *Reason* always begins with abstractions. The listed principles of a *World Peace Order* are examples of such abstractions. Abstraction is the indispensable means of pure *Understanding*, which *Reason* must use: no clarity without abstraction, without thinking in distinction and contrast. But abstract thinking, according to Jaspers's argument, becomes untrue if it does not return to reality and if it does not become concrete, fulfilled, vivid, and meaningful thinking. The disastrous consequences of abstraction detached from reality can be seen everywhere, including in the departmental thinking of politics: with its insistence on "responsibilities," it leads to the absolutizing of one's own limited actions, it grows like a tumor in the living body to the detriment of the "spirit of the *Whole*."[60]

The double movement toward the abstract and back to reality illustrates the double movement of every *Conversion*, the movement of ascent and descent. This double movement is the "basic constitution" of *Reason*:

> Through *Reason* alone we gain distance from ourselves and from things, but in such a way that we live in them with passion as ourselves (instead of standing before them skeptically or with disgust or unaffected). *Reason* prevents us from getting caught up in limitations that falsely become the *Whole*, in finite things that falsely become *Absolutes* (. . .). It teaches us to be modest and to seize what is possible, and it keeps us in the tension of not missing what is given to us as an opportunity.[61]

Statements like these make it clear why, for Jaspers, *Reason* and power of judgment are inseparable: the ascent to reason must go hand in hand with the awareness of "the one concrete, historical time" and the judgment of what must be done in the here and now, so that "no moment is lost, no opportunity is missed."[62]

This places him in opposition to Plato: Plato—still ignorant of biblical religion and its radical idea of the creation of the *World* out of nothing—"knows nothing of historicity. He does not know of the one history in which irrevocable, eternal decisions are made, but he is at peace with infinite time, in which divine providence will one day bring about what is failing today."[63] Thinking non-historically, he tries to draft "laws for an unchangeable state"; thinking non-historically, he can therefore so easily "abandon the present task of concrete political reality (. . .) in favor of a withdrawal of the philosopher from the hopeless world."[64]

## THE DECISION FOR DEMOCRACY AND AGAINST TOTALITARIANISM

The main difference between Jaspers and Plato is triggered by a fundamental question: to whom is the way of *Reason* open in the first place? For Plato, it is "a few selected people, proven and matured by decades of education," who should therefore also be the rulers, while the rest of the population remains excluded from this path and therefore also from government. "They must obey and be governed." "Plato," according to Jaspers's criticism,

> forgets: all men always remain men. The men who govern are men again. Plato presupposes men who are like gods or who have become gods. Since men are always ruled by men, and all men without exception, if they have power, can

> also abuse it, we must develop everything that leads to a common will among men: Talk to each other, not just listen and obey. Always entrust government to the elected only for a limited time; keep everyone, without exception, under mutual control.[65]

But we—and by "we" Jaspers means not only the Federal Republic of Germany but also the entire free world—have chosen a different path: We "have trusted in the possibility of forming, with the peoples, states that are called democratic. With Plato, only dictatorship is possible; with us, political freedom." The model for us "is the political thought of Kant and the thought and action of the recognized founders (among the Anglo-Saxons, the Swiss, the Dutch)."[66]

The crossroads with which Jaspers is concerned is—in relation to today—the fundamental choice between *Democracy* and *Totalitarianism.*

Jaspers lists as the ideal-typical characteristics of a *Totalitarian System:*[67] An elitist party that pretends to be identical with the people and declares any opposition to be directed against the people, as treason against the state, and persecutes it with all means; a state leadership that has the power of disposal over all means of production, instrumentalizes the legal system, and subjects it to the arbitrariness of the ruling elite; the invocation of the "true doctrine," which is constantly defended by the ruling elite against dissenters and revisionists, but also reinterpreted as needed, and which serves the leadership to justify its monopoly on education, censorship, and pervasive propaganda. The truly devastating aspect of *Totalitarianism* is this last point: where the truth is suppressed and distorted, and the radical lie becomes the principle. Here is the limit where lies and truth are indistinguishable, where speaking itself becomes deception, where it is only a matter of how to obfuscate and deceive others, with the result that everyone ends up obfuscating themselves. The bond that unites people, the common search for truth, is torn apart.[68] But without truth, according to Jaspers's programmatic sentence in his speech accepting the Peace Prize of the German Book Trade in 1959, there is no freedom, and without freedom, there is no peace.[69]

Our "salvation" can only lie in the realization of the principle radically opposed to *Totalitarianism*: the principle of *Democracy*. Jaspers is not thinking here of institutional questions, not of a specific form of government, but of the form of government which Kant called the *Republican type of Government* and which he contrasted radically with the *Despotic Type*.[70] Its essential features are: it protects freedom and makes freedom possible. It protects freedom in the negative sense, by allowing the individual only so much freedom as can coexist with the freedom of others, and no one who obeys the laws need to fear the violence of others or the violence of the state. It grants freedom in the positive sense by giving everyone the same right to participate in the common decision-making process and the opportunity to exercise their will and insight. The protection of freedom is guaranteed by the rule of law, while participation is the hallmark of *Democracy*. The right to participate is realized through voting and elections. Decisions are made on the basis of prior public and unrestricted discussion, in short, by talking to each other. There is not just one worldview and one party but also a multitude of opinions and parties. Therefore, there is a strict separation between politics and ideology. This prevents violence and allows for the intellectual struggle of opinions.[71]

But *Democracy* is never finished. There will never be "a final, universally satisfactory state of democratic political liberty."[72] The *Republican Type of Government* is an *Idea*, a regulative principle, as Kant would say, which we are called to realize, but which we can only ever realize gradually and never completely. But what is really decisive is that, as a counter-principle to *Totalitarianism*, it pursues the opposite goal: it does not want deception, but knowledge; not useful lie, but truth, even if it is uncomfortable and painful. Its first battle is therefore against lies in all their forms. It wants to know what justice means and how justice operates in society, because it wants justice to be real and not just the appearance of it.[73] The *Unconditional* and comprehensive will to know and to understand must therefore be the highest goal of the *Democratic* state.

But who tells us what is true and what is important? There is no one who already knows, and that is why we must all go on a search together. Jaspers' conclusion to Plato's provocative thesis is, therefore: "Plato is right: without the combination of politics and philosophy among the rulers there is no salvation; but, we add, this combination must also embrace the people, so that it (. . .) becomes a people of philosophers."[74]

However, as Jaspers admits, this demand only becomes understandable if philosophy is not understood in the sense of a specialized discipline "practiced by professors of philosophy at the universities"—this "school philosophy" is a mere "hobby" of specialists who write only for specialists. Rather, what is meant is philosophizing, which is the concern of every human being, because everyone philosophizes "without being aware of it, without calling it philosophy."[75] What is required is that we do better what we have always done: "Let us learn to philosophize better. Then we will become better human beings and better politicians at the same time."[76]

What does this philosophizing consist of? Jaspers's answer sounds modest. It means nothing more than becoming more insightful, more serious—more *Reasonable*:[77] "*Reason* must penetrate the people if it is to be effective and lasting. That is why *Democracy* is inevitable. Its purpose is the elaboration of *Reason* in the common thought and action of a people and of peoples among themselves."[78] The elaboration of *Reason* means—as one can probably interpret it—to find out together what is to be considered true and what is to be made true by giving reasons and counter-reasons and by opening up the widest possible horizon. And to know what we are doing when we are doing it this way. But (for us finite beings) this process will never be completed. The thinking of *Reason* is always in motion, it demands criticism of every position once reached, and it fights against the natural "tendency to free oneself from further thinking by definitively fixed thoughts."[79]

The will to self-criticism pushes *Reason* toward the other, the foreign, the unknown, in order to give it a language and allow it to come into its own; nothing should remain unexamined, nothing should be excluded from the outset. *Reason*, then, goes hand in hand with an "unlimited will to communicate"[80] that seeks to understand and appropriate everything that has already been thought and said. For *Truth*—understood here not as a specific content, but as the struggle for *Truth*[81]—is bound to communication, but not to communication in the sense of a "one-sided proclamation. I do not bring the truth, but I seek the truth with the person I meet, listening, questioning, trying."[82]

## STATE PEDAGOGY: ABOUT DEMOCRACY AND SELF-EDUCATION

The great question remains: How does *Reason* reach the people? There can be only one answer to this question, and not only for Jaspers: through *Education. Education* is the key question of every political regime. For every regime, even the most *Totalitarian*, depends on consent. Rulers gain consent only if those they rule believe that it is good for them to be ruled in this way. Generating this belief must therefore be a fundamental concern of every state. In order to achieve this, the state itself must become pedagogically effective: through an appropriate *State Pedagogy*, that is, a form of *Education* run by the state, promoted by it, or at least permitted by it.

The basic question of any *State Pedagogy*, regardless of its form, is: Who educates the educators? For a *Totalitarian Regime*, the answer is clear: the true educators are the rulers themselves, or those they appoint as educators. Since the rulers believe that they already know what is true, the only thing that can be done in this system of education is to make everyone—even those who do not want to believe—believe that what the rulers think is good is good. Whatever serves to reinforce this belief is welcome: fairy tales, lies, propaganda, indoctrination, even brainwashing if necessary. In any case, the goal is to close the mind and silence questions. A historical example—the Jesuit church education in absolutist France. As a black utopia: George Orwell's *1984*, as a dark reality: *State Education* under Hitler, Stalin, and Putin, a regime of mullahs as in today's Iran.

The *Democratic State* seems to have a hard time with the question of who educates the educators: Since no one has the truth and no one can be considered educated, there is no one to educate the educators. But the *Democratic State* makes a virtue of this necessity: since there is no one to educate the educators, there is only one thing left for its citizens to do—they must educate themselves, all of them together. *Self-education* becomes the key term for Jaspers when he speaks of *Democratic Education*, but for him *Self-education* is also the epitome of all democratic politics. It not only presupposes *Self-education*, it is in itself a *Self-education to Reason.*[83]

*Self-education* is not a new term. Jaspers borrowed it from the reform pedagogy of the 1930s and the postwar period. At that time, it replaced the concept of *Self-formation* (*Selbst-Bildung*), which had been used since Humboldt at the latest to capture the *Idea* central to the neo-humanist concept of *Education:* that ultimately all *Education*—since the purpose of man is in himself—must lead the individual to "educate himself."[84] The reference of *Self-education* to a republican understanding of *State Education* is not new either. Even in the liberalism of the early nineteenth century, the state was supposed to protect the "freedom of *Self-education.*"[85] What goes further, however, is the consistency with which Jaspers does not limit *Self-education* to compulsory school, but extends it to all ages and equates it with the politics of the *Democratic State.*

For Jaspers, it is obvious that *Self-education* per se can never be completed, *and Self-education* in a *Democracy* cannot end, because *Democracy* is a form of politics that has never been realized and is constantly threatened anew. It would therefore be fatal to assume that the sovereign of the people is "wise, good, or even divine." It must first become *Reasonable.* It is only on the way. Only if the perversions of *Democracy* are constantly fought against and overcome by the individuals themselves can *Democracy* exist, that is, as the fundamental process of freedom in which it first becomes. "Where this freedom does not really assume the responsibility that belongs to it in the individual, *Democracy* must perish."[86]

## THE PRECONDITIONS FOR DEMOCRATIC SELF-EDUCATION

Jaspers highlights the need for *Democratic Self-education.* It begins with the claim that the individual makes on himself. For Democracy is "first and foremost not the claim that people make on the state, but the claim that each person makes on himself, the fulfillment of which enables him to participate in *Democracy.*"[87] No less daring is the second premise, that everyone is in principle capable of *Self-education*—if only they want to—and that differences in talent between people should play no role in this. Giftedness is relevant when it comes to the development of specific abilities, although we must always be careful not to see talent as something to be taken for granted.[88] Moreover, "One must not confuse training for the purpose of technical ability with awakening to the *True Human Being*. Both are necessary, but in such a way that purposeful training remains or returns under the guidance of the human being."[89]

*Self-education* aims at the latter. It refers to the way we lead ourselves and is therefore an *education in Reason*. Questions of *Reason*, however, are not questions of what is rationally right, but of what is intrinsically important; they refer to what concerns us all, what is common to us all, and "what everyone should and could understand."[90] Jaspers's hope that a nation could become a "nation of philosophers" is based on this premise.

To accept such assumptions requires an *Unconditional Faith* in human beings. This *Faith* can never be proven, neither by empirical evidence nor by history. But Jaspers is not concerned with proof, but with "the question of what we want in politics and what we set as our goal." And for him, it is clear: "Basic trust in man, in the people" is the "condition of a meaningful life." For what would be the alternative? "Mistrust, taken to the extreme, means that human existence is an episode, a process of self-destruction that may soon come to an end." However, the trust in man that Jaspers demands is not optimistically naive: it does not refer to man as he is, but to "what he can become."[91] And no one, not even the individual himself, knows in advance what he can become.[92]

There is only one way to know what one can become—by trying.[93] *Democracy* must dare. For Jaspers, this is the only possible answer to the "inextricable knot" of *Democracy*, namely that *Democracy* must always presuppose *Reason* in the people, "which it is supposed to produce."[94] This "inextricable knot" of *Democracy* is one of the antinomies of our *Dasein* that we must endure and that we can only face in one way: By continuing to believe in *Reason*, even when all seems hopeless, and by helping to bring *Reason* into the world.

## THE ROLE OF THE STATESMAN AND THE ROLE OF THE PHILOSOPHER

How does Jaspers's quasi-grassroots democratic understanding of a common *Self-education* of all relate to his apology of political leadership, which he maintained from *The Spiritual Situation of the Time* of 1931 to his last political writings?[95] This may only appear to be a contradiction if one ignores the distinction, important for Jaspers, between two fundamentally different kinds of *Equality*: Equality before the law and Equality of opportunity, which are indispensable for any *Democracy*, on the one hand, and the never possible "equality of natural endowments, the power of personal *Existence*," "ethical reliability," and "the moral quality of judgment and *Reason*," on the other.[96]

*Equality* in the first sense requires that everyone be granted the same right to political participation and co-determination, combined with the right to think and judge for himself or herself. *Equality* in the second sense, on the other hand, is the *Equality* that can never be expected in regard to the willingness and ability of individuals to comply with this demand and to exercise their power of judgment. These factual inequalities give rise to the unmistakable differences in rank that exist between human beings. Although no one has the right to claim such a difference in rank in relation to others, sincerity requires us to recognize these differences where they exist. Not in order to submit to those of higher rank and place our destiny in their hands, but, as Jaspers puts it, to experience through them what we ourselves want, to become "stronger" in the "love of the greater" that speaks from them, in "the love of the better" in ourselves.[97] The selection of the "best in all areas of life" must therefore be the main concern of a *Democracy*.[98]

The best should show us what is important to us. The main responsibility of elected leaders, on the other hand, is to win the consent and "participation" of the people. "If they want a policy of freedom, they must inform the people as much as possible, make them think along with them, justify their goals to them, show them ways and means, and thus educate them."[99] The greatest statesmen are therefore always the greatest educators of their people.

But is this not personality worship or, worse still, *human idolatry* by the back door, far beyond ordinary *Self-education*?

Against this objection speaks not only Jaspers's admonition not to see in great men more than people like us[100] but also—and this is decisive—his fundamental conviction: The person who thinks that he can determine himself directly out of himself is deceived; he confuses freedom with arbitrariness, with caprice, with random decisions. What man lives from and what guides him is always more encompassing than anything he can recognize and justify himself. It approaches him from the outside, as a power that at the same time grasps and carries him from within.

What speaks from the individual—and in a great way from the great man—is always more than himself, it is the overarching powers of *Faith* in whose service he stands. What draws us to the other—or repels us from him—is the commonality or the difference of these powers that determine us.[101] The *Supra-Political Ethos*, the *Idea of Democracy*, or the *Idea of the University* may serve as examples of such overarching Spiritual wholes that determine our lives and thoughts. Where these find inner approval, they become what Jaspers calls *Authority*.[102] Without reverence for *Authority*, according to his pedagogical credo, "no *Education* is possible"; it is the "substance of all *Education*." Reverence therefore prevails in each of the three ideal forms of *Education*: reverence for tradition in *Scholastic Education*, reverence for the personality of the teacher in *Master Education*, and reverence for the *Idea of the infinite Spirit* in *Socratic Education*.[103]

*Socratic Education* and its form of reverence is not only the one appropriate to the *Idea of the University* but also the universalized model of *Democratic Self-education*. For only it can be the answer to the "fateful question" of the "politically free world" at a time when all previous, unquestioningly accepted authorities have collapsed: How can an *Authority* become effective in this world that "contains within itself freedom" and establishes a new "community of *Faith* in the possibility of a *Human Order of Dasein*"?[104] The only power that fulfills this condition is *Democracy*, "which educates to the freedom and responsibility of all."[105]

The *Substantial Whole* on which all *Education* must be based is therefore today none other than the *Supra-Political Ethos* of sincerity and truth that corresponds to the *Idea of Democracy*.

The greatness of a statesman lies in the fact that he is the purest expression of the will to truth, and thus becomes the "exponent of a greater spirit and will."[106] Because he is dedicated to freedom, he invites criticism and explains his motives openly. There must be no blind, misplaced trust. Therefore, criticism must meet criticism: "It reaches its zenith in free discussion, which is still critical of itself, and which strives in public purely for truth."[107] The *Reasonable Statesman* will never want to be the only voice. He knows:

> Personalities must appear in whom the people recognize themselves, who tell them what is and what is desirable and what should be done. And several people say this, in different ways, for the consideration of the people. In this way, each individual among the people, spiritually alive, should learn to ask questions and think politically. They should become aware of the situation in their own area and on a large scale, and realize what they want.[108]

To conclude, the answer to this objection is that the recognition of ranks and greatness obviously has little to do with the cult of personality.

What about the voice of the philosophers, or, more precisely, of the "professors of philosophy who make philosophy a teachable profession"?[109] In their role, not as Platonic rulers—for only the renunciation of power guarantees their independence—but as advisors in the Kantian sense, they must speak out, just like journalists and political writers. But they have a special significance: as "true philosophers" they were always denied what is generally denied to us today: to live unquestioningly within an authority. The only way left to them, therefore, was that which is expected of everyone today:

instead of wanting to possess the truth and proclaim truths, to take the path of *Reason* and to examine what we can take to be true.[110] According to Jaspers, therefore, the special task of all those who have made the teaching of philosophy their profession is to encourage others to use *reason* and to support them on this way, a task which he himself took on with verve in the last years of his life, even at the risk of "losing his head and neck."

The purpose of this task is "to transmit the thoughts of the great philosophers, not to allow the manifestations of their personalities to be forgotten, to take young people there so that they can see what was there and what happened." To the extent that such teaching is successful, philosophers must ensure that it "takes a simple form and reaches a broad section of the population." For, as Jaspers hopes, "such teaching can bring greater clarity to the philosophizing that comes to man as man and is always already there in him."[111]

Clarity is especially needed in political-philosophical thought. The purpose of political-philosophical thought, from the Greeks to the present day, is none other than "to preserve this thought in its multiplicity, in its contradictions, in its constant struggle. Disorder and anarchy of thought must be dared so that order and unity can be restored in their original form." But this must be done "in truthfulness, not in the compulsion to cultivate a technique of thought with dogmatically fixed content." Only the "vitality of unrestricted free thought (. . .) makes possible the language in which the statesman can say what he wants and in which the peoples, becoming transformed by such thinking, can understand what they themselves want."[112]

## EDUCATION FOR SELF-EDUCATION

However, it is not enough to say that "all great politics (. . .) in the community is a *Self-education to Reason*"[113] and can be effective in each individual. The process of *Self-education* must be made permanent. For this to succeed, as Jaspers emphasizes, there is nothing more important in a *Democracy* than the *Education* of future generations. "*Democracy*, freedom and *Reason* depend on this *Education*. Only through this *Education* can the historical content of our existence be preserved and our life be fulfilled as a generative force in the new world situation."[114]

But how should this *Self-education* take place? In the world of the state, *Self-education* becomes concrete only when institutions are created that serve this purpose. And if we are looking for such an institution, we do not have to go very far. It is the one Plato invented: the *Academy*, or, in its present form, the *University*. Probably not the actual *University*, but the *Idea* of what a *University* should be (and which in modern times was conceptualized by Humboldt, following in the footsteps of Friedrich Schleiermacher and philosophers of idealism such as Johann Gottlieb Fichte and Friedrich Wilhelm Schelling).

The *Idea of the University* can serve as an illustration of *Self-education* in its purest form.[115] If we follow it, we can see once again how deeply Jaspers's thinking is rooted in the Socratic tradition. The *University* has a single, overarching goal: knowledge, comprehensive knowledge. Its mission is to explore and investigate all that there is to explore and investigate. Such an unconditional and comprehensive will for knowledge requires one condition: *Freedom*. There must be no restrictions about what is to be explored and for what purpose it is to be explored, no biased guidelines, no ideological reservations.

The principle is: everything that can be studied and investigated must be studied and investigated, and politics has no place here except as the object of investigation itself. There are no expectations as to what the result should be, no rules about what should be considered or proclaimed to be true in every case, but only this one thing: that what one says can actually be considered true. But when can something be considered to be true (and not just an opinion)? The only test is that, as we already know, as long as no one can convincingly prove that what is said to be true is false. Anyone who wants to know whether what he claims to be true is true must therefore do everything in his power to make his claims known, that is, to make them public, so that all those who are concerned with the truth have the opportunity to object.[116]

This is the concrete form of *Self-education* of which we have just spoken and was first historically exemplified by Plato in his Socratic *Dialogues*. The search for dialogue is therefore the be-all and end-all of a *University* dedicated to knowledge.

But the dialogue is not only with the current generation but also with the next generation, because that generation needs to be empowered to continue the discussion. It will be up to the next generation to sit in judgment and decide whether what we say today will still be valid tomorrow. This is the basic idea behind the concept of unity of research and teaching. Teaching is part of the dialogue that every researcher must have with the next generation. For students and junior faculty, teaching is a form of practice in this dialogue. Humboldt described this relationship between professor and student with a memorable formula: "The professor is not there for the student, but the student is there for the professor, and both are there not for themselves, but for science."[117]

The *Idea* that Humboldt pursues here is part of a long tradition. It is the old *Idea* of *Liberal Education*, which in turn was inspired by the Socratic *Idea* that only an examined life is a life worth living. Examined means a life that allows me to free myself—from the shackles of habit, traditional opinion, and prejudice. The studies that serve this purpose are called by the Romans *studia liberalia*, and in the Anglo-Saxon world, *Liberal Education*.[118]

What distinguishes it is its contribution to life, or more precisely, to a way of life that deserves to be called *human*. This is the deeper reason why liberal education is also called *humanistic*. Its principle of permanent self-examination and self-criticism, however, is none other than the basic principle of the "republican way of thinking" that Jaspers, following Kant, called for, and to which there is still no alternative that we can wish for.[119]

But the price we pay for this way of life is high. It requires that we dare to stand up for ourselves and resist the comforting feeling of being confined to the narrow circle of our own group. That we think against ourselves and, if necessary, against the opinion of others, always ready to break new ground. Humboldt once again used the memorable phrase *Freedom and Solitude* as the fundamental principle of the *University*.[120] The examined life is not only the way of life of the *University* but also, more generally, that of the *Democratic* or *Socratic State*.

But what exactly defines this form of life? The answer seems simple. It is a life driven by the unconditional will to know for its own sake. This unconditional will is initially negative: in conscious distance from the opposite natural tendency to subordinate the will to know to the purposes of life and survival, and above all, to the social or economic benefits that new technologies might bring. Humboldt's concept of science owes much to the polemic against the utilitarian thinking that dominated the Enlightenment and did not accept any knowledge that was not directly useful for life and usable for social needs.

The polemic of Humboldt and the idealist philosophers allied with him is therefore vehemently directed against the type of scholar that Friedrich Schiller, in his famous inaugural lecture of 1789, contemptuously apostrophized as *Bread Scholars*. The *Bread Scholar's* clientele are the *Bread-and-Butter Students*, as the philologist August E. Wolf put it, who know no higher goal than the "ordinary exam" and getting into some kind of office as quickly as possible.[121]

The antithesis of the *Bread Scholar* is what Schiller called the *Philosophical Head*, the scholar who lives for science,[122] and who, as Schelling makes clear, understands science *inwardly*, in order to reproduce it in its context and to grasp it sharply and correctly in all its relations, to judge it according to principles, and to put it together independently.[123] Schiller's *Philosophical Head* is—without doubt—that of the philosophy of German idealism, and in this respect, he is a very time-bound figure. But it can certainly be transformed. There are three moments in particular that can be emphasized as characteristics of such a *Philosophical Head* dedicated to science: The awareness

(1) that only a disciplined, methodically regulated process can move us forward in our searching and testing;
(2) that there must be an inner connection between all knowledge;
(3) that there can be no knowledge without reflection on what one is doing, without reflection on why it can be considered knowledge in the first place, and what it should be used for.

These three moments—methodological awareness, the pursuit of unity, and reflection—are still philosophical in the medium of scientific thought and define the attitude of the scientist.

None of these moments can be dispensed with, but the first moment rightly comes first: the question of method.[124] Anyone committed to science will accept that only a methodical approach allows us to answer our questions. Controllable answers that can be seen and repeated by everyone. This is the only way to ensure that everyone can understand what has been found in the same way as if they had found it themselves.

But there is no awareness of methods without the awareness that every investigation is always linked to preconditions and can only be carried out on the basis of them. These basic conditions of every science are:[125]

(1) the rules of logic; it would be impossible to recognize if one were to deny the theorem of contradiction;
(2) that science should exist at all, and that science has its value, even if it cannot prove this value;
(3) that the object being studied is actually worth studying.

These presuppositions, which precede all science and cannot be gained by any science, make clear what science cannot do. It cannot explain the meaning of its actions, it cannot explain why it should be the case, and it cannot tell us why we do not want deception and prefer clarity to concealment.

This shows that science is always rooted in something else that transcends it and constitutes the truly philosophical in all sciences. The philosophical is concerned with the question of the first conditions of our thinking and acting in general, according to which we can understand the whole in which we stand and the ultimate end of our actions.

## SCHOOLING FOR SELF-EDUCATION

Jaspers' references to the possibilities and limits of pedagogical action are significant in relation to *School Education*.[126] First of all, these are the limits of all *Education*. Like *Caring*, *Education* is a kind of action that lies between free communication and technical making: "the other is still treated as an object, but at the same time recognized in its own being."[127] One waits "for an *Originality* in the other (. . .); goals and methods are developed towards the educated person, listening and being guided by him, without him knowing it." Therein lies the "limit of this action": "The autonomy of the other remains the condition of the purposeful setting of goals on the part of those who nurture or educate."[128] A "new revelation of the autonomy of his object" can lead him to change not only his method but also his goal. The outcome of his actions is therefore always uncertain, and the least certain is "man, who, as a historical being, changes with every experience he makes and of which he becomes aware, and therefore does not become a fixed object; it is in his nature that his knowledge changes him in an unpredictable way."[129]

In the final perspective of *Self-education*, everything depends on what the other person makes of himself in freedom and how the "spirituality of *Ideas*" affects his situation.[130] The only thing that remains here is the always new undertaking "in continuous, constantly renewing and changing contact" with the other person.[131] This makes *Education for Self-education* completely unpredictable, contrary to the taken-for-granted assumptions of pedagogy, which thinks in a "one-line causal connection"—"as if the educator already knew what the right education is, what its content is and how it should be planned."[132] Teachers, too—and this is the above-mentioned plight of *Democracy*—cannot be regarded as already educated; they too must undergo the "self-education process of all."

> The assumption that the teacher is educated and passes on his knowledge to the uneducated children is, on the whole, as absurd as the assumption that the adult population is educated and therefore correctly judges all things. Only those who are still being educated by means of communication can be educated. Only those who are trained for *Self-education* in the medium of strict and persevering learning are correctly educated."[133]

This "circle of educating and being educated" does not become more fruitful by constantly coming up with new reforms and methods—in an intensified "educational enterprise." It only becomes fruitful—according to Jaspers's basic conviction—"if it is filled with the content of *Faith*, knowledge and ability." The "content of *Faith*" is the comprehensive belief in man and *Reason* outlined above, and "knowledge and ability" refers to the "clarity of knowledge" that enables the teacher to admit every objection and "to speak and answer in free discussion."[134]

According to Jaspers, however, what is decisive always happens indirectly—in philosophy at any rate, but also in *Education*, because what is decisive is "the educational world founded on *Faith* as meaningful, the image of man, everything that is not taught directly, but is realized in teaching by example and by the selection of learning and practice material."[135] What educates, then, is not didactics based on psychology, but being with the subject itself: supported by the believed *Authority* of the traditional content.[136]

And what is this traditional content? For us Europeans, the "deepest human content in its purest form and simplest version," according to Jaspers's answer, is still that of the first, *Greek Humanism.* Familiarity with the writings and art of antiquity, but also with the Bible, is therefore still the path of Western *Education.*[137]

## NOTES

1. This chapter includes a revised and expanded version of Anton Hügli, «Erziehung zur Selbsterziehung oder: wie Demokratie und Bildung zusammenhängen,» *Studia Philosophica,* 71/2012, 155–180.

2. In today's language, this means: "Political power always requires legitimation, i.e. a justification that is accepted, or at least tolerated, by those subject to power, regardless of their motives" (Jürgen Habermas: *Ach, Europa* (Frankfurt a.M.: Suhrkamp, 2008), 173).

3. See, for example, the now classic distinction between *Power* and *Violence* by Hannah Arendt, *Macht und Gewalt* (München: Piper, 1970), 44 ff.

4. A 207f.

5. UZG 209f.

6. AB 48.

7. GSZ 82.—A passage in his letter to Hannah Arendt on the occasion of the delivery of his book *Die Atombombe und Zukunft des Menschen* (*The Atomic Bomb and the Future of Man*) shows how much Jaspers was concerned in his actual political writing to redeem the claim he made in the 1930s of wanting to go the whole way: "My attempt can only be valid as an attempt to fundamentally go the whole hog" (BAJ 386).

8. Aut 79.

9. GPhil 319.

10. GPhil 316.

11. AB 21.

12. AB 22.

13. AB 37.

14. See Karl Jaspers, «Die Atombombe und die Zukunft des Menschen» (1956), in ders.: *Hoffnung und Sorge. Schriften zur deutschen Politik 1945–1965* (München: Piper, 1965), 153–172, 157f.

15. See Karl Jaspers, «Die Atombombe und die Zukunft des Menschen» (1956), in ders.: *Hoffnung und Sorge. Schriften zur deutschen Politik 1945–1965* (München: Piper, 1965), 153–172, 158f.

16. AB 40.
17. AB 20.
18. AB 23.
19. Karl Jaspers, «Die Atombombe und die Zukunft des Menschen» (1956), in ders.: *Hoffnung und Sorge. Schriften zur deutschen Politik 1945–1965*, (München: Piper, 1965), 153–172, 162.
20. Karl Jaspers, «Die Atombombe und die Zukunft des Menschen» (1956), in ders.: *Hoffnung und Sorge. Schriften zur deutschen Politik 1945–1965*, (München: Piper, 1965), 153–172, 163.
21. AB 294.
22. AB 473f.
23. UZG 189f.
24. AB 319, 404.
25. AB 468.
26. AB 467, 460ff.
27. AB 49.
28. AB 478.
29. AB 471.
30. AB 472.
31. See AB 27–30.
32. AB 49.
33. AB 89.
34. AB 89.
35. GSZ 111.
36. See Ph 1, 261.
37. See W 39.
38. Karl Jaspers, „Was ist deutsch?," in ders.: *Hoffnung und Sorge. Schriften zur deutschen Politik 1945–1965* (München: Piper, 1965), 346–371, 360f.
39. Karl Jaspers, „Was ist deutsch?," in ders.: *Hoffnung und Sorge. Schriften zur deutschen Politik 1945–1965* (München: Piper, 1965), 346–371, 359–365.
40. AB 49.
41. See Ph 1, 258–262, esp. 259: The purpose of the *Supra-Political* is to find that unconditional *Faith* in one's own "God" that helps man break through the "political self-legality."
42. This is clearly stated in AB 283: "At the turning point, therefore, a twofold process is to be accomplished: First, from planning, from certain knowledge of the possibilities of events, to philosophical thinking from the *Encompassing*;—and then from there back to thinking in that world of knowledge and planning. The first turn in thinking leads to the transformation of man by this thinking, the second to the effect of this transformation in the world, with the consequence of the new direction in the course of events."
43. These are the three interwoven parables: the sun parable, the line parable, and the cave parable (cf. Plato, *Politeia* 506 b—509 b, 509 c-511 e, 514 a- 517 a).
44. Plato's parables may have been one of the sources of inspiration for his image of the two wings, the wing of *Reason* and the wing of *Existence*, both of which must swing if we do not want to fall.

45. GP 276.
46. GP 276f.
47. GP 277.
48. Ph 1, LII.
49. The willingness to sacrifice can be especially necessary when life or freedom is at stake, and in a situation of violence, it can go to the extreme: that the individual sacrifices his life for the sake of a life worth living—in the awareness that there is more than mere *Dasein*. Jaspers refers to the soldier's willingness to sacrifice and to those awakenings in the history of mankind in which peoples rose up for their freedom and were prepared to sacrifice everything for it, as the Hungarians did in his time (AB 91).
50. AB 52.
51. AB 299.
52. AB 76/77.
53. AB 308.
54. AB 309.
55. Cf. VWZ 34.
56. VWZ 35.
57. This also corresponds completely to Kant's concept of *Reason*, which Jaspers adopted. See Immanuel Kant, "Metaphysik der Sitten," in *Akademie Ausgabe*, hg. Königlich Preussische Akademie der Wissenschaften, Bd. 4 (Berlin, 1903, reprint 1968), 385–464, 396: *Reason* is not the organ that we can use for self-preservation, for the promotion of our well-being, but is there solely to "bring forth an intrinsically good will."
58. VWZ 36.
59. VWZ 36.
60. AB 290f.
61. AB 299.
62. GP 302.
63. GP 302.
64. GP 305.
65. A 209. Jaspers's criticism is directed against the traditional image of Plato, which was also the target of Karl Popper's great reckoning with Plato in the first volume of *Die offene Gesellschaft und ihre Feinde* (*The Open Society and its Enemies*), which was based on the same motives. Richard M. Hare (*Plato*, (Oxford; New York: Oxford University Press 1982), 26, 62f., 65–69) has made it clear that there could also be another reading of Plato with his distinction between the authoritarian *Plato* and the liberal *Lato*. For an interpretation of Plato that consistently follows the liberal reading, see for example Peter Stemmer's monograph on Plato's dialectic (*Platons Dialektik. Die frühen und mittleren Dialoge* (Berlin: de Gruyter, 1992). Jaspers himself probably also has these two possible readings of Plato in mind when he celebrates Plato as a "groundbreaking and liberating philosopher" who puts everything in abeyance, but in the "written realization of thought" shows more and more "the tendency to dogmatic conclusion" (GP 308).
66. A 209.
67. AB158f.
68. AB 159–162.

69. Jaspers, Karl: "Wahrheit, Freiheit und Friede," in ders.: *Hoffnung und Sorge. Schriften zur deutschen Politik 1945–1965* (München: Piper, 1965), 173–185, 174: "First: No external peace can be maintained without the inner peace of people. Second: Peace is only through freedom. Thirdly, freedom is only through truth."

70. AB 426.

71. Cf. on the whole UZG 202–220.

72. UZG 212.

73. See the key sentence of Socrates in Plato, *Politeia* 505 d: "But it is not enough for anyone to have only apparent good, but everyone seeks what is good, and everyone despises appearances."

74. A 210.

75. A 208.

76. A 210.

77. See A. 209: "We must ensure that the peoples, who are no longer illiterate, become as reasonable, as sensible, as serious as possible."

78. A 419.

79. VWZ 33.

80. VWZ 36.

81. See, for example: "Wahrheit, Freiheit und Friede," in Karl Jaspers: *Hoffnung und Sorge. Schriften zur deutschen Politik 1945–1965* (München: Piper, 1965), 173–185, 176: "Truth does not lie first in the content, but in the way in which it is thought, pointed out and discussed: in the way of thinking of *Reason*." Or: FW 262: "Truth is not on the table. No one possesses it. It is real only because it is struggled for. Truthfulness does not cease to examine each particular truth anew."

82. VWZ 36.

83. A 444. See A 446: "In the *Idea of Democracy*, politics itself is *Education*."

84. Humboldt, Wilhelm von, „Das achtzehnte Jahrhundert," in *Akademie Ausgabe*. I/2, ed. A. Leitzmann (Berlin: de Gruyter, 1904), 2–112, 68.

85. Carl von Rotteck, "Bildung," in Carl von Rotteck/Karl Theodor Welcker (ed.), *Staats-Lexikon*, 2 (1837), 572. For the history of the term with further evidence, see Menze, Clemens, "Selbstbildung," in *Historisches Wörterbuch der Philosophie*, ed. Joachim Ritter and Karlfried Gründer, Bd. 9 (Basel: Schwabe 1995), 379–383.

86. AB 440: To perish means that the rule falls back into the hands of a few people.

87. AB 441.

88. IU (1961) 130.

89. AB 337.

90. AB 330.

91. AB 330.

92. See IU (1961) 131.

93. In the debate about the Federal Republic, Jaspers therefore also opposed the common thesis that the German people were not yet ready for democracy: "A people must begin with itself as it finds itself, or it never begins" (A 130).

94. AB 423.

95. Cf. the polemical article by Norbert Kapferer, "Paternalismus und Erziehung zur Demokratie," in *Philosophie—Erziehung—Universität. Zu Karl Jaspers'*

*Bildungs- und Erziehungsphilosophie*, ed. Kurt Salamun (Frankfurt a. M.: Peter Lang, 1995), 75–91.

96. AB 442.

97. See AB 442. The figure in which Jaspers himself experienced greatness is not only biographically significant: "Among my contemporaries, the reality of greatness, historically distant men, became tangible to me in a unique and wonderful way through Max Weber" (Aut 20; also: "Karl-Jaspers—ein Selbstporträt" (1966/67), in *Schicksal und Wille. Autobiographische Schriften*, ed. Hans Saner, 15–38 (München: Piper, 1967), 33).

98. AB 443.

99. A 129.

100. See GP 33: "Reverence for greatness is not idolatry of man."

101. This also sets limits to any mutual understanding. I am always already a party; by considering an authority as an authority, I have already chosen it (Ex 44). An example of this is Jaspers's dispute with Jean-Paul Sartre (see Anton Hügli, "Sartre und Jaspers zur Frage nach der Transzendenz. Ein Aufriss der grundlegenden Differenzen zwischen Jaspers und Sartre aus der Jaspersschen Sicht," in *Karl Jaspers und Jean-Paul-Sartre im Dialog,* ed. Anton Hügli and Manuela Hackel (Frankfurt a.M.; Bern: Peter Lang, 2015), 7–23, esp. 32–35).

102. See Anton Hügli, „Karl Jaspers und die Erziehung," in *Karl Jaspers. Grundbegriffe seines Denkens*, ed. Hamid Reza Yousefi u.a. (Reinbek: Rowohlt, 2011), 289–304.

103. IU (1946) 49.

104. PGO 69.

105. PGO 450.

106. Thus Emerson, whom Jaspers quotes approvingly in his reflections on greatness (GP 34).

107. GP 34.

108. A 332.

109. A 208.

110. Cf. Ex 46f.

111. A 208.

112. AB 336.

113. AB 444.

114. AB 444.

115. The clearest development of the *Idea of the University* is still due to Karl Jaspers, who at three different points in his life referred to it: first in 1923, then in 1946, and finally again in 1961, each time under the title *Die Idee der Universität.*

116. This is the guiding principle under which Habermas, with recourse to Schleiermacher, still sees the university today: "'The first law of every University based on knowledge directed endeavor [is]: Communication; and in the impossibility of anything even on its own, without language, nature itself has created this law quite clearly [. . .]' I rely on this one of Schleiermacher's "Occasional Thoughts on the University in the German Sense' without sentimentality, because I

seriously believe that it is the communicative forms of scientific argumentation that ultimately hold university learning processes together in their various functions" (Jürgen Habermas, «Die Idee der Universität—Lernprozesse," in ders.: *Eine Art Schadensabwicklung, Kleine politische Schriften IV* (Frankfurt a.M.: Suhrkamp, 1987), 71–99, cit. 95).

117. Wilhelm v. Humboldt, „Über die innere und äussere Organisation der höheren wissenschaftlichen Anstalten in Berlin," in *Gesammelte Schriften*, hg. von der Preußischen Akademie der Wissenschaften, Band 10 (Berlin: de Gruyter, 1905), 250–266, 252.

118. On the tradition of *Liberal Education*, see, for example Martha C. Nussbaum, *Cultivating Humanity. A Classical Defense of Reform in Liberal Education* (Cambrige, MA; London: Harvard University Press, 1997), 15–49.

119. For further clarification of these connections, see Anton Hügli, «Erziehung zur Selbsterziehung oder: wie Demokratie und Bildung zusammenhängen,» *Studia Philosophica,* 1/2012, 155–180.

120. Thus in: „Der Litauische Schulplan," in *Gesammelte Schriften*, Band 13, ed. Königlich Preußische Akademie der Wissenschaften, 276–283 (Berlin: de Gruyter, 1905), 280: "The University is reserved for what only man can find through and in himself, the insight into pure science. For this self-actus in the most genuine understanding, freedom and helpful solitude are necessary."

121. F. W. J. Schelling, «Vorlesungen über die Methode des akademischen Studiums" [1802], in *Sämtliche Werke*, ed. K. F. A. Schelling, Abt. I, Bd. 5, 207–352 (Stuttgart; Augsburg: Cotta, 1859) 212; see also 239ff.

122. Friedrich Schiller, „Was heisst und zu welchem Ende studiert man Universalgeschichte?" [1789], in *Werke*, Bd. 2, 956–970, München: Droehmersche Verlagsanstalt, o. J, 958f.

123. F. W. J. Schelling, „Vorlesungen über die Methode des akademischen Studiums" [1802], in *Sämtliche Werke*, ed. K. F. A. Schelling, Abt. I, Bd. 5 (Stuttgart; Augsburg: Cotta 1859), 241–242.

124. On the significance of method, see for example Friedrich Nietzsche, *Menschliches, Allzumenschliches*, Kritische Studienausgabe, Bd. 2, (München: dtv, 1999), Part I, §635, 360: "On the whole, scientific methods are at least as important a result of research as any other result: for the scientific spirit is based on insight into method."

125. Cf. IU 1/946), 22–23.

126. An impression of the extent to which Jaspers dealt with the question of upbringing and education is provided by the anthology: *Was ist Erziehung? Ein Lesebuch*, ed. Hermann Horn (München; Zürich: Piper, 1977, 3rd ed. München 1982—new edition 1992) (= WErz).

127. Ph 1, 118.

128. Ph 1, 119.

129. Ph 1, 119.

130. Ph 1, 120. See, for example AB 52: *Conversion* cannot be forced. Whether something happens in the individual through what education can do—pointing out

realities and "letting the demanding voice of the millennia speak"—"is left to the freedom of each individual already at an early age."

131. Cf. Ph 1, 120.

132. AB 444.

133. AB 445.

134. AB 447.

135. Karl Jaspers, "Freiheit und Autorität," in *Philosophie und Welt*, 41–64 (München: Piper 1958), 49.

136. Karl Jaspers, „Von den Grenzen pädagogischen Planens," in *Philosophie und Welt*, 28–40 (München: Piper 1958), 36f.; see also W 798.

137. Karl Jaspers, "Über Bedingungen und Möglichkeiten eines neuen Humanismus," in *Rechenschaft und Ausblick*, 312–344 (München: Piper, 1958), 332.

# Summary for the (Not-Too-Fast) Reader

Means and channels of communication are multiplying daily and worldwide. Never before in the history of mankind have there been so many ways to connect with other people as there are today. However, it seems that the willingness to talk and listen to each other has never been as low as it is today. It is not only the connection between the living that is in danger of breaking down but also the communication with the history of mankind, with the dead who have been cast into the sea. People insist on their unquestionable opinions, plunge into irrational delusions, and wage a campaign of destruction against all those who disagree. The inability to communicate extends to all areas of life: from questions of public services, vaccination or non-vaccination, for example, to social and political problems, to ideological and religious issues. In any case, it seems hopeless to ever reach agreement on these issues. They open up not just divides, but chasms.

This lack of communication is more disastrous than all the other dangers threatening humanity today. It is the driving force behind every other doom that hangs over humanity like a portent, first and foremost climate change, the loss of biodiversity, and the danger of nuclear self-destruction of mankind, which has not been averted for a long time. How can we meet these dangers if we cannot talk to each other and form a common will?

*So the question of all questions is: Is global understanding possible at all? If so, under what conditions? And in what way?*

This question lies beyond the horizon of any science. Whoever tries to answer it will always be confronted with another, even deeper question, the question of what kind of beings we are, what is possible for us humans, and what is impossible for us. This is a philosophical question—not just one among others, but the question in which all philosophical questions converge. Among contemporary philosophers, there is one in particular who has linked the question of man with the question of the possibility of communication: Karl Jaspers. More than any other philosopher, he suffered from the lack of communication, and more than almost anyone else, the will to communicate became the driving force behind his philosophizing, and making communication possible the goal of his philosophy. More than almost anyone else, he has sharpened our awareness of the extent to which communication has been part of philosophy from the very beginning: in that it urges communication, wants to express itself, and be heard.

Understanding the other person is one thing; agreeing with him is another. The will to communicate is the will to agree. Agreement can only come about when I realize that what the other person is telling me is not only true and correct but also important.

But how can I find agreement if the other person does not also seek the truth and does not truthfully say what he himself believes to be true?

Everything depends on the will for truth and the truthfulness of those who communicate with each other because truth only exists with the other person. The reason for this is that there is only one way to test whether what we believe to be true is true: by measuring our judgment against that of others. This requires that we communicate what we believe to be true and why we believe it to be true and see if others can contradict us with good reasons, point out things that we have overlooked or not noticed, or that we were not aware of. These others are not just those we happen to be able to reach but, in principle anyone who can speak and understand—and who, like us, wants to know the truth. In fact, it should be everyone (those present as well as those still absent) because there could still be one person who comes through the door and proves us wrong.

This is the reason why, where truth is important to us, we demand publicity for our judgments. Anyone who wants to should be able to answer. Therefore, anyone who wants to must have the opportunity to learn about my judgment. What has not yet been contradicted can be considered true. This is true even if we refer to direct perception and our own experience. As soon as we try to communicate what we ourselves have experienced or perceived, it becomes indirect or communicable and, like everything that is communicated, needs to be verified. Everything so-called given, everything factual, is, as Goethe says, already theory.

It follows: If you want truth, you must want communication. And vice versa, if you want communication (with the goal of reaching agreement), you must want truth—in truthfulness. But truth is not just truth. Depending on the context, the encompassing whole in which we stand, truth has a different meaning.

What are these holistic contexts, these modes of the *Encompassing*, as Jaspers says?

(1) We are biological beings in a struggle for *Dasein*. True is what benefits us; untrue is what diminishes our interests in power and existence. Solidarity exists only to the extent that I see the other as a comrade-in-arms and not as an enemy. Communication is measured by vital interests: say and do only what serves your vital interests, and deceive and lie when it seems more advantageous. Nevertheless, we ultimately need an overarching concept of truth: What I believe to be in my best interest must actually (and not just seemingly) serve my interest.

(2) The overarching concept of truth (which only becomes apparent when we go beyond the struggle for *Dasein*) is that of *Consciousness in General* purified of all interests of life: the I in me that wants nothing but knowledge. What is true here is that which is right for everyone, that which is evident in itself, that which, by virtue of its evidence, imposes itself on everyone who has understanding and understands it. This is independent of time and person: the fact that two plus two equals four is and remains timelessly true throughout all time. When I become certain of the rightness of this equation, I am a pure thinking self, fully *Consciousness in General*. Performing the arithmetic operation forces me to believe that the matter is and must be as I think it is. This is why Jaspers speaks of *Compelling Knowledge*. Here, as in the borderline case of mathematical insight, absolute agreement is possible.

(3) We are all *Consciousness in General* when we want to know what the case is. Those who consciously make this their task, or even their life's work, must face up to the disciplinary and methodological demands that the search for knowledge requires according to the standards of contemporary research in this field. Those who do so place themselves at the service of an *Idea*, the *Idea of Knowledge*, which has its reality in institutions such as the university and which binds together as a community all those who have followed and are following this *Idea* today.

(4) To be guided by *Ideas* is what Jaspers calls *Spirit* (*Geist*). We all follow *Ideas* when we choose a task or a social role: when we want to be a doctor, an artist or a gardener, a friend or a lover, a citizen or a good person. In the spiritual world of *Ideas*, truth has a different meaning. In *Consciousness in General*, truth consists in the fact that reality is as we think it is, but participation in *Ideas* it is about the truth of reality itself; it is true if it corresponds to what the *Idea* requires: if a person is not just a friend but a *true* friend, not just a doctor but a *true* doctor, and so on. But again, in order to determine the extent to which an Idea has become real, I need to be aware of whether things are really as I think they are, according to the demands of *Consciousness in General*.

(5) More than that. It also demands that I am willing to take on my task true to its *Idea*. And this presupposes the will to be true to myself, not

to give in to illusions, not to deceive myself, but to want to know what I really do and what I really want—not just occasionally, but unconditionally, absolutely. But where does this *Unconditional Will* come from? It is undoubtedly not a natural drive of our biological *Dasein*, but rather directed against all natural drives, because wanting to know the truth about myself is usually anything but happiness and life-giving. The *Unconditional Will* also cannot come from *Consciousness in General*, which is itself guided by my will. Nor does it come from an *Idea*, because *Ideas* only lead to something if I have made them my own. Only if I want to be a friend am I under the imperative to do what friendship demands. As a religious person, I could still say that my *Unconditional Will* is the will of God. But the will of God—if I know it at all—can only become my will if I will to obey God's commandments.

(6) But what do I mean when I say that *I* am the one who wants or doesn't want something? What kind of I is it that decides to want something absolutely? Is it the *I* of *Dasein*, the *I* of *Consciousness in General*, or the *I* of a social role in a practice determined by an *Idea*? If the *Modes of Encompassing* that have been shown so far—biological *Dasein*, *Consciousness in General*, and *Spirit*, are already all there is, then the hypothesis of such an unconditional *I* is an illusion. For in a world of causalities and conditionalities, how can there be such a thing as an *Unconditioned Will*? A will that sets an absolute beginning and therefore can be called free? It is, we should honestly say, a beautiful belief, but not knowledge. The only thing that can support this belief is whether I have already experienced something like an *Unconditioned Will* within myself, combined with the philosophical insight that the belief in the possibility of an *Unconditioned Will* is at least not contrary to all Reason.

As far as the experience of the unconditional is concerned, there are at least testimonies of people who, like Luther with his words "Here I stand, I can do no other," have made known what can be understood as the expression of an unconditional will—if such a will is considered possible at all. And isn't there this awareness deep within us that we could make a start of our own—if only we wanted to?

That the possibility of something unconditional cannot be excluded was demonstrated by Kant in an irreversible way: Everything that we regard as reality is reality only for us, reality only insofar as we are able to grasp it with our senses and our intellect. In short, the world exists for us only insofar as it *appears* to us. What eludes our cognitive faculty is as if it were not there. But it must be there; it is the *Ultimate Reality* and not a Nothingness. We experience it in the effects it has on us and in its resistance when we try to influence it. We do not know what this *Ultimate Reality* is, only that it is there, and that it must be such that everything that appears to us in it must be possible. That it is there is simply a fact that cannot be attributed to anything else. It is something that is no longer conditioned, just as everything in the phenomenal world is conditioned but—unconditional.

The unconditionality that we think we feel in ourselves is just that. There is the voice of the *Categorical Imperative*, which tells me that there can only be peaceful coexistence if everyone, and that means me first and foremost, obeys the moral law, which requires us to obey only those rules that we want everyone to obey at all times. There is also the unconditionality in the voice of love, which tells me that this person and this task in the world are something I must stand up for and take care of, if only because it is the way it is.

Should I not now conclude that the *Ultimate Reality* from which everything that appears in the phenomenal world originates is also the origin of the unconditionality that I experience in the moral law and in my love? But if my unconditional will has its *Origin* in this *Ultimate Reality*, this would mean that my will itself is not something that I can will, but something that is *given* to me and out of which I can will in the first place. This could also explain why those who believe they have an *Unconditional Will* always speak of a *Must, a Necessity*: they could not do otherwise than what they want to do. But such a way of speaking is, in short, a paradox: Anyone who submits to such an *Unconditional Will* must surely want to submit to it, but how can he do so if his will is "caused" by this *Other*? And conversely, if a person did not feel such unconditionality in himself, would it then not be due to him, but again, to the *Other*?

Jaspers coined the formula for this paradox: "I am given to myself." And it can always be the case that I "can remain out of myself." But this "Self" given to me is what I am, my reason and origin at the same time; it is my true Self. This possibility of being myself by unconditionally wanting the unconditional is what Jaspers calls *Existence*, or more precisely: *Possible Existence*. The Other, the *Ultimate Reality*, by which I am given to myself, he calls *Transcendence*. And to express the fact that the one cannot be without the other, he uses the basic formula: *no Existence without Transcendence*. *Existence* is the *Mode of the Encompassing*, which encompasses me in my empirical appearance; *Transcendence* is the *Encompassing*, which encompasses me and the world as a whole.

The struggle to be my-self sounds like a rather lonely affair: I alone with "God." It is, of course, true that I have to be able to bear the loneliness of being on my own. But all the more, I need the other person who fights with me in solidarity for my selfhood, a beloved adversary who helps me on my way and relentlessly opposes me when I want to take it too easy and surrender to my self-deceptions. Jaspers calls this form of communication *Existential Communication* and speaks of it as a *Loving Struggle.*

But what is the point of such thoughts about *Existence* and *Transcendence*? In what sense, if any, can they be "true"? There can be no question of knowledge here because we are talking about things that lie beyond all appearances and therefore elude our sense-bound mind. Nevertheless, they are thoughts that we can feel compelled to think. And not only can we think them, but they have been thought in one way or another ever since human beings have asked themselves questions such as, "What is *True Being*? Where do we come from? Where are we going?" The *Ultimate Reality* has been sought under many different names: as True Reality, as God or Deity, as the Original Being or the Primordial One, and so on. But these are all just names, and we do not know what they really mean, or what this something might be that they seem to denote—except that it is of such a nature that it cannot be grasped by any of the categories and concepts with which we tend to grasp the objects of our cognition, and which are the only ones available to us. And yet we cannot stop thinking about the unthinkable.

What allows us to do this? It is a special faculty of reason that urges us to ask again and again how everything we can think and imagine can be brought into unity, into an overall context. We involuntarily follow the *Idea* that in the end, all must be *One*, although we cannot say what this *One* could be, because we can only think in terms of distinctions—that something is or is not, that it is this way or that way, etc. Therefore, we can never even intend the *One*, because as soon as we begin to think about it, we do not have the *One*, but the seeming *One* and the other that it is not. So we think what is not thinkable.

Kant called this faculty that allows us to think the unthinkable *Reason* (*Vernunft*). Reason urges us to constantly search for the *One*, for unity. This is where it differs from *Understanding (Verstand),* which is only ever concerned with recognizing the particular many (as it appears to us). *Understanding* can only say whether something is right or—in terms of purpose—whether something is expedient. *Reason,* on the other hand, looks for the whole, the context, and asks how important rightness is at all, and whether it makes sense to pursue these and precisely these ends. *Reaso*n, one might say, is the search for meaning in the whole and of the whole—for the meaning of life, for the meaning of the world, for the distant and unknowable *One* in whom we can find support. *Reason*, therefore, is never satisfied; it is always searching for that which ultimately matters, that which is truly important, that which has rank and greatness. This thinking of *Reason* is the thinking that has been called *Philosophy* since the Greeks.

But what about truth in the realm of *Reason*? And what about communication? Because *Reason* is boundlessly open and tries to grasp even the unreasonable and the absurd, it must leave nothing out. It must embrace everything that is and everything that has already been said, thought, and done. For this reason, those who follow *Reason* must go wherever people (even if they had no name for it) have asked themselves philosophical questions and tried to answer them—breaking through the authoritative proclamations of religions—on the basis of their *Reason* alone, in communication with each other, questioning each other, struggling with each other, and often fighting against each other. But always with one goal in mind: to find the one unconditional *One* who can give meaning to their lives and guide their thoughts and actions.

In his search for the origins of philosophy, Jaspers discovered that there was not only an occidental origin of philosophy but also an independent and simultaneous Indian and Chinese origin. He calls the period in which this breakthrough in the thinking of *Reason* occurred in world history the *Axis Time*, and dates it himself to the time between 800 and 200 BC. These different philosophical currents have since merged, and today, according to Jaspers's vision, we are on the way from Western philosophy to a future *World Philosophy*. It is a never-ending worldwide dialogue, and wherever people ask themselves philosophical questions (and there is no one who remains completely untouched by them), this dialogue continues.

But unlike the sciences, which focus on phenomena in the world, there is no progress toward truth that everyone can find for himself or herself. Those who set out to answer these questions must do so from their own place, and each individual must decide for himself what he believes to be true. Truth for him is the *Faith* by which he will live his life.

The only criterion by which philosophical ideas can be judged is whether they help or hinder communication. Any effort to wall oneself up in one's thoughts, to believe that one has found the truth that is truth for all, is hostile to communication. The imperative of *Reason* is to break through all mental barriers, not to be satisfied with any answer, and not to be dominated by one's own thoughts. Therefore, it is crucial in the use of *Reason* to be clear about how one thinks and where the possibilities and limits of one's thinking lie.

But how does this go together, being open to everything and yet finding a *Faith* that you can live with? It only goes together because there are two opposing demands that we have to satisfy: the demand of *Reason*, which urges us to think beyond all horizons, and the demand of *Existence* to be oneself, to be present, and to gain reality in the here and now. I need the vastness of *Reason* in order to determine where I stand in the whole that encompasses me, or, what is synonymous for me, in the whole of the constructions with which we try to illuminate the ultimate possibilities of meaning—always aware that what we take to be the ultimate point of view cannot yet be the ultimate point of view.

But if there is to be unconditionality in my life, I cannot want many things; I can only want one thing at a time. So I have to decide where I want to be in the realm of possibilities. Such ultimate possibilities of meaning that challenge our decision are, for example,

(1) Accepting the *Immanence* of the phenomenal world as the *Ultimate Reality*, or believing in *Transcendence*.
(2) Seeking the brightness of *Reason* or submitting to an authority that appears in the world.
(3) To dare to communicate without limits, or to cut off communication and wall ourselves in with dogmatic opinions.
(4) Wanting to be ourselves or wanting to live as we are used to.
(5) Taking the risk of independent thinking or clinging to objective certainties.
(6) Opening oneself to the ultimate possibilities in the abysses of life, or being comforted by the deceptive hopes of this world.

This list may give the impression that it is possible for us to adopt a superior standpoint from which we can then make a sober decision in favor of one alternative or the other. But this appearance is deceptive. We grow up in a certain tradition, we always find ourselves on a certain side, we are always already a party and as such in a struggle against the other party. It is as if these alternatives were superordinate powers, themselves at war with each other, drawing us into their struggle. Even when we construct possibilities of meaning, it is always from the side on which we stand. Therefore, it will never be possible for us to have an overview of all points of view. There is no God's point of view from which we can look down on the *Spiritual World* and understand all points of view equally. But seeing the respective opposing power helps us to see more clearly where we ourselves stand, what we want, and what we don't want.

But where is the unifying factor when we are always at war with each other? What unites us human beings is our common human fate: that we are thrown into a world from which we cannot escape, condemned to suffer and struggle, to become guilty and to die, and faced with the alternative of despairing or finding a place where we can find support, be it by following the promises of salvation made by religions or by choosing the philosophical path of independent thought. But in order to make any decisions at all, one thing above all else is required of each individual: the sincerity to recognize, without self-deception, what their destiny is and to ask themselves what they want to find their meaning in. This clarity and sincerity cannot be achieved without following the path of *Reason*. And *Reason* opens the space in which we can meet in our search for the *One* who encompasses us. It is the bond that ultimately unites us in our historical diversity.

To make use of *Reason*, to use it to shed light on what we do when we think, to make clear to ourselves what we know and what we cannot know, and to approach the *One* in whom we have our common origin: this is the task that *Reason* sets for us. But in order to accomplish this task, we need world-wide communication, not only with those who are alive today but also with all those before us who lived to bring *Reason* into the world. The memory of their deeds and works can help us educate ourselves to *Reason* and follow their example in our own historical path.

But the place where we have to do this is in the here and now of our physical *Dasein*, and communication out of freedom is only possible when everyone is free, free inwardly, but also free politically. Because inner freedom is only possible when there is also political freedom. To contribute to political orders that make freedom possible for all thus becomes a further project for Jaspers—in addition to all his monumental philosophical projects. Even at the risk of losing his "head and neck," he took up the fight against all forms of *Totalitarianism* and for *Democracy*, which he understood as the never-ending project of the *Self-education* of peoples on their way to the *One* by creating peace and unity in the world. He worked tirelessly to awaken the shift in consciousness that the thinkers of the *Axial Time* brought about for the first time in human history, and which must now become the change of consciousness of the many if we are to have any chance of averting the imminent nuclear and climatic self-destruction of humanity. Jaspers's battle is the same one we must fight today, under different circumstances and in an even more catastrophic situation.

# Bibliography

## BIBLIOGRAPHIES

*Karl Jaspers. Basic Philosophical Writings, Selections, edited by Leonard H. Ehrlich, Edith Ehrlich and George B. Pepper, 543–556. Athens, OH; London: Ohio University Press, 1986.*

*Karl Jaspers. Eine Bibliographie.* Bd. I. Die Primärbibliographie. Bearbeitet von Gisela Gefken und Karl Kunert. Oldenburg, 1978.

*Primärbibliographie der Schriften Karl Jaspers'.* Im Auftrag der Karl Jaspers Stiftung auf der Grundlage der Bibliographie von Gisela Gefken und Karl Kunert völlig neu bearbeitet und herausgegeben von Christian Rabanus. Tübingen und Basel: Francke, 2000.

*The Philosophy of Karl Jaspers*, edited by Paul Arthur Schilpp, 2nd augmented edition with section on Heidegger, 871–904. Lasalle: Open Court, 1981. [Bibliography of the Writings of Karl Jaspers to 1957, compiled by Kurt Rossmann, revised and continued from 1958 to 1973 by Gisela Gefken.]

## REFERENCES

Arendt, Hannah. *Macht und Gewalt.* München: Piper, 1970.

Arendt, Hannah. *Über das Böse. Eine Vorlesung zu Fragen der Ethik.* München; Zürich: Piper, 2006.

Aristoteles. *Metaphysik.* Berlin: Aufbau Verlag, 1960.

Augustinus. *Der Gottesstaat*, edited by Carl Johann Perl, 3 Bde. Salzburg: Otto Müller, 1952.

Ballanti, Roberto Celada. „Die Augustin-Deutung von Karl Jaspers." *Studia Philosophica*, 67/2008, 251–264.

Diels, Hermann. *Die Fragmente der Vorsokratiker*, Bd. 1, 5. Aufl., edited by Wilhelm Kranz. Berlin: Weidmann, 1934.

Frankfurt, Harry G. *The Reasons of Love*. Princeton, NJ; Oxford: Princeton University Press, 2004.

Frankfurt, Harry G. "Über die Bedeutsamkeit des Sich-Sorgens." In *Freiheit und Selbstbestimmung*, edited by Monika Betzler and Barbara Guckes, 98–115. Berlin: Akademie Verlag, 2001.

Goethe, Johann Wolfgang v. "An Lavater (20. 9. 1780)," *Gedenk-Ausgabe*, edited by Ernst Beutler, Bd. 18, 533.

Habermas, Jürgen. „Die Idee der Universität – Lernprozesse." In ders.: *Eine Art Schadensabwicklung, Kleine politische Schriften IV*, 71–99. Frankfurt a.M.: Suhrkamp, 1987.

Habermas, Jürgen. *Ach, Europa*. Frankfurt a.M.: Suhrkamp, 2008.

Habermas, Jürgen. *Auch eine Geschichte der Philosophie*, 2 Bde. Berlin: Suhrkamp, 2019.

Halfwassen, Jens. *Auf den Spuren des Einen. Studien zur Metaphysik und ihrer Geschichte*. Tübingen: Mohr Siebeck, 2015.

Halfwassen, Jens. „Karl Jaspers als Metaphysiker." In *Jaspers. Stationen seines philosophischen Wegs*, edited by Anton Hügli, 173–192. Basel: Schwabe, 2021.

Hare, Richard. "Could Kant Have Been an Utilitarian?" In Richard Hare: *Sorting out Ethics*, 147–166. Oxford: Clarendon Press, 1997.

Hare, Richard. *Freedom and Reason*. Oxford: University Press, 196I.

Hare, Richard. *Plato*. Oxford; New York: Oxford University Press, 1982.

Hare, Richard. *Sorting Out Ethics*. Oxford: Clarendon Press, 1997

Hart, H. L. A. "The Ascription of Responsibility and Rights." *Proceedings of the Aristotelian Society*, 49 (1948/9), 171–194.

Hersch, Jeanne. «Karl Jaspers als Lehrer.» *Erinnerungen an Karl Jaspers*, edited by Klaus Piper and Hans Saner. 59–61. München; Zürich: Piper, 1974.

Höffe, Otfried. *Kants Kritik der praktischen Vernunft. Eine Philosophie der Freiheit*. München: Beck, 2012.

Hügli, Anton. «Das Nahe und das Ferne, das Einzelne und das Allgemeine, das Zeitliche und das Ewige. Über die Grundpolarität in Jaspers' Denken.» In *Karl Jaspers: Filozofia Wieczysta – Filozofia Czasu*, edited by Czeslawa Piecuch, 15–36. Krakow: Wydawnictwo Naukowe UP, 2021.

Hügli, Anton. „Erziehung zur Selbsterziehung oder: wie Demokratie und Bildung zusammenhängen." *Studia Philosophica*, 71/2012, 155–180.

Hügli, Anton. «'Grenzsituationen erfahren und existieren ist dasselbe' - eine Meditation über einen Satz von Karl Jaspers», *Swiss Archives of Neurology, Psychiatry and Psychotherapy*, 2/2020, 1–7.

Hügli, Anton, ed. *Jaspers. Stationen seines philosophischen Wegs*. Basel: Schwabe, 2021.

Hügli, Anton. „Jaspers' Darstellung von Philosophie – eine Form der indirekten Mitteilung?" *Jahrbuch der österreichischen Karl Jaspers Gesellschaft*, 28/2015, 9–36.

Hügli, Anton. "Jaspers, Karl (1883-1969)." In *Bloomsbury Philosophy Library*, 2020 (https://www.bloomsburyphilosophylibrary.com/article?docid=b-9781350962200&tocid=b-9781350962200-0007&st=Karl+Jaspers).

Hügli, Anton. „Karl Jaspers und die Erziehung." In *Karl Jaspers. Grundbegriffe seines Denkens*, edited by Hamid Zeza Yousefi u.a., 289–304. Reinbek: Rowohlt 2011.

Hügli, Anton. „Malum (Böses, Übel, Schlechtes). Neuzeit.» In *Historisches Wörterbuch der Philosophie*, edited by Joachim Ritter and Karlfried Gründer, Bd. 5, 611–706. Basel: Schwabe 1980.

Hügli, Anton. „Mitteilung, Mitteilbarkeit, indirekte Mitteilung." In *Historisches Wörterbuch der Philosophie*, edited by Joachim Ritter and Karlfried Gründer, Bd. 5,1424–1431. Basel: Schwabe 1980.

Hügli, Anton. „Die Instrumentalisierung des Malum in der Philosophie der Neuzeit.» In *Die Wirklichkeit des Bösen. Systematisch-theologische und philosophische Annäherungen*, edited by Friedrich Hermanni and Peter Koslowski, 159–183. München: Wilhelm Fink, 1998.

Hügli, Anton. "The Relevance of Karl Jaspers' Philosophy of Religion Today." *argumenta philosophica, Revista de la Encyclopaedia Herder*, 2/2016, 35–50.

Hügli, Anton. „Søren Kierkegaard – Der Einzelne, das Ethische und die Freiheit." In *Klassiker der Philosophie heute*, edited by Ansgar Beckermann and Dominik Perler, 439–458. Stuttgart: Reclam, 2004.

Hügli, Anton. „Sartre und Jaspers zur Frage nach der Transzendenz. Ein Aufriss der grundlegenden Differenzen zwischen Jaspers und Sartre aus der Jaspersschen Sicht." In *Karl Jaspers und Jean-Paul-Sartre im Dialog*, edited by Anton Hügli and Manuela Hackel, 7–23. Frankfurt a.M.; Bern: Peter Lang, 2015.

Hügli, Anton, Kaegi, Dominic, Weidmann, Bernd, ed. *Existenz und Sinn. Karl Jaspers im Kontext.* Heidelberg: Winter, 2009.

Humboldt, Wilhelm v., „Das achtzehnte Jahrhundert." In *Gesammelte Schriften*, Band 1/2, hg. von der Preußischen Akademie der Wissenschaften, edited by Albert Leitzmann, 2–112. Berlin: de Gruyter, 1904.

Humboldt, Wilhelm v. „Über die innere und äussere Organisation der höheren wissenschaftlichen Anstalten in Berlin." In *Gesammelte Schriften*, hg. von der Preußischen Akademie der Wissenschaften, Bd. 10, 250–266. Berlin: de Gruyter 1905.

Humboldt, Wilhelm v. „Der Litauische Schulplan." In *Gesammelte Schriften*, Band 13, hg. von der Preußischen Akademie der Wissenschaften, 276–283. Berlin: de Gruyter, 1905.

Jaspers, Karl, „Freiheit und Autorität." In ders.: *Philosophie und Welt*, 41–64. München: Piper 1958.

Jaspers, Karl. „Die Idee des Arztes" (1953). In ders: *Philosophie und Welt*, 169–183. München: Piper, 1958.

Jaspers, Karl. „Über Bedingungen und Möglichkeiten eines neuen Humanismus." In ders: *Rechenschaft und Ausblick*, 312–344. München: Piper, 1958.

Jaspers, Karl. „Was ist deutsch?" In ders: *Hoffnung und Sorge. Schriften zur deutschen Politik 1945-1965*, 346–371. München: Piper, 1965.

Jaspers, Karl. «Immanuel Kant. Zu seinem 150. Todestag.» In *Aneignung und Polemik. Gesammelte Reden und Aufsätze zur Geschichte der Philosophie,* edited by Hans Saner, 242–250. München: Piper, 1968.

Jaspers, Karl. «Kierkegaard. Zu seinem 100. Todestag.» In *Aneignung und Polemik. Gesammelte Reden und Aufsätze zur Geschichte der Philosophie,* edited by Hans Saner, 312–329. München: Piper, 1968.

Jaspers, Karl. «Max Weber: Eine Gedenkrede (1920).» In *Aneignung und Polemik. Gesammelte Reden und Aufsätze zur Geschichte der Philosophie,* edited by Hans Saner, 409–423. München: Piper, 1968.

Jaspers, Karl. «Das Unbedingte und das Böse.» In *Das Wagnis der Freiheit. Gesammelte Aufsätze zur Philosophie,* edited by Hans Saner, 86–96. München, Zürich: Piper, 1996.

Jaspers, Karl. «Wo stehen wir heute? (1960).» In *Das Wagnis der Freiheit. Gesammelte Aufsätze zur Philosophie,* edited by Hans Saner, 185–198. München, Zürich: Piper, 1996.

Jaspers, Karl. «Unsterblichkeit (1957).» In *Das Wagnis der Freiheit. Gesammelte Aufsätze zur Philosophie,* edited by Hans Saner, 336–341. München, Zürich: Piper, 1996.

Jaspers, Karl. «Die Atombombe und die Zukunft des Menschen (1956).» In *Hoffnung und Sorge. Schriften zur deutschen Politik 1945-1965,* 153–172. München: Piper, 1965.

Jaspers, Karl. „Wahrheit, Freiheit und Friede." In *Hoffnung und Sorge. Schriften zur deutschen Politik 1945-1965,* 173–185. München: Piper, 1965.

Jaspers, Karl. "Karl Jaspers – ein Selbstporträt (1966/67)." In *Schicksal und Wille. Autobiographische Schriften,* edited by Hans Saner, 15–38. München: Piper, 1967.

Jaspers, Karl. *«Antwort auf die Frage: Aus welchen Kräften leben Sie?* (1962).» In *Philosophische Aufsätze,* 238–247. Hamburg: Fischer, 1967.

Jaspers, Karl. «An Jean Wahl.» In *Schriften zur Existenzphilosophi. Karl Jaspers Gesamtausgabe I/8,* 164–167. Basel: Schwabe, 2018.

Kant, Immanuel. «Träume eines Geistersehers." In *Akademieausgabe,* edited by Königlichen Preussischen Akademie der Wissenschaften, Bd. 2, 315–384. Berlin: de Gruyter, 1905, Neudruck 1968.

Kant, Immanuel. *Kritik der reinen Vernunft,* edited by Raymund Schmidt, 2. Aufl 1930, Neudruck. Hamburg: Meiner, 1956.

Kant, Immanuel. „Metaphysik der Sitten." In *Akademie Ausgabe,* edited by Königlichen Preussischen Akademie der Wissenschaften, Bd. 4, 385–464. Berlin: de Gruyter, 1903, Neudruck 1968.

Kant, Immanuel. „Kritik der praktischen Vernunft." In *Akademie Ausgabe,* edited by Königlichen Preussischen Akademie der Wissenschaften, Bd. 5, 1–164. Berlin: de Gruyter, 1908, Neudruck 1968.

Kant, Immanuel. „Kritik der Urteilskraf." In *Akademie Ausgabe,* edited by Königlichen Preussischen Akademie der Wissenschaften, Bd. 5, 165–486. Berlin: de Gruyter, 1908/13, Neudruck 1968.

Kant, Immanuel. „Was heißt: sich im Denken orientieren?" In *Akademie Ausgabe,* edited by Königlichen Preussischen Akademie der Wissenschaften, Bd. 8, 131–148. Berlin: de Gruyter, 1912, Neudruck 1968.

Kant, Immanuel. „Über eine Entdeckung, nach der alle neue Kritik der reinen Vernunft durch eine ältere entbehrlich gemacht werden soll." In *Akademie Ausgabe,* edited by Königlichen Preussischen Akademie der Wissenschaften, Bd. 8, 185–251. Berlin: de Gruyter, 1912, Neudruck 1968.

Kant, Immanuel. "Über das Misslingen aller philosophischen Versuche in der Theodicee." In *Akademie Ausgabe*, edited by Königlichen Preussischen Akademie der Wissenschaften, Bd. 8, 253–272. Berlin: de Gruyter, 1912, Neudruck 1968.

Kant, Immanuel. „Über den Gemeinspruch: Das mag in der Theorie richtig sein, taugt aber nicht für die Praxis." In *Akademie Ausgabe*, edited by Königlichen Preussischen Akademie der Wissenschaften, Bd. 8, 273–314. Berlin: de Gruyter, 1912, Neudruck 1968.

Kant, Immanuel. „Logik." In *Akademie Ausgabe*, Bd. 9, 1–150. Berlin: de Gruyter, 1923, Neudruck 1968.

Kapferer, Norbert. „Paternalismus und Erziehung zur Demokratie." In *Philosophie – Erziehung – Universität. Zu Karl Jaspers' Bildungs- und Erziehungsphilosophie,* edited by Kurt Salamun, 75–91. Frankfurt a. M.: Peter Lang, 1995.

Kierkegaard, Søren. *Tagebücher*, Bd. 1, edited by Hayo Gerdes. Düsseldorf, Köln: Diederichs, 1962.

Kierkegaard, Søren. *Krankheit zum Tode*. edited by Emanuel Hirsch. Düsseldorf: Diederichs, 1957.

Kierkegaard, Søren. *Abschliessende unwissenschaftliche Nachschrift zu den Philosophischen Brocken, Zweiter Teil*, edited by Hans Martin Junghans. Düsseldorf/Köln: Diederichs, 1958.

Koselleck, Reinhart. «Jaspers, die Geschichte und das Überpolitische.» In *Karl Jaspers, Philosoph, Arzt, politischer Denker*, edited by Jeanne Hersch, Jan Milic Lochmann, Reiner Wiehl, 292–303. München: Piper, 1986.

Lamping, Dieter, *Karl Jaspers als philosophischer Schrifsteller. Schreiben in weltbürgerlicher Absicht.* Stuttgart: Metzler, 2018.

Lübbe, Hermann. «Die Masse, der Nationalsozialismus und die Atombombe. Karl Jaspers als politischer Moralist.» In *'Wahrheit ist, was uns verbindet.' Karl Jaspers' Kunst zu Philosophieren*, edited by Reinhard Schulz, Giandomenico Bonanni, Matthias Bormuth, 391-410. Göttingen: Wallstein, 2009.

Marquard, Odo. „Kompensation. Überlegungen zu einer Verlaufsfigur geschichtlicher Prozesse." In *Historische Prozesse,* edited by K. G. Faber and Christian Meier, 330–362. München: dtv, 1978.

Marquard, Odo. "Kompensation." In *Historisches Wörterbuch der Philosophie*, edited by Joachim Ritter und Karlfried Gründer, Bd. 4, 912–918. Basel/Stuttgart: Schwabe, 1976.

Menze, Clemens. „Selbstbildung." In *Historisches Wörterbuch der Philosophie*, edited by Joachim Ritter und Karlfried Gründer, Bd. 9. 379–383. Basel: Schwabe, 1995.

Nagel, Thomas. *The View from Nowhere*. Oxford: Oxford University Press, 1986.

Nietzsche, Friedrich. «Menschliches, Allzumenschliches.» In *Kritische Studienausgabe*, edited by Giorgo Colli und Mazzino Montinari, Bd. 2. München: dtv, 1999.

Nietzsche, Friedrich. «Die fröhliche Wissenschaft.» In *Kritische Studienausgabe*, edited by Giorgo Colli und Mazzino Montinari, Bd. 3, 343–652. München: dtv, 1999.

Nietzsche, Friedrich. «Jenseits von Gut und Böse.» In *Kritische Studienausgabe*, edited by Giorgo Colli und Mazzino Montinari, Bd. 5, 9–244. München: dtv, 1999.

Nussbaum, Martha. *Cultivating Humanity*. Cambridge, MA; London: Harvard University Press, 1997.

Platon. "Apologie." In *Werke*, edited by Gunther Eigler, Bd, 2, 1–70. Darmstadt: WBG, 1990.

Platon. "Gorgias." In *Werke*, edited by Gunther Eigler, Bd, 2, 268–503. Darmstadt: WBG, 1990.

Platon. "Laches." In *Werke*, edited by Gunther Eigler, Bd, 1, 219–286. Darmstadt: WBG, 1990.

Platon. "Politeia." In *Werke*, edited by Gunther Eigler, Bd, 4, Darmstadt: WBG, 1971.

Plotin. *Enneaden*, übers. von Hermann Friedrich Müller, 2 Bde. Berlin: Weidmann, 1878–1880.

Popper, Karl, *Der Zauber Platons*, in *Die offene Gesellschaft und ihre Feinde*, Bd. 1. Bern: Francke, 1957.

Ratzsch, Tolga. *Karl Jaspers und Plotin. Eine Untersuchung zu den Quellen von Jaspers' Metaphysik der Transzendenz*. Baden-Baden: Alber, 2023.

Rotteck, Carl, von. »Bildung«. In *Staats-Lexikon*, edited by Carl von Rotteck and Karl Theodor Welcker, Bd. 2 (1837). Frankfurt a.M.: Keip, 1990.

Salamun, Kurt, ed. *Philosophie – Erziehung – Universität. Zu Karl Jaspers' Bildungs- und Erziehungsphilosophie*. Frankfurt a. M.: Peter Lang, 1995.

Salamun, Kurt. *Karl Jaspers. Physicist, Psychologist, Philosopher, Political Thinker*. Berlin: Palgrave Macmillan (Springer), 2022.

Saner, Hans. *Kants Weg vom Krieg zum Frieden*, Bd. I: *Widerstreit und Einheit. Wege zu Kants politischem Denken*, München, 1967.

Saner, Hans. *Jaspers*. Reinbek: Rowohlt, 1970.

Saner, Hans. «Die politische Bedeutung der Natalität bei Hannah Arendt.» In *Erinnern und Vergessen. Essays zur Geschichte des Denkens*, 33–58. Basel: Lenos, 2004.

Saner, Hans. „Kunst als Antizipation der Grenzsituationen." In *Existenz und Sinn. Karls Jaspers im Kontext*, edited by Anton Hügli, Dominic Kaegi, and Bernd Weidmann, 23–36. Heidelberg: Winter, 2009.

Saner, Hans. „Auf der der Suche nach einer philosophischen Polemik." In ders.: *Erinnern und Vergessen*, 169–182. Basel: Lenos, 2004.

Saner, Hans. "Foreword to Karl Jaspers' Principles for Philosophizing." In *Philosophical Faith and the Future of Humanity,* edited by Helmut Wautischer, Alan M. Olson, and Gregory J. Walters, 9. Dordrecht: Springer, 2012.

Schelling, F. W. J. *Vorlesungen über die Methode des akademischen Studiums [1802]*. In Sämtliche Werke, edited by K. F. A. Schelling, Abt. I, Bd. 5, 207–352. Stuttgart; Augsburg: Cotta 1859.

Schelsky, Helmut. *Einsamkeit und Freiheit. Idee und Gestalt der deutschen Universität und ihrer Reformen*. Reinbek: Rowohlt, 1963.

Schiller, Friedrich, „Was heisst und zu welchem Ende studiert man Universalgeschichte?" [1789]. In Werke Bd. 2, 956–970. München: Droehmersche Verlagsanstalt, edited by O. Güntter, G. Witkowski. Leipzig: Hesse, 1910.

Schiller, Friedrich. *Musenalmanach für das Jahr 1797*, Nr. 84. Nationalausgabe, Bd. 1. Weimar: Böhlau Verlag, 1992.

Searle, John R. *Mind, Language and Society. Philosophy in the Real World.* New York: Basic Books, 1999.

Seneca. *Briefe an Lucilius*, edited by Ernst Glaser-Gerhard, Bd. I. Reinbek: Rowohlt, 1965.

Stemmer, Peter. *Platons Dialektik. Die frühen und mittleren Dialoge*. Berlin: de Gruyter, 1992.

Tilliette, Xavier. „Begegnung mit Karl Jaspers." In *Erinnerungen an Karl Jaspers*, edited by Klaus Piper and Hans Saner, 269–280. München: Piper 1974.

Tugendhat, Ernst. «Retraktionen zur intellektuellen Redlichkeit." In ders.: *Anthropologie statt Metaphysik*, 85–113. München: Beck, 2007.

Walters, Gregory J. "Karl Jaspers on Democracy and the Relevance oft the Supra-Political Element in Politics." In *Karl Jasper's Philosophy*, edited by Kurt Salamun and Gregory J. Walters, 115–146. New York: Humanity Books, 2008.

Weber, Max. „Wissenschaft als Beruf." In *Gesammelte Aufsätze zur Wissenschaftslehre*, edited by Johannes Winckelmann, 582–613. Tübingen: J. C. B. Mohr, 1988.

# Index

# About the Author

**Anton Hügli**, born in Switzerland in 1939, was Professor of Philosophy and Education at the University of Basel, having previously taught at the Universities of Münster and Bielefeld. He has published numerous studies on Karl Jaspers and, as president of the Karl-Jaspers-Stiftung in Basel, is currently involved in the preparation of the commentary edition of the published and unpublished works and letters of Karl Jaspers. His books include *Die Erkenntnis der Subjektivität und die Objektivität des Erkennens bei Søren Kierkegaard* and *Philosophie und Pädagogik*. He was co-editor of the *Historisches Wörterbuch der Philosophie* and editor of other lexical and philosophical-historical works and of the *Studia philosophica.*

www.ingramcontent.com/pod-product-compliance
Lightning Source LLC
LaVergne TN
LVHW102012210926
848483LV00011B/339

* 9 7 8 1 7 9 3 6 4 9 1 2 6 *